INHUMANITY

NICHOLAS BARKER

HANGAR 1 PUBLISHING

CONTENTS

1

INTO DARKNESS

I awoke in the sleeping compartment, still not sure of anything that had happened over the past few days. The bumping of the boxcar along the tracks, the sounds of the world racing by as we barreled down the tracks, the darkness that surrounded the car was never-ending. Another sleepless night and all I could wish for was the inevitable rising of the sun. If I could not rest with efficiency, then I would wait for the morning to come. This particular car of the train was reserved for only the wealthiest clients. The mahogany walls with their lavish gold light fixtures seemed to only add to the restlessness of my mind. The bed, if it could be called such, was a very thin mattress outlined in a mahogany shell, the base supported on the floor by seemingly crude bolts. I had supposed that there was no way to hide the fixture, for it was ever important to the stability of the bed. No expense was spared for my travel as I was an honored guest of the rail line's owner, Mr. Bertram. Mr. Bertram had been an important client of the Northeast Bank, and I had honored him with my efficiency as his personal banker for years. In fact, if I had not taken that deal, I would still be an apprentice, waiting hand and foot on some stuffy man with crude tastes, just wishing to make money and for nothing else.

Years passed and I felt more and more discomfort at the hands of the master banker, Mr. Taveshy. Though he appreciated the help and rightfully needed it, he was a very crude and unpleasant man, never allowing any apprentice the joy of closing a deal or helping a client with an investment deal. All apprentices only filed paperwork and sorted papers on their clients. Every day that passed, I always wondered about any of that time wasted upon monotonous paperwork.

Even though it seemed a waste of time, I still loved the opportunity to meet the new clients. I knew that one day I would get the chance to take on an office of my own and broker deals just as Master Taveshy had done. It was Mr. Taveshy's misfortune that he stepped out one afternoon to talk to a few attractive patrons when Mr. Bertram walked into the building. He carried himself like a man with the world in the palm of his hand, a man who knew what he wanted and achieved his goals by any means necessary. With his charcoal-black top hat and his fancy gold pocket watch, he was a man to be honored and thanked for the money that he would bring to our bank. I sat casually behind Mr. Taveshy's desk scripting orders for other clients on the ledger paper. He looked at me with reserve as if he knew that I could not possibly be Master Taveshy. I was but a young man of eighteen years. I had barely begun my career. Mr. Bertram looked around the upper bank offices and noticed that I was the only person there, besides himself, of course. He strolled into the office and gently rapped on the door. I looked at him with a smile, arose, and shook his sturdy hand. "Good day, sir. My name is Mr. Price," I said. "How may I help you today?"

Mr. Bertram met my smile with a hearty laugh and, with a booming voice, said, "My name is Mr. Bertram. I would like to invest money into your bank."

"Well, Mr. Bertram, come in and have a seat. Let me grab some fresh ledger paper and I will start a file for you, sir." I rushed to clear the papers from the desk.

Mr. Bertram just sat there looking perfectly intent to wait. I slid the drawer open, gently removing five fresh sheets of ledger paper. I carefully wrote out Mr. Bertram's personal information, placing elegant lettering in each space. Each line had to be written carefully to make sure that nothing was left to the imagination. The lines of numbers went on and on as I had to track all that was being written on the ledger. I then started calculating the full amount of interest as well as the full amount of the final investment. I provided Mr. Bertram with only the best information on his investment. I then placed the ledger in a seal with the official bank name. Mr. Bertram waited patiently as I continued to calculate each detail and to write it subsequently on the ledger. Everything had to be tracked and written in its own space.

Once I had written out the ledger and begun calculating each item, Mr. Bertram asked, "Well, son, you seem to have a keen aptitude for this work."

"Yes, sir," I said. "The hours are long, but with a keen mind anyone can perform my exact duties."

Mr. Bertram laughed energetically and pulled a handkerchief from his pocket to wipe his forehead.

I finished the calculation and signed the document. "Mr. Bertram, would you look over the ledger and confirm that it is to your satisfaction?"

He read the ledger in its entirety, only scoffing at one item.

"Is there something wrong, sir?" I asked.

"No, sir, but I do have an issue with the interest."

"Very well, what is the issue?"

"I was under the impression that the interest would be greater for an amount this large."

"Oh yes, sir, it is a greater amount," I stated. "With the current amount of maximum interest that can be accrued, this amount of money would be complimented with a five percent interest."

"Very well, if that is the maximum interest that can be given, I will take the ledger to be final."

"Very good, sir!" I jubilantly said. "Then I shall file this ledger and get your money into the safe downstairs. Please, if you would follow me." I led Mr. Bertram out of the office and down the stairs to the vault itself. I turned the dial to the correct series of numbers and unlocked the latch. I pushed the latch hard at first to slide it out of its normally permanent position. "Mr. Bertram, would you be so kind as to come to the back of the safe and place your money into a deposit box?"

Mr. Bertram stated, "It would be my pleasure to do so, sir."

"Thank you," I replied. I took Mr. Bertram to the back of the vault and opened the deposit box for him. Mr. Bertram then cautiously placed his money into the deposit box. I quickly resealed the deposit box with the key and placed it on the corresponding shelf. "Thank you for your investment, Mr. Bertram," I said emphatically.

"I am sure that it will be well taken care of, young sir."

I replied, "Yes, sir, it will be safe with us." I led Mr. Bertram to the front of the bank and shook his hand strongly. "Have a good day, sir, and safe travels to you."

Mr. Bertram smiled and said, "Yes, sir! And you do the same!"

When he walked out of the door, Mr. Taveshy approached me, exclaiming, "What have you been up to, apprentice?"

I turned to Mr. Taveshy and said, "I have performed my duties as I should have, sir."

At this statement, Mr. Taveshy flew into a rage and stomped upstairs, proclaiming, "Never shall an apprentice show me up! I will have your job, young man!" I waited patiently at the bottom of the stairs for Mr. Taveshy to return. When he finally came loping down the stairs with his belongings, he looked at me with hatred in his eyes. "Fools, women and you men pretentious as you in this profession frustrate me to no end! You all think that you can do whatever you like, but I am the master banker here!" With that Mr. Taveshy stormed past me, shoving me out of his way. "I quit!" he exclaimed.

Every soul in the office stared at him as he stormed across the street and into the bar. We all found this to be very humorous. A few days later I was named the master banker of the branch.

. . .

The previously mentioned investment led me to a career as a master banker. I did not, however, treat my apprentices any such way as Mr. Taveshy had to my fellow apprentices and me. Mr. Taveshy did, in the most unreasonable way, end his career after that deal was finished. Mr. Bertram liked my style of presentation so much as to completely disregard Mr. Taveshy as the master banker. When Master Taveshy realized that he had not been included in the deal, he objected by attempting to burn the bank to the ground later that day. The result was my being placed as the master banker and he was placed in jail. Though my career has had many accomplishments, I never knew in any capacity that one day I would broker such a deal as the Morrison deal.

A wealthy merchant by the name of Calvin Morrison started the deal by request through one of his many secretaries. This secretary, Mr. Johnston, came to my office to inquire about a deal that could be struck with our bank. The investment would consist of an unusually large sum of money being placed in the exclusive care of the Northeast Bank. When I heard these words, I calmly but swiftly began to write an outline of the conditions of the deal. Upon hearing and subsequently writing the terms of the contract, I had no choice but to accept the terms of the deal. The outline of the investment was to place two million dollars into a deposit account to draw interest over a period of ten years. The interest on this transaction alone would be enough to operate the bank in its entire need.

After some terms were laid out, Mr. Johnston stated, "I do believe, my good man, that we have a deal. Mr. Morrison will be by in a few days to sign and register the transaction in full with a cash sum of two million dollars."

I had no choice but to say, "Mr. Johnston, I would be honored to receive your employer merrily on that day."

Mr. Johnston ended on, "Good, Mr. Price, the deal shall be finalized in four days. Thank you for your time, Mr. Price."

"Likewise, Mr. Johnston," I replied. With that, Mr. Johnston left the bank and leaped aboard a small coach awaiting his return just beyond the door of the bank. I quickly scurried back to my desk and read the terms once more. I was astonished at the amount that was to be deposited for the bank to have in its vault. It was an enormous amount of money of which I had never previously seen. I could only baffle at how this merchant, Mr. Morrison, had come across this much money. And to that thought, how would he be willing to trust our bank with such a large amount? I quickly signed off on the ledger after calculating a few figures. The deal would be the largest that the Northeast Bank had ever seen. Immediately the paperwork was neatly filed in Mr. Morrison's personal registration account. After which I quickly collected my coat from its rest on the coat rack and hastily shut the door to my office on the way out. The door slammed with a thud, causing most everyone to look at me with reserve as though I was enraged. I quickly gave them a smile and said, "Good day! I shall see you all tomorrow!" I rushed down the stairs and walked out the door. I had the feeling that could only be found in the company of a good woman—a seeming release of all the recent frustrations that I had faced.

The day was gray with a slight smell of moisture. Most had already outfitted themselves with these coats to protect from the rain. I did not, however, bother with any such thing. I briskly strolled across the street to the bar. I burst through the door and with a quick look at the bartender said, "Good day, sir! I would like the best scotch that you can offer in an ornate glass, please!"

The bartender looked at me with excitement, as of a king arriving at a house of peasants. I do not hold myself in such reserve, however, but it was nice to see his enthusiasm at my request. The bartender yelled, "Yes, sir! I shall have it to you in the second!"

I quickly responded, "Thank you, sir! I shall not forget your pleasant haste!"

The bartender quickly grabbed the bottle of his finest scotch and poured it into a blue-tinted ornate glass. It seemed as if the man had found a new love of the day. He accented the glass with a slight flavor of vanilla, as of an elegant touch to a magnificent drink. The bartender rushed out from the bar and ran quickly up the small steps to my side. He placed the drink in my hand and proclaimed, "If you don't mind my asking, what is your name, good sir?"

I stated that my name was Mr. Benjamin Price and that I was a master banker at the Northeast Bank across the street. To this, he replied, "Well, sir, it was nice to make your acquaintance. You are welcome here any time, and please let me know if you need anything else."

I smiled slightly and said, "Yes, sir, I will. Thank you very much!" I sat in peace and sipped on my scotch. I thought about the day and the amazing turn of events that had brought me to the present moment. Each sip of scotch was more delicious than the last. It brought a fire in my stomach that burned like the excitement that I was currently experiencing. All the hard work that I had undertaken prior to this moment had finally paid off in full. I was to be one of the most successful bankers in all of the Americas.

I sat back in my seat, reveling in my success. I could finally relax in the face of all the previous day's trials. My mind raced with all the wealth I was about to acquire, the scotch smoothing each thought into perfection. I could not think of anything but finally purchasing my own company. I had longed to be an entrepreneur since I was an early child. Nothing had given me greater satisfaction than to receive requests and to deliver packages neatly wrapped in silver bows and colorful paper to my clients, to assist my customers in purchasing the many items that I had to offer. This was my fondest dream. I had begun to act upon this dream when I found my interest in accounting and banking at the university. I had enrolled for a hefty sum of money paid on debt to my honor with the Northeast Bank. When I spoke with the banker at the time, Mr. Willows, he took a great interest in my aptitude for numbers. Mathematics, he had called it, was of interest to me. No successful businessman could ever hope to deal with large numbers without mathematics. I immediately seized upon the opportunity to be employed for a tidy sum so as to pay my debts while taking courses in business and accounting at the university. Nothing had made me more proud to see all my hard work pay off.

I sat there thinking of the merriment that I would engage in every day after the finalizing of this deal, drinking the expensive scotch, the taste of smoking the finest cigars; the true mark of a wealthy master banker was to show his wealth with expensive tastes. It all seemed so relaxing until the bartender quietly strode up to my side. "Would you like more, Mr. Price?"

I sat up in the chair. "Why, yes, I would, my good man!" He gave a pleasant smile as he poured the smooth liquid into my glass. I smiled at him, saying, "Thank you, sir, but what is your name? I am quite sorry that I was not polite enough to ask earlier."

He said, "Oh, Banneker, sir. Alfred Banneker!"

"Well, Alfred," I said, "thank you for your hospitality!"

"Oh, it was my pleasure, Mr. Price!" He finished pouring my drink and briskly walked behind the counter to attend to the other customers.

I drank a small sip of scotch, noticing a man with a somber look on his face entering the bar. He looked like a delivery man, carrying hundreds of letters in his bag. He walked with a gait that suggested he was in a hurry, but still somber. I saw him walk to my table. I started thinking, *What could this man want?* He approached my table and said, "Mr. Price?"

"Yes, sir," I replied.

"I have a letter for you. It was addressed in the most urgent manner."

"Oh! Thank you," I replied.

He looked at me for a moment and then walked out the door that he had entered the bar through. I could not understand what had just happened. I did not know if I was to receive news of grave proportions or simply receive a notice from the bank itself. I looked at the front of the letter and read the sender's location.

"North Carolina?" I whispered. "Who could have written me from North Carolina?" I quickly realized that it must be from my extended family. I immediately opened the letter.

"Dear Benjamin Price,

My name is Percy Merivel. I am writing you this letter on behalf of your aunt Caroline. I regret to say that your aunt has taken sick and is getting worse every day. She is being kept comfortable, but the doctor does not know if she will recover. Please, Benjamin. Come to visit your aunt with all haste. She has been asking for you by name. I am sorry that I am writing you now, but it took me a few days to find your address and get the letter in order. Please visit as soon as you can.

Sincerely, Percy."

I could not understand. My aunt had been doing so well. She had never had a sickness that would warrant this kind of haste. In that moment I realized that my day had been shattered. I could not fathom that my aunt would have fallen ill without my knowledge until this time. How could this be? I had written her last month, and she had replied very quickly to me. I felt as though I had lost my joy. I sat there staring at the glass with my scotch. I put the glass to my lips and took a sip. What once had contained a spicy liquid of celebration now contained a sinister hint of misery. I drank little by little, remembering what it had been like to visit my aunt. She was sweet to me when I was a child. I would go to North Carolina to escape the harsh winters as a youth. My mother would take me in a carriage that my father had built. We would ride all the way from Massachusetts to Hillsborough, North Carolina. The trip would take many weeks, so we would start our journey at the end of the growing season. My mother would leave my sister to care for my father and tend to the preparation of his meals.

I seldom would go on this journey, however, because of the poverty of our family as farmers, and also because of my father needing every available member of my family to help with the harvest. At that time the years were harsh to our crops, causing them to yield far less than needed to survive the winter and make money for the things that we needed. The summers would be cool with a good amount of rainfall. The air was cold yet and would cause anything that grew to lose its crop. My father every summer would continuously curse the world, screaming on and on every afternoon that he would die a broken and poor man. He of course had been drinking when he would do this. My mother would stand at the door watching in amazement as my father acted like a child. And on the days when he would rest, she would bring him water from our well to quench his thirst, should he wake.

When the growing season would come to a close, my mother would ask, "Father, may I take Benjamin to visit his relatives?" To which he would reply, "Yes, Mother, the harvest will be small this year." I would almost leap for joy. I absolutely loved my aunt and her manor home in North Carolina. That afternoon I would help my father and mother make preparations for our journey. My father would pack extra food for my mother, saying, "Don't worry, I will hunt this winter. I won't have enough to eat anyway." She would always look at him with a slight disapproval, knowing that she could not tell him anything different. She would kiss him and then go into the house to prepare dinner.

Those were days that would shape my life. Our journey was long and treacherous. Often we would try to drive on as much as possible, pushing ourselves to the brink of fatigue. My mother was one of the best carriage drivers I had ever seen. She always knew the roads and how to go through wooded passes with ease. She always packed for safety as well. She had her own sense of style with a shotgun at her side, ready to defend us if she needed. The journey was always smooth, though. Never was there a time that I saw her shoot anyone or anything. When we arrived in North Carolina, we would always stay at my cousin's cottage on the border with Virginia. It was a small cottage. The fire was always raging in the corner. Delicious meats were cooking with vegetables in a pot. Simmering sounds could be heard loudly as we sat there talking with my cousins. I would stay there talking with them until I could not take it, and I would ask, "Excuse me, ma'am, but may I have some food?" She would always smile at my adolescence and say, "Yes, you can, Benjamin. Here, let me get you something to eat. Here, take this cup and go outside and get a drink of water." The water in that area was delicious. I always loved the earthy taste of it. It almost made me think of candy. I would always enter the cottage again seeing all the food in my bowl and say, "Thank you, ma'am." She would nod and go back to talking to my mother with vibrant enthusiasm. I would sit for hours eating my stew and drinking my water. I never left anything on the plate or any water in the cup.

The cottage was so cozy that I would immediately go to bed, even if the sun was still shining. There was always a nip to the cool air, which made me sleep so well. My mother always told me it was because of the water in the area surrounding the cottage. The water would make the wind colder until it cut through you like a knife. The thick timber walls of the cottage would usually prevent the air from rushing through you, though it did allow a small amount of the wind to blow through the cracks between the timbers. I would sleep for hours until first light. Then I would be awoken by my mother, and she would tell me that we had to go.

The rest of the journey was short but interesting. The beautiful colors in the trees, the air whipping across the Appalachian Mountains, the mist rising early on the fall mornings usually covering the road, but leaving to the imagination what would come next in the journey. My mother knew the country of North Carolina well. She had lived there most of her life until she met my father. It was then that she moved with him to Massachusetts.

When we arrived at my aunt's manor house, she would greet us with a smile and a wave. She was always happy to see me, and I, to see her. My aunt would invite me to have sweet tea and sit on the porch to watch the rest of the evening go by. I would sit there for hours just waiting for the sun to go down and see all the bugs come out in the cool air. The breeze would blow through the trees, moving them in such a way as to greet me. I really felt at home there among the forests. Then my mother would emerge from the house and say, "Benjamin, it is time to come inside and eat." I would jump down from the chair and rush inside. I was so excited to eat. My aunt would always prepare greens and chicken with a small portion of potatoes. I always loved the way that she would put the food on the plate. It always made my mouth water, watching as she would gently lay the greens on the plate. Gently pressing the chicken with a knife to make sure that it was prepared properly, she would always make the juices run out of the meat onto the plate. I was so hungry by the time she would lay the plate before me. I would devour the food and look at her with a smile, saying, "Ma'am, may I have another helping?" She would smile and laugh a little but would ultimately give me more than I had before.

My mother would chat with her for hours about everything that was happening on the farm and what it was like living in Massachusetts. I would sit by the fire listening to their conversation and think about the things that I would do the next day. There was an endless amount of land to explore and so many things to see. I would always dream about a creek just below the house. It always bubbled out of the ground with a gentle sprinkle and run over the rocks. I could play in the small waterfall that trickled down just below the start of the spring. I would jump in the water and play with the rocks there; I had all the time in the world to play and enjoy myself. Every day was like that.

In the night my mother and aunt would call me to come and eat, and I would race across the meadows to meet them on the porch. I would eat slowly, trying to listen to what they were saying. In the end, I would go to bed well-fed and relaxed from the conversation. My mother would prepare a bed for me in the sitting room near the fire, and I would beg her to tell me a story before I went to bed. My mother would always smile and say, "I will tell you a story about your aunt when she was a child." I would always look her in the eyes with excitement, waiting to hear the story. The fire would crack and pop, and I would hear my mother's soothing voice as I slowly drifted into sleep, the world around me slowly fading into blackness, and sometimes I could feel the sensations of a beautiful dream, dreams of the world around me and the ever-needed extra time to play. Oh, how I would love to play in the meadows of my mind. I would drift from knoll to knoll, singing and playing as I skipped along. Nothing in the world would interrupt my peace and joy. I would play in my mind until the sun came up.

At sunrise I would hear my grandmother's sweet voice, calling me to awake from my slumber and get some breakfast. She would always prepare gravy with biscuits, eggs, and bacon. I never went a morning without a full belly. I would always listen to the world going by outside as I ate. I heard the birds sing and the wind gently drifts through the trees, carrying a soothing rustling sound with it. My aunt's house was always a refuge for me, but as I got older, I lost interest in the summer travels to North Carolina. I had traveled there so many times that it seemed to not be worth the trouble. Since I was seventeen, I had not been to see my aunt. Now some five years later I was returning. It all seemed like a dream to me now.

Two days ago I was working on the biggest banking deal the Northeast had seen. I was to be the master banker for the deal. Now it all seemed to flow away from me like the little stream of which I was so fond. All the work, all the late nights I had spent working on the arrangement. Now it was so long ago in my mind. I sat there in the darkness thinking about the days that led to this spontaneous trip. I thought about my aunt and how she must be suffering, just waiting to see me again. I saw her in my mind as she once was. Such a sweet lady, she would always offer me anything that I needed to be comfortable as a child. Now all she could do was lie in a bed, waiting for the sickness to end.

The train rocked and creaked as it rushed down the tracks. The wind howled by outside, and the only thing that I could do was wait for the sun to emerge from the horizon to relieve the world of this reflective darkness. I could feel myself slipping into sleep as I sat there. This situation had become all that I could think about. I could not imagine that my aunt would become ill so easily. How could she just feel so bad? I always remembered her as the life of the conversation. She always wished to be involved in what she could to help others. I sat there for a few minutes more, thinking about my aunt and how I could have gotten into this situation. I stood up and began fixing the bed. I might not fall into sleep tonight, but I would be comfortable in case I do. I lay down on the bed, slightly drifting under the sheets. The cold sensation that ran along my skin as I corrected my relaxed posture from the sheets was amazing. It was as if my skin almost tingled from the sensation. I felt so relaxed, just waiting there for the sun to arise, calling me forth into the next day.

I closed my eyes and gently drifted into a trance-like state. I let my mind wander ever deeper into the image that had come to mind. I could see the train rushing down the tracks. I could feel the sensation of the wind, but I felt strange. The sky was darkened with clouds that were so thick it seemed the sun would never shine. As I felt a terrible sense of urgency I could not understand, my mind drifted over the ground as if it were a part of the train. The sky rumbled, and rain began crashing onto the car. I gazed through a window to where I was lying. I could feel a terrible sense of dread. The car seemed darker than it had been when I lay down. A pressure rushed over to me and began forcing down onto my chest. The sense was cold as if something containing so much malice wished to oppress me in my dream. I felt the hatred as it stung my chest. I could feel a sharp pain coursing through my flesh. At that moment I could feel an obstacle pressing down around me. I opened my eyes in a flash and tried to sit up. I could not. Why could I not control my own body? In my brief moment of relaxation, had I become paralyzed? I felt drained of my energy, and I could not bear it. I screamed out in terror at this sensation. When my eyes opened and my breath was taken from my chest, I felt a pressure pushing me back down. I could feel the hatred and malice ever stronger the more that I struggled. Something in this compartment wished me harm. I fought and fought when suddenly I heard a slight laugh as of a deranged man. I felt the breath of this creature rushing across my face. It was laughing in my face as if to say that I should not continue. I fought ever harder. Wiggling more and more under the sheets, I finally fought free of its grasp. I launched myself into an upright position, feeling the terror slowly sink inside. I could hear it laughing from the doorway. In that moment I froze, realizing that this creature was here as a warning. I am unsure as to what warning it was trying to convey. I sat there for a minute in silence as the creature just lingered in the doorway. I could feel its gaze upon me, daring me to move. I stared back, but into darkness as the creature's form was unseen.

I felt a peace rest upon my shoulders; however, it did not last long. I called out, "Who are you, and what do you wish for me?" The creature did not respond for some time. I sat there waiting for the answer, not knowing what would happen next. In an instant, I heard a voice coming from the doorway as of darkness itself. There was a very gruff tone to it, but with a brutality that I had never imagined. I sat there listening as it spoke on.

"I am your fear!" the creature said. "I have come to terrify your very soul!" I could feel the creature smiling as it spoke these words. There was a sense of twisted pleasure in this act. "If you continue to pursue us, we shall devour your soul, for all hell to hold!" An instant passed and the doors flew open, the creature rushing out of the room and out of the car itself. There was a distinct sound of maniacal laughter as the creature fled the car. I felt an instant drop in temperature, but the pressure and fear were gone. I sat there wondering what would come next. I thought about that sentence. Who would devour my soul? Whom would I pursue? To what end would this creature deem to devour my soul? I did not understand any of this. I lay there feeling the peace that surrounded me once again. I felt as if all my fatigue had left. The night moved slowly by, and I found myself sitting in the chair situated at the foot of my bed. I sat there watching the door, waiting. I could not know if this beast would return, or if I would simply sit there alone. If it did return, what would happen? Would that mean that my time had finally come? Would I be guided into hell as the beast spoke? I did not want to find out at all. I wished to simply wait for whatever would happen next.

I prayed in part of my mind that the sun would come. In a way, I felt as if light would make everything better. The other part of my mind wished to face this beast, to understand it. I felt the car moving violently at times as if it were tipping off the tracks. I felt myself slowly drifting into a trance, trying to understand what was happening. I knew that it was all in my mind. There was no plausible explanation for this occurrence. Creatures such as this don't exist. I thought for an instant that I could be insane. My mind rejected this theory, knowing that I was of sound mind when all this occurred. I knew that I was not dreaming entirely. If I had, I would not have felt the creature as it tried to pin me down. On the other hand, this all had to be a dream. How could something so utterly inexplicable happen? There was no more cause for alarm, yet I felt a terror that had been left deep inside my heart. I could not understand it, but I felt as if I could not continue on this path. "I must continue!" I thought. Whatever this creature could have been was a dream. Nothing happened last night, nothing at all! I quickly refocused on my situation.

The sun shone in with an intensity that I had never felt. The light told me that today would be an unusually hot day. I got up from my chair, watching the air filter through the light. Time seemed to stand still in that moment. I paused, thinking about my aunt. I could not return to New York; I had to continue on. My aunt needed me, and I could not refuse such an invite, especially given the circumstances. I immediately walked over to the wardrobe, opening the doors with caution. I knew there was nothing to fear anymore, but I could feel as if there might be something that I had to avoid. I pushed the feeling to the back of my mind and opened the doors quickly. The doors slid open with a thud as they smacked against the walls. I reached into the darkly lit space, feeling my clothing in my hand. My suits had all been pressed and neatly put away before I even reached my compartment. I pulled the suit out of the wardrobe, gently unfolding the arms. I could feel that the suits had been neatly pressed and placed carefully into the wardrobe. I glanced over the pieces of the suit with caution, looking for stains or creases that were out of place. Nothing had been neater than my suits, with no creases or blemishes the eye could see. The rest of the compartment was in shambles. I had not attempted to unpack anything other than what was handed to the stewards upon my arrival. I had become content with this lifestyle, however.

The day was shining brightly into the compartment from all angles as I dressed myself. One door gently slid open, and I leaned to one side with a cautious look. "Mr. Price?" the man said.

"Yes?"

"I am here to make sure everything has been taken care of for you, sir."

"Oh, everything is perfect, I assure you," I said.

"Great, sir," said the man with emphasis. He looked at me with a puzzled look, and I had to ask. "Sir, did you hear anything coming from this compartment last night?"

He began with a look of interest, "No, sir, I did not." Upon hearing this, I quickly ended the conversation. "Sir, I am also here in case you have any other requests. Please feel free to let me know of anything that crosses your mind."

"Thank you," I said. "I have no other requests at this time."

"Great, sir, thank you for choosing Northwest Rail," the man said.

"Thank you for your hospitality. It has been much appreciated."

"It was my pleasure," the man said with a smile. He then gently pressed the doors back together, smiling as he went. I could not help but wonder if he had, in fact, heard anything last night. Surely there was no one that could not hear such a disturbance.

I finished straightening my tie and rinsed my hands in a nearby bowl. Today would prove to be yet another adventure. I was sure that I would make the acquaintance of the other guests. Nothing brought more pleasure for the morning than to chat with other members of the higher society. Bankers, lawyers, and wealthy merchants, all with the need to socialize—men in such a line of work would always enjoy meeting others from similar backgrounds. I glanced in the mirror again to make sure that everything was perfect. I slipped out the door into the hallway of the car. I would have to walk through three cars to get to the dining hall, and at this speed, it would prove difficult. The cars were always rocking back and forth, swinging on a balance point, and at times you would feel like the whole car would roll off the tracks. The high amounts of wind that blew against the car were not comforting either. I have never seen a train car blown off the tracks by wind, but the wind seemed determined to make that happen today.

I briskly walked to the door of the car and stepped out onto the walkway. I could see the world rushing by with a swishing noise as if someone was cutting the air with a sword. Without thinking I moved quickly across to the other door. I felt an uneasy presence at that moment as if the beast had returned. I turned and glanced back with nothing there, not even another soul. I felt as if I was losing my mind. I gently rubbed my forehead with my handkerchief and entered the car. The door crackled slightly as I shut it back. It felt in my hands as if it would simply fall off the car and onto the tracks. Perhaps it was just my nervous mind. I had not been out of my car the whole time I had been on the train. My mind had been a torrent of thoughts since I boarded.

I walked down the middle of the aisle of the car and into the dining area. The space was small yet cozy. Leather seats lined each wall with beautiful white tablecloths covering the oak table surface. The tables had been set perfectly with the finest china. I was amazed at the luxurious nature of the dining car. The lights dimly lit the space but with windows accompanying them to give the car a light I had never seen. This was truly the work of a perfectionist. I casually walked forward and sat down in the first available seat. I waited for some time before the waiter came over and set a cup of fresh coffee in front of me. I thanked him and asked for a chance to look over the menu. I sat there in the dim light, simply glancing out the window and occasionally over to the menu. Nothing could make me happier this morning than to just sip my coffee and watch the world pass. I did know, however, that my time would be well spent eating some actual food.

I looked over the menu, quickly noticing the grand breakfast menu. Scones, muffins, and roasted meats, everything seemed so delicious. I could almost taste the roasted pork as I thought about it. I sat there for a minute just thinking about my destination. I stared into the window with a slightly frightful look. I could feel the misery in that creature still. I lingered there for a bit before my food came, and I could not help but feel that somehow something did not want me to arrive at my destination. I did, however, enjoy my breakfast as the train wound headlong into North Carolina.

2

PROGRESS

The train came to a complete stop with a screeching of the wheels. The stop was a little rough as I gathered my things. I would have allowed the stewards to gather my things, but I could not linger for too long. I rushed to cram all my clothing into my bags and prepared myself to exit the car. The sun was just beginning to rise above the train depot; the rays of light shone down onto the train from a seemingly mystical position in the sky. I had never seen the great city of Raleigh in my life. I had never cared to venture that far south, but railways would carry anyone where they wanted to go. No matter how far south or north the traveler would go, the railways would accommodate all; unfortunately, the railways only had a few stops of which you must travel. I looked forward to seeing this great city, however. Nothing would please me more than to see the central location of all industries in North Carolina.

I exited the car with a gentle step. Though my bags were heavy, I still managed to maintain my grace and easy-footedness. When I looked up from my concentration to not fall from the train's steps, I saw a beautiful city covered in modern brick and beautiful roofs on all the buildings, no matter how important or the lack thereof. I was simply impressed that North Carolina was not just a farmer's paradise; it could also attract the avid businessman. The streets were kept in a very orderly fashion, even with the wet clay surface that the carriages and horses would carve with each step and roll of the wheels. The sun rose in such a way as to add an almost heavenly appearance to the city. Each building stood in a neat fashion so as to allow the traveler to easily find his bearings in this magnificent city. I stepped from the platform into the building and was taken in by the many travelers passing through this depot. I had heard in New York that Raleigh was a beautiful and vibrant city, but now I was sure that I had found a city of the south that one day might compete with the popularity and sophistication of New York City.

I strolled to the window in the station and presented my documents. The clerk simply looked at me with a rigid style. He smiled and said, "Good morning, sir. May I help you?"

"Yes, sir," I said. "I would like to inquire about the coach that was to meet me at this very station."

The clerk looked at my documents and said, "Well, Mr. Price, I am pleased to tell you that the coach checked in just a few minutes ago and should be waiting outside." The man pointed to the door and smiled as if saying, "Please move along."

I smiled and thanked the man and then strolled casually to the door. Not long after I had exited the station, a man waved at me and said, "Mr. Price, please let me help you with your bags!" I thanked the man and followed him to the coach. "Mr. Price, let me welcome you to Raleigh, North Carolina. It is my pleasure to take you as far as you need to go." He smiled and bowed to me as he opened the door to the coach.

I entered the coach and said, "Thank you, sir."

He smiled as he looked me in the eye and walked to the front of the coach where he placed my bags on top of the coach and subsequently clasped them to the roof. He sat at the reins of the coach, and we were traveling as fast as I had arrived. I looked out the windows of the coach and took in all the splendors of the city. Shops, with open doors and beautiful displays, invited customers to shop in them all day. Pedestrians wandered from door to door, gazing through the windows and commenting on the displays, which were placed in such a way as to make you really want to buy whatever the shops were selling. The people here looked so similar to the gentlemen that usually walked the streets of New York City, though the suits they wore were not expensive; in many respects, the suits seemed amazingly well sewn.

The carriage moved steadily through the streets with the wheels bumping and clacking across the road. The driver rode close to the middle of the street until he had to move. I gazed at each new building that we passed, wondering what could lay inside and perhaps for what each building could be used. Each door seemed different with similar people scurrying from the steps to the streets, everyone hurrying in anticipation of the coming evening, rushing to finish what was left to be done. Raleigh was a world away from New York City, but so similar even in the actions of the people.

I continued to watch the people walking on the street as we approached the postal office. "Driver, stop here, please!" I exclaimed. I exited the carriage swiftly and briskly walked up the steps and into the postal office. The door was a massive wooden construction that was elegantly coated to bring out the shine of the wood. I pulled the door open and walked to the desk. "Good day, sir," said the teller.

"Good evening, I would like to send a letter."

"Very well, where would you like to send it?"

"I have already marked the address on it, but I would like to buy postage as well."

"Very well, just one moment, sir." The teller briskly searched for the correct postage. The sound of papers shifting and small objects being moved emanated from below the desk that was in front of me. The man emerged from below the desk with a sheet of the postage and examined the letter. "Sir, are you sure that you want to send a letter to this location?"

"Yes, I need to inform my cousin that I will be arriving in a couple days."

"Very good, but the reason that I ask is that it will have to be delivered directly to the recipient's residence, which will be expensive."

"Expense is of no consequence to me at this point, sir. I will pay the balance in full."

"The total will be two dollars."

I handed the man the money and thanked him for his help. I turned to leave the postal office when I heard someone speak from behind me.

"Excuse me, sir, but are you a Mr. Benjamin Price?"

I turned back to the man and nodded in assurance.

The man looked at me and said, "I have a letter for you here that was postmarked as important." The man rushed off through a small door and out of sight. Once again I heard the shifting of papers and packages. The man rushed from the doorway and handed me a letter.

"Thank you, sir," I said and turned toward the door. I left the postal office and entered the coach once more. I sat in the luxurious seat, looking at the letter for a moment before I opened it. I read the letter with haste, which outlined that my aunt had passed away the night before. I felt a crushing alone feeling as well as a feeling that I had failed in my mission to visit my aunt before she passed. I immediately thought about the house and what I would do now to sell it. It was now permanently my property since my aunt's passing. The longer I thought about selling the property, the more exhausted my mind became. I regressed to my previous activity of watching the citizens of Raleigh as I noticed that the city was quickly coming to an end. I used that time to focus more on the actions of the people I observed.

The road began to change from orderly streets outlined by a master designer to a hodgepodge of dirt and the roots of trees. I looked behind me, observing the city slowly vanishing before my eyes. I wondered at this moment how long this journey would last. It seemed like an eternity since my departure from the station in New York. Oh, how I missed my home, and now the only reminder of civilized culture crept ever out of my sight. The carriage with its driver and I as the passenger rolled faster and faster down the road at a seemingly rapid pace. The sun had risen to a good position in the sky as to light the way for the carriage driver. Trees seemed to dance past us as we continued down the road. I particularly noticed the difference in the trees here as opposed to the city. The birds played and glided along, seeming to soar to and fro while displaying an almost humanlike desire to keep pace with the carriage, which gave me a grand opportunity to observe nature in this region of the south as of my childhood. The wind gently blew through the openings in the carriage, giving me refreshing air as I sat back in the seat, imagining a fine dinner in the uptown district of New York City. Nothing could compare to the way each meal was delicately prepared to the liking of each customer. I could taste succulent steak and chicken, served with a savory herb sauce and potatoes roasted and seasoned to perfection. I could feel the breeze blowing across my face as I thought about the aromas of the cuisine mixed with the fine perfumes of well-to-do people, each couple sitting perfectly mirroring each other in proper fashion, all while delicately sampling each bite of their meals. Nothing fascinated me more than to immerse myself in high society. The streets would always be full of people, strolling from shop to shop, sometimes glancing into the windows and taking notice of new merchandise in each window. Children would exclaim at the sight of a new toy, while women would gawk at the sight of the latest fashions of Paris and other such exotic destinations.

It was at this moment that the carriage took an immediate right down a dusty trail in the forest. I gazed out of the window, wondering where we could be going in such an abrupt way. Deeper and deeper into the forest we traveled as the light dimmed until I could barely see the edges of the trail. The farther the carriage rolled, the more curious I became until we reached a clearing. The sun shone brightly over gentle hills of grass and small shrubs. I watched buildings in the distance grow larger as we traveled on.

The driver yelled, "I am sorry, sir, but we will have to stop and let my horses rest!"

I did not respond but held my reserve as we came ever closer to a house with barns all around. We rolled swiftly over a little hill in the road and turned onto an entranceway to this quaint little farm. Grasses sprang up on the edges of the entranceway, clinging to short stone walls as if to reclaim the ground on which the wall was built. A little wooden gate had been opened, and a man motioned the carriage over to the barn. Horses bayed and stammered as they grazed on hay that had been arranged so as to make it easier to feed the horses at once. People walked from the house to the barn and back again yelling about what needed to be done and delegating the responsibilities of the younger men. Dogs barked in the distance as herds of cows wandered around pastures of beautiful green grasses both long and short. The barn gleamed with the sun's rays bouncing off the side of the deep brown and rustic wooden side facing the entranceway to the farm. Men carried load after load of hay to pile in front of the horses that had lined up to graze. The farm was a true picturesque glimpse into the country life and all that it has to offer.

The driver stepped down from the seat of the carriage and began talking to an older gentleman who was delegating jobs without hesitation. I imagined that he would talk for a little while, so I climbed out of the carriage to enjoy the time that I could have to stand. I glanced around for a minute, just taking in the layout of the farm as well as a place to smoke. I pulled my pipe from my pocket and began wiping the outside to wipe away the lint from the pipe. I walked and packed my pipe to smoke and all the while taking in the sights of the country. I placed my tobacco back into my pocket and lit my pipe. I walked and puffed for a little time until I had walked to the other side of the house. I stood there taking in the breeze and the wisps of pipe smoke that wafted into my range of smell. I could feel something else like the air was hanging with tension. I felt as if something was pulling me farther into the field in front of me. I walked closer to the edge and gazed across the horizon. I gazed farther and farther until the grass could not be seen, but there was nothing there. Still, the feeling lingered as if something was controlling my gaze beyond my ability. This emotion gripped my heart deeply, and I began feeling weaker. I took another deep puff of my pipe and tried to ignore the situation, but I could not. The world slowly went dimmer until I felt my face hit the ground. I awoke in darkness, only hearing the sound of a thousand people breathing, but I could see nothing. I held my hand in front of my face, and my vision remained dim. I could not feel anything. "You cannot know what you are searching for, Mr. Price! I will be your death!"

"Who is there?" I asked. I received no response from this voice. "Who are you!" I yelled louder and louder, but still no response. I felt as if I was strangely drawn to crawl farther into the darkness. I continued to reach out, even to touch nothing. I felt as if nothing would save me from this blinding darkness. That I would remain obscured from the world that I had left, only to remain in whatever hell this vision had become. Farther and farther I crawled, beckoning to be released from this madness, but in return, I only heard the sounds of breathing. Nothing was going to save me. The despair would become too great, and then I would be met with the end.

I crawled a little farther, only to awaken in a strange room. The doors were wooden and the walls as well, but nothing here was familiar to me, nor to my way of life. I lay on a couch in the far corner and stared longingly into the distance. There was a door across from me, but a door that I feared for whatever strange reason that my mind could process. I gazed around the room, looking in each corner for any signs that I was not alone. Yet there was nothing, no one, and no object besides myself and the couch that I lay upon. I looked closer toward the door and perceived that it could be a possible exit from the room. I thought a little longer and a little harder. I only thought about my escape from this foreign space in which I had been purposely placed.

I eagerly placed my hand on the couch and prepared to dash for the door. My hand entered the fold of the couch until it struck the board on which the cushion rested. I gathered all the will in my heart and forced the fear and confusion further out of my mind. I placed one leg on the floor and with all my strength forced my body upright and dashed toward the door. I ran faster and faster, still glancing around the room so as to prevent anything from surprising me. I could hear my feet thudding upon the wood floor and the echo of each step that sprawled closer to the door in question. The room seemed to be never ending. The walls seemed to stretch on and on until in the ever-increasing distance, I could see the other wall and the door. Though I could not know exactly how big the room truly had become, I did not care. My only option was to reach the door and hope that I could burst through to the other side and to my freedom.

I finally seemed to be making progress, when suddenly I was thrown to the ground. I was dazed as my feet had not been obstructed, but I had been pushed by an unknown force that I could in no way perceive. My heart raced as I crashed to the ground. I lay there for a few seconds and then forced myself onto my back. I looked up as if expecting to see someone there trying to harm me, but nothing. No one else was in the room, and there were no obstructions to be sure. I had simply been pushed while still managing to be completely alone here in this room. It was in that moment that I heard a strange creaking sound. The creaking grew louder and louder and was accompanied by the occasional popping sound. The room seemed to be filled with this sound. I yelled as loud as I could until I realized that the sounds were coming from behind me, from the door that was to be my exit. I slowly and cautiously turned my head until the door was partially in view. I was horrified at what I was witnessing. The door, which moments before was a simple and unassuming door, began to grow arms as if something was pushing through the wood itself. Hands grasped and clinched toward me as if to try to snatch my clothing and drag me closer. The creaking was a horrid sound, but the hands reaching and grasping were far more terrifying.

I scrambled to my feet and tried to create distance between myself and the door. The room did not stretch at all, and the floor did not seem so harsh against my feet. Turning to face the door, I winced at the thought of seeing such a sight, but nothing was there. The door had returned to normal, and still, not another soul had entered the room. I stood in amazement for a few minutes and tried to come to terms with what I had just witnessed. The door stood staring back at me, and the walls had returned to normal. Nothing was out of place in this strange room. Yet I felt a feeling of uneasiness as I stared at the door. Would this be the opportunity to rush the door again? Could I make it to the door without such a strange occurrence happening again? Where would this door lead exactly? Where could I appear? Yet if I didn't try to escape, then I shall remain here for an eternity.

I made up my mind and prepared myself for the escape. I stood poised to rush the door for an instant then sprang into action. I charged more furious than the last, determined to exit this empty space. I let out a roar as I rushed the door to give myself extra energy so as to reach the door faster. The room did not seem to stretch or distort in any way. Nothing changed at all except my closing of the distance to this imposing door. The closer I came to this door, however, the more my mind seemed to race. My mind wondered if I would finally be able to escape this room or if I would be subjected to more horrors that I could not fathom. I raced as hard as I could toward the door. Finally, I grasped the handle of the door and opened it, only to find a void of more darkness. I tried to grasp the wall, but I could not control the force with which I charged the door. My own weight threw me into the nothingness. I seemed to fall and fall, only to burst forth from a strange bed. I fell onto the floor, which was wooden but different from the room I had escaped. I rolled to my back and felt hands grasping me as I fought to survive. I kicked and rolled and punched as if fighting to prevent my own demise. I kicked as hard as I could one last time, only to hear the shriek of a woman as she toppled to the ground. Startled, I sat up on the floor and tried to realize what was happening. I looked around and noticed that I was in the farmhouse that I had walked toward. The women of the house were trying to bring me back to reality until I attacked them. The woman sat there looking at me as I apologized repeatedly. Everyone else seemed to understand what had happened. Yet the lady and I still seemed to be misunderstanding exactly what had happened. I looked up at the wife of the farm owner. She stood over me cautiously as if waiting to see if I attack her. Once she realized that I was still unsure what was going on, she helped me to my feet and the others rescued the woman that I had kicked. The woman looked at me with embarrassment and rushed out the door and down the wooden stairs. I looked at the farmer's wife inquisitively.

"I am sorry," the woman said. "She is just a little embarrassed that she fell to the ground. You must forgive her, sir, as she is just a girl."

I looked into the woman's eyes and said, "No, my good woman, it was my fault, but I am confused as to what actually happened."

The woman seemed amazed as she said, "Well, sir, you were having a dream or something like it. You looked as if you were having an awful time dealing with it. We have been concerned for hours."

I walked to the window and gazed out onto the farm. "I am sorry that I scared all of you, but I don't know what came over me. I was looking out to the end of the field when I felt strange and then I..." At that moment the driver burst through the door.

"Are you all right, sir?" he asked.

"Yes," I said and simply shrugged off the whole incident. The world outside looked as if nothing had ever happened. People were still walking here and there, trying to complete the tasks that were given to them. I turned to the woman and said, "I thank you, miss, for your help, but I really must be traveling on. I have a long journey ahead and much to accomplish."

The woman looked at me with intrigue and nodded. "I understand, good sir," she said.

With that, I walked briskly out of the room and down the stairs. The girl that I had kicked stood in the doorway to the kitchen with her head slightly lowered. "I am sorry I assaulted you. I did not mean you any harm. I was simply confused." She smiled at me and looked into my eyes. She too nodded, and I walked down the hall and out the door of the farmhouse. The door creaked open, and upon walking onto the porch, I could feel a rush of air. The breeze was unusually cold for this time of year in North Carolina, but I buttoned my jacket and braced myself against the wind.

The driver had reclaimed the carriage with its horse from the stables and sat in the entrance to the farm, waiting for my entrance into the vehicle. I walked as quickly as I could to the door of the carriage and ducked to enter.

"Are you sure that you are well, sir?" asked the carriage driver.

"Yes, sir, I am. I am also eager to start our journey."

With that, the man nodded and snapped the reins of the horse. "YAH!" he yelled, and the horse began walking with a sense of urgency out onto the road that had brought us to the farm.

I sat there watching the farmhouse and beautiful meadows slowly pass away. I had no need to stay, especially with all that had happened in a few short hours. I still did not understand what it all meant, but I had a feeling that nothing would be easy from here until my destination. My stomach sank at the thought of that room and all that had occurred there. Those hands, grasping as if to pull me closer —it had all been a nightmare that was all too real. I could not shake the sense of dread that still lingered, but I hoped that the girl would be well. Nothing in my life could prepare me for such a strange incident to happen. I could not fathom that it was brought on by any medical condition. Yet I could not reason anything else as being the cause of my episode. It was all as if I had been transported to another world, and in an instant was lost.

The sun had risen further, and in a few more hours we would be forced to travel these winding roads under cover of night. This was something that I feared and was only exacerbated by the fact of what I had witnessed at the farm. I could not hope with more gusto than those events or none such like them would occur again. Yet with all the hopes I had had before it still happened, and I would have to come to terms with that. The driver snapped the reins again as we sped ever fast down the little dirt road. The trees grew thick again, but the sun was at our backs. The world seemed to change for me from a pleasure to experience each day to an unrelenting fear of what could occur. Unlike the journey here, there were no animals playing to and fro. Nothing seemed to be alive in this forest. The path grew a little darker with each passing of trees. The carriage reached the main road, and we turned right to continue our journey west.

The road seemed to have met with rain. There were puddles of water and mud with each rotation of the wheels. The road that was once relatively smooth was now filled with holes and bumps. I did not see a cloud in the sky, yet still, there was water on the ground. The driver and the horse, which drove the carriage, seemed to mirror my same confusion in their actions. Our pace slowed, and the driver looked around cautiously. I leaned out the window to the carriage and looked ahead to see about any trouble that had arisen. The driver guided the horse around puddle after puddle and looked both at the sky and the trees to see any signs of rain having fallen. The horse dodged as quickly as possible and with great agility pressed on through the puddle-filled road. I too looked at the trees closely for signs of rainfall but to no avail. The limbs seemed to be as dry as when we had passed here before.

The farther we traveled, the more the water had soaked the ground, but still, no trees showed signs of rainfall. The sky was not even darkened or gray at all. Nothing seemed to have caused this water, but we still traveled on. Eventually, we all forgot about the strange water covering the ground without any cause. The journey resumed as normal, and we turned onto the road to travel north. The whole way we had spied no other souls on the road. Even with the fact that this was the quickest route to Hillsborough, there still seemed to be no one wanting to take it this way. We had even passed a few farmsteads and houses that had been built in the woods just off the road. Yet not another soul traveled the same road. No matter how strange, the carriage still wound around each curve and ever closer to our destination.

The sun sank further in the sky until we could barely see where we rode. The driver lit his lantern and yelled to me, "We are going to stop soon to take on another man. It will only take a moment to load everything, and we will resume shortly, sir."

I yelled to the driver my approval, and he returned his focus to the road. The night had fallen quickly, and I wondered what surprises awaited us as we traveled on. Nothing could be more suspenseful than wondering what could happen next. My mind raced with fear, and my blood seemed to thicken at the thought of what might occur. I did not want to consider the fact that we might have to interrupt our quest to deal with an unsightly horror. Nor did I want to consider that I might have another episode. I thought deeper and deeper into this subject until the carriage fell into a small rut in the road and I jumped with fear at the jarring of the vehicle. I could feel my blood rushing to my legs as if to indicate that I should run. Yet I said nothing. I did not want anyone to know that I feared this night. I simply sat back and tried to calm myself. Nothing had happened, but my body was ever prepared to deal with whatever might come our way. I held on to the door for a bit to make sure that any more jars of the carriage would not release the latch and send me falling onto the road. I could not read or write anything in this time for I did not possess a source of light. My personal bag sat across from me as if it had become another passenger. The space was darkened, and only the light of the driver's lamp and the moon shone into the compartment.

The carriage slowed and turned onto a little path that led directly to a cottage. The cottage was made of wood and dimly lit in the night. No one seemed to be inside at first glance, but the closer we came to the cottage, we could see people walking by the window with a seeming hurriedness. We rode up to the cottage path and stopped. The driver jumped down onto the path and walked to the door. One knock after another could be heard on the door in the night. The inhabitants of the cottage rushed around the tiny one room. Children played near the beds, and the fire roared in the background. I sat there admiring the craftsmanship of the cottage as the driver loaded the other man's things. The man did not speak to me, nor did he have many possessions to be loaded. The cottage doorway was filled with the silhouette of a curvy, vivacious woman. She kissed the lips of her husband and said goodbye. The children ran to the door and saw their father off. The man then walked to the carriage and climbed onto the driver's seat with the driver. The horse seemed to acknowledge the man as if he was a familiar sight, and we were off on our journey again.

The two men sat on the driver's seat talking and laughing. Stories were shared and recollections passed with a fond embrace of better times. The two men clearly had history, but nothing that I cared to join. I simply lay in the seat and tried to rest as well as I could over their banter. My eyes closed, and I was greeted with complete darkness, save the occasional bright flicker of the lantern. The carriage bounced slightly as if turned onto the main road and continued north. My mind drifted from reality as I started to drift to sleep. The carriage would wind on through the forest. The driver and his friend would relay stories of time lost and life in general. Nothing seemed to be more important to either man than watching the road and telling stories. I let my mind drift further until I found myself thinking about the girl.

She was of a good age and fair-skinned. Never had I seen such beauty in my life. I felt the embarrassment of kicking her rolling back and forth in my mind. She looked at me and smiled with such innocence and intrigue. Though now it seemed a dream. I would never see that girl again, and I would never bother her family with my oddities that seemed to follow me. Perhaps it was for the best that I not see her again. Her family was helpful indeed and decent beyond limit, but I could not help but feel that I had overstayed my welcome. I drifted back and forth for a few moments, first to the girl and then to thoughts of my aunt and her passing. Nothing would be the same when I arrived in Hillsborough. I could imagine the loneliness that surrounded her home and the land. This would be the first time that I would visit with nothing to look forward to but silence. I would sell the home and the land around it, then return to New York and forget about this trip. I would try to forget the innocent girl that I had met and the hardships that I had endured.

At that moment my mind flashed to the event on the train. Could the two events be connected? Could there be a simple explanation? I feared for my sanity and health, for nothing could be a greater focus for worry. The tighter that I closed my eyes and the deeper I traced my thoughts, the more the carriage lunged and bumped down the little dirt road. No matter what I wanted, soon I would be in Hillsborough and the last leg of my journey would begin. I had hoped that I would be able to simply sell my aunt's estate and leave with haste. I did revel in finally meeting my extended family, especially those that were related to my aunt. The excitement of meeting new portions of my family was gaining, but the tribulations of selling the home gave me pause and a sense of reality. I lay my head on the cushion of the couch and forced my mind to quiet. I was finally calm enough to sleep for the night. I would finally be able to rest well and alleviate this drained feeling.

My head became filled with dreams of the days that I had spent with my aunt. She was a strong woman whose heart was filled with love for all in our family. She did not care, however, for those that sought to sell her items or to whom she had to be unpleasant. My aunt was an interesting woman, even in my dreams. She never bore children, nor did she have a husband or suitor of any sort. No one seemed to be interested in this tall, beautiful woman whose only thoughts were on family and community as a whole. My mother had told me often when I was a child that my aunt did not care to meet men. She did not care to be with anyone that could change her life or to whom she would be bound by any means. She always cared for her farm and the workers therein, and nothing else would matter.

I loved my aunt, and I especially loved her sense of humor and the vibrant tones that she would use when she told her stories. My aunt had always lived in North Carolina but had moved to Hillsborough only in her twenties. Many had assumed she moved away because of a potential partner, but I refuse to believe this opinion. Why had she chosen to live alone? Why would any woman of community stature and grace seek to simply isolate herself from others? I dreamed about the days that I would see my aunt sitting on her porch. She would make items for the house and others in the community and especially loved to knit winter scarves. She also took on a peculiar trade for women of her time, which was carpentry. My mother would tell me stories of how my aunt would send a worker in the afternoon to fetch wood for her to make furniture. She would often sell these pieces of furniture or donate them to new members of the community. She would often be seen caring for the grounds around her home during the day or helping the workers harvest crops. No matter what was said about my aunt, she would always work the days that she was able and care for those in need.

My dreams were drifting from topic to topic on my aunt, each new recollection more beautiful and sweet than the last. In that moment my dreams shifted from pleasant thoughts with beautiful undertones and graceful thoughts to dark images that I had never seen before. I could make out each portion of the dreams now as if I were there. I saw my aunt standing before a great fire in an area that I had never seen. I could not understand what she was saying, but she threw some sort of liquid into the raging fire and would chant a few words. It was as if I was being shown an evil side of my aunt that I had never known. I could feel the weight of dark magic hanging in the dreams. She had a sinister look on her face, one that I had never seen before. I could not understand why I was being shown these things. Surely none of these actions occurred. I watched as if helpless to look away as a young man approached her. She looked at him and grabbed each side of his head. She chanted strange words for a few moments, and then she took a dagger from her belt. I was horrified to see my aunt gripping the dagger in such a harsh manner. She held the dagger over the fire as if blessing it. She then grasped a cup from one of her work-ers. She held the cup to the boy's chest and with one quick strike opened his neck as if with no effort. Blood poured from his throat as he was clearly gasping for breath. Two of her other workers rushed to the boy's side and held him up as all the blood was drained through his neck and into the cup.

I began trying to call out in my dreams as if I were next in line to be slaughtered. I could not understand why, if these events were true, my aunt would partake in such a strange ritual. No matter what I tried, I was trapped in the dream. I saw my aunt turn to me, and her face seemed to change to that of a demon's. She laughed maniacally as the dream abruptly ended. I opened my eyes in an instant, feeling a mix of terror and confusion. I saw before me the young man whom the driver had stopped for last night. He was shaking me heartily as if he thought that I might be dead. I pushed him away and sat up in the seat. I felt the rush of blood through my veins as if I were ready to attack the man, but I stopped short when I realized that I had slept through the night. I looked into his eyes and said, "Is everything all right, sir?"

The man nodded and, with a startled look, spoke, "I am sorry, good sir, but the driver has asked me to wake you for breakfast." I was confused by this as I did not bring any extra food, nor did I remember the carriage stopping for the night. I turned my head to the right toward the open door. The driver was nowhere to be seen, but a rather large inn stood beside the carriage.

"Thank you, sir," I said, and with that, I exited the coach and walked casually into the inn.

The door opened with ease and without the slightest hint of creaking. The room was filled with the smell of pipe tobacco and a raging fire that had been fed pine for fuel. I looked around the room, taking in all the sights. A rather large man stood behind the little bar that was constructed directly across from the entrance. The man looked at me with a sense of curiosity, but I thought nothing of it. None of the other men in the inn were dressed quite like I had been dressed. Each new person that came into my field of vision seemed to be dressed in the traditional garb of the trapper. Every man in the inn seemed to carry a rifle as well, which was indicative of a typical hunter in the rugged regions of North Carolina. No one seemed to carry themselves with any importance either.

The room was covered with tables and chairs that had been roughly fashioned out of local trees. Most of these tables were empty with the occasional full table. I could smell the perfume of breakfast of some kind cooking on the fire. I could not make out exactly what the food consisted of, but the smell was pleasant enough for my empty stomach to growl. I looked to my right and to my left for the carriage driver, but I could not spy him in this room. I walked briskly to the small bar where the innkeeper stood cleaning his cups and utensils. He looked sternly at me and said, "What can I do for you?"

I was rather taken aback by the man's rough voice and cautious demeanor. "I am looking for the man that drove my carriage. I was told he would be waiting for me here with breakfast."

"Yes, he is over there in the private room. He clearly asked for a private place, not sure why though."

I thanked the innkeeper and walked in the direction the man

had pointed. I came to a tiny opening in the wall where the driver sat at a small table with two plates of what appeared to be eggs and venison. No doubt the evening catch or a quick meal that someone had brought to cook. I walked into the room and sat in front of the man.

He looked up at me and graciously offered the seat across from me. "I saved a plate for you, sir," he said.

I sat down and immediately started to eat. "We are not far now from our destination now, sir," he said excitedly.

"I am glad to hear it, and I thank you for taking me such a long way from the city. It has been a privilege to be a passenger."

"Why, thank you, sir. I have enjoyed the journey, and I too have passengers to gather in Hillsborough."

I sat there eating my breakfast and talking to the driver for a moment. We talked about Hillsborough and the people that lived there. I asked him about his relationship with the area and if he had any family there.

"No, sir, I have no family there, but I knew a woman that lived there once. She took me in on a cold and rainy night."

"Tell me about this woman, my good man."

"Well, she was a nice enough woman at first, but there seemed to be something strange about her."

"What do you mean?"

"Well, sir, she was dressed nicely and her house was a beautiful manor, but she kept disappearing at random times. I knew that she was not leaving the house for it was raining much too hard. She would appear in different parts of the house in doorways and would scare me half to death."

"What do you mean by appear?" I asked.

"It was like she was not there, but in an instant, she would be and she would speak with a gloomy tone. I stayed the night, but in the morning, I left before seeing her again. I think she lived in the Tourney Manor house on the outskirts of town."

"Are you sure it was that manor in which she lived?"

"Yes, sir, why?" the driver asked.

"My aunt lived in that house until a month ago. She was not a strange or gloomy woman at all. When did you visit the home?"

"Ah...it was about three years ago, sir."

I looked at the man with a shocked and puzzled look. "You must be mistaken, sir. My aunt has lived in that house since she had it built and had been bed-bound since seven years before today."

The man dropped his utensil onto his empty plate and gave me a look as if he had seen a ghost.

"I am sure you could not be talking about the same manor in which my aunt lived."

The man simply agreed with a very silent nod and immediately grabbed his plate. He stood looking at me for an instant and then swiftly exited the room. I did not see the driver until I had finished eating and walked outside. Perhaps he was confused, but who was I to judge?

I cleaned my plate and took it to the innkeeper. I thanked him and complimented him on his cooking abilities. After a short conversation with the innkeeper, I walked to the carriage and climbed inside. The carriage ride quickly resumed, and we were back on the main road to Hillsborough.

We rode through more trees and took caution in the darker portions of the forest. I sat looking out the window, trying to spy animals playing in the trees and on the ground, but I saw no animals in sight. I sat looking for a while, but at no point did I see any signs of life. This took me by surprise as I realized this was too deep into the forest not to hear animals traveling in the forest and playing. The forest should be alive with all sorts of sounds and signs that animals inhabited these woods. This silence hung heavy over the whole forest, it seemed. Perhaps the animals heard the breathing of the horses or the banter of the driver and his helper. I simply brushed the thought aside as we entered the darker part of the forest. I sat there for a few more seconds looking out the window, trying to spy any further signs of life in the forest. The trees began casting a shadow that seemed deeper than any I had seen. It was as if the sun had faded to a darker tint. I started to lose interest in the forest around us.

Just then I heard a loud noise just beyond the carriage window. It sounded like a tree was falling. Neither the driver nor his helper seemed to notice it, but they had changed their conversation to the darkness that seemed to hang in the forest. At that moment I noticed a goat simply standing in a clearing in the forest, looking directly at me. The closer we came to the goat, the more it seemed to be a normal goat. I was confused by this but dismissed this as simply another strange occurrence. The goat did not make a noise, nor did it move at all. It had a rather indifferent look on its face but did not even hint at moving.

We continued riding until I was directly parallel to the goat. All of a sudden, the goat changed into a strange-looking creature that darkness partially covered. It had deep red eyes that peered out of the darkness at me and stood brooding in the darkness. I could not make out the details of the creature, but it was fearsome, and the way it stood raised the hair on the back of my neck. I tensed and blinked my eyes to see if it was just an illusion. When I opened my eyes, the creature lunged rather fiercely toward me. I did not have enough time to react except to throw myself to the other side of the carriage. The creature let out a bloodcurdling scream as of nothing that I have ever heard. The eyes grew deeper red and the figure became so large that I thought it would attack the carriage to get to me. I still could not see the creature for the darkness, but we passed it as it seemed to vanish.

I yelled so loud, and the driver started to ease the reins. I yelled at him to continue as swiftly as possible. The young man peered into the front opening of the carriage to make sure that I was all right. I looked into his eyes with what I would imagine was a look of absolute terror. The boy yelled to me, "Are you all right, sir?" I simply nodded to him and was unable to speak. I could feel myself go cold as I felt the blood drain from my skin. I appeared as white as a sheet in my mind but prayed to God in my head that the driver would not stop the carriage until we reached town. The boy looked concerned but seemed to understand that I would be fine as long as the carriage did not stop. He started talking to the driver, and immediately the driver hurried our pace.

The veil of darkness lifted abruptly, and I seemed to lose the sense of caution that I had previously felt. A weight seemed to lift from my chest, and I could breathe well again. The driver began driving harder until we started going over a hill. The carriage topped the hill, and the driver worked to slow the horse slightly so as to not tip the carriage. The sun shone over the trees as the helper yelled to me, "We have arrived, sir!"

I sat back in my seat and thanked God for the safe journey, but still feared what other strange things might happen.

3

THE TROUBLE BEGINS

The carriage bumped and bounced as we rode toward the town area of Hillsborough. There weren't many buildings, but I could see one or two houses scattered around. I saw one building as we left the road and turned onto the entrance to a coach house. The building was not big but looked like a courthouse or town meeting center. I did not see too many people walking around the building, but clearly, there was something going on inside. The carriage rode to a small post just beside the coach house. We came to an easy stop, and the driver and his helper jumped to the ground. The driver opened the door to the carriage and gestured for me to exit the vehicle. I stepped out onto the soft soil. The ground seemed to mush under my feet, yet there was no water on the ground. I had finally understood the meaning of "Tarheel mud." I walked toward the rear of the carriage and peered around the edge as if the creature that I had witnessed in the woods would be there. I stood staring into the forest from which we had traveled. I saw nothing but trees and a gentle breeze that rustled the leaves. I could not imagine what had actually happened in the forest or why some unidentifiable creature would appear to me.

I stood there for a moment before I stepped out of the carriage. I decided that the creature was not there and nothing would come to harm me. Perhaps it was a dream as well, but I doubted that theory. I looked up into the canopy of the forest for a moment. I began feeling a sense of wonder at what was happening to me. At that moment I felt someone grasp my shoulder with a firm grip. I turned as fast as I could to meet this being. I had half expected to see that goat-like creature staring back at me. I jumped back when I realized it was not the creature but the driver. He gave me a strange look and said, "Sir, are you all right? I did not mean to frighten you, but your things have been unloaded from the coach."

"Thank you, sir," I replied. I handed the man ten dollars. The man graciously accepted and did not seem to care that anything strange had occurred. He simply shook my hand and sprang back to work. I strolled to where my things had been set on the ground. I grasped the handles of my luggage firmly and started walking toward the coach station. The building was small and unassuming. There had been a mediocre labor to construct the building because of how small and rustic the building had been. I walked onto the porch and grasped the door after shifting my luggage to my other hand. The door opened stubbornly but with no creaking or any sound at all. I peered into the building to understand where I should walk. I walked in and stood before a large wooden desk. The man behind the desk looked like a normal clerk for the day and had a clerk's usual positive demeanor.

"May I help you, sir?" the clerk asked.

I walked to the desk and set my luggage on the ground. "Yes, sir, I would like to know if there is any way that I could get from here to the Tourney Manor."

The clerk responded, "Why yes, sir, there is a way to get there, but you will have to take a horse, or there is a man that has a wagon just across the street. I am sure that he will take you where you need to go."

"Thank you, sir. I will surely ask him. Who would I ask about the wagon ride?"

The clerk pointed out the window to a rather reflective-looking man perched beside a pole on the porch of the building across the street. I thanked the man and stated that I would definitely ask this man for a ride to the manor. The clerk smiled in return and nodded in acknowledgment. I then left the coachhouse and began walking across the street toward the wagon driver. I had walked to the middle of the street and heard the rumble of thunder in the distance. The air hung thick with moisture, and I was sure that at any moment rain would pour down from the sky. I walked ever quicker to the porch where the man was perched.

The man did not seem to care that I was even alive. He did not acknowledge that I was walking toward him. He simply stood there puffing on the pipe in his hand and blowing smoke rings. He was dressed in a black-and-white rancher's suit with fine leather boots. His success was apparent as he seemed to also carry himself with importance. I stepped onto the porch just beside the man as the boards under my feet cracked and creaked. "Good morning, sir," I said optimistically.

The man looked at me and stood upright. "Good mornin' to you as well, sir," the man said cautiously.

I looked into his eyes and seemed to recognize him in some way.

"My name is Benjamin Price, and I would like to know if you would take me to Tourney Manor on your—"

The man broke the sentence immediately and said, "Yes! Mr. Price! My name is Percy Merivel. I am the man who mailed the letter to you in New York."

I excitedly shook Percy's hand as he greeted me with a heartiness that I had only known from my own family.

"I am Caroline's assistant. I hope that your journey here was comfortable and you traveled with ease."

I looked at the man with surprise at his manners and asked, "Mr. Merivel, have you been here on this porch waiting for my arrival?"

Percy nodded and said, "Yes, I was expecting that you would arrive sometime soon. I decided to be here in case you needed any help getting to the manor. I know the coaches don't like to run to the country parts of town."

"Thank you, Mr. Merivel," I said hastily.

"Pardon me, Mr. Price. I imagine that you are eager to gather your things and begin the ride to the manor," Percy said thoughtfully.

"Yes! I am quite prepared to travel now if that is all right with you, sir."

Percy nodded and looked past my shoulder. "Where is your luggage, Mr. Price?"

I replied, surprised, "Oh yes! I left the luggage at the clerk's desk in the coach station. I was not sure if you would be willing to take me to the manor."

Percy seemed more interested in hurrying to grab my luggage. "Well, Mr. Price, let's gather your things and we will be on our way before the rain starts."

I replied, "Thank you, Mr. Merivel, and you may call me Benjamin."

"Very well, Benjamin." With that, we were walking toward the coach station with haste. Percy walked at the same pace as I but did not say anything at all. We entered the station and grabbed my luggage.

"Benjamin, allow me to extend the offer of lunch with my family and I," Percy said excitedly.

I thought for a moment and replied, "Oh yes, Mr. Merivel. I would be honored to join you and your family for lunch."

Percy seemed overly happy at my response. "Very good. We will take your things to the manor, then we will head to my family's farm-stead for lunch."

I smiled and said, "Yes, that will be fine. I am quite famished from the journey here."

Percy tipped his hat to the clerk and, without any other actions, began walking out the door. I followed him closely but looked toward the sky briefly to check the clouds and for rain. Nothing had begun falling, but the sky was definitely more gray than a few moments ago.

Percy placed my luggage under the roof of the porch and said, "Wait here, Benjamin, and I will return shortly with the wagon."

I thanked Percy, and he walked toward the building across from the station. I stood there looking around and wondering what sort of people Percy's family would be. I did not want to assume anything for that would be rude. I did, however, wonder whom I could count on in this town. I had not been to Hillsborough in some time, at least not since I was a child, almost a teenager.

Percy emerged from the opposite side of the building across the street. I could hear the clacking of the feet of Percy's horses and the grinding of the wheels. The wheels bumped over the muddy ground as they rolled in my direction. The horses pulled the wagon just in front of me, and I began placing my luggage into the back of the wagon.

Percy smiled at me and said, "I did not think that it would rain today, or I would have brought my cover for the wagon."

I smiled in return and spoke, "That is quite all right. I understand that a man cannot predict the weather, and for that matter the future. That is an ability reserved for only God himself."

With that Percy laughed heartily and leaned his head back as if laughing into the air. I was a little puzzled as to why he would laugh so heartily but decided it was simply his way. Percy assisted me in placing my luggage quickly into the back of the wagon. He then motioned for me to sit on the driver's platform. I did as such and patiently waited for him to sit in the driver's position. He took the time to make sure my luggage was secured then walked quickly to the front of the wagon. Taking the reins firmly in his hands, Percy rapidly popped the horses on the rear. The wagon was jerked slightly by the horses beginning to walk.

I sat in silence as Percy drove the horses to turn the wagon in the opposite direction. We rode swiftly away from the coach station and out into another stretch of forest. The trees here did not seem to carry the same silence as the forests before. There was no darkness except the grayed-out sky. Animals once again were playing to and fro between the limbs of each tree. Nothing seemed to be out of place, and a sense of relaxation swept over me. My mind finally could rest as the thought of such normalcy took the place of the fear that I had felt before. The leaves wafted in the wind and rustled under each move that every animal made. Squirrels seemed to follow the wagon for a bit and then plunged deeper into the forest so as to hide from us, it seemed.

Percy seemed to realize that I was looking about the forest and said, "The forests here are beautiful, aren't they?"

I nodded and said, "Yes. I rather enjoy seeing the wildlife running about in the forests. There is really a sense of serenity here."

Percy chuckled and spoke with a tone of sincerity. "You are welcome to stay in the town as long as you like. I know I was not looking to settle here until I was captured by the peace and silence of the area. Also, no one seems to look into others' lives, but always try to help each other in the community."

I gave Percy a look of agreement as we continued to travel farther down the road. It seemed apparent to me that I would enjoy my stay. I wondered for how long these dark things that seemed to follow me would stay at bay. I did not want to evoke darkness upon myself or upon anyone else.

The road met us with a sharp turn to the left. Percy struggled to make the turn as smoothly as possible but to no avail. The wagon thudded violently as the wheels slid over rut after rut in the muddy road. I could imagine the wheels simply snapping off and falling into the road. It was all that I could do to hold on to the wagon and hope that my luggage did not fall from the wagon. Nothing seemed to move even with the violent thudding. The road straightened again, and our journey resumed its peaceful pace. The occasional hill and bump were all that we had to face now.

I looked toward Percy as he returned my look with that of regret. "I am sorry, Benjamin. I didn't mean to scare you."

I laughed slightly and said, "Everything is perfectly fine. I am just glad that none of my luggage was lost, sir."

Percy smiled and turned his head back to the road. He seemed to be a man that had many secrets but would not share them easily with anyone. He sat there with a stature of rigid strength as he fought the wagon over bump after bump. His face was wrinkled with thought or worry. I could not understand why he would have this look on his face. I dismissed it as an action that he performed every day. Perhaps this look was his normal expression, or he truly was deep in thought about many things. I wanted to ask, but I thought it might be a little out of the normal. I barely knew this man or his family, and I surely would not be impolite to a new friend.

I refocused my attention on the forest around us. I sat there watching animals playing in the forest and leaves rustling in the wind. The sky remained gray but began to release drops of rain inter-mittently. I looked to the rear of the wagon and held my arm in the air. I could feel drops of rain hitting my arm, but not terrible enough to worry.

Percy glanced at me with the most peculiar of looks. He seemed to focus for an instant on my actions as if he were worried that I might be insane. I gave him a look of reassurance and said, "It is starting to rain. I do hope that we will make it to the manor before the rain really beings to fall."

Percy nodded and gave a half smile. He spoke with assured authority, "We are very close now, Benjamin. I would like to know if anyone had told you about the manor and the property that it included."

I thought for a moment and replied, "No, sir. I have not heard any specific details of the property."

Percy shook his head with a seeming disgust and said, "Mr. Price, I will take you around the property on a better day and show you your inheritance."

I chuckled to myself silently. "Thank you, Mr. Merivel."

He nodded then pointed to the right. "The house right through those trees is my farm. I helped Caroline with her farm for so long that I decided to arrange a farm of my own."

I smiled and fondly thought of my youth. I remember the magic of spending time on a farm. "I would imagine that you miss her very much as I do. What was it like working for my aunt?"

Percy tilted his head to reminisce about better days, it seemed. "She was warm and caring and really placed importance on taking care of all those that helped her. She was a very strict supervisor of all the work that was done on the farm. She always seemed to have a smile no matter what had happened that day. I really miss Caroline, but I miss her farm the most. I would have loved to own that area, but it was not for me to have, I suppose." His words seemed to be filled with regret as he gazed forward to the road ahead.

The wagon continued forward down the road. "Just a little farther and we will arrive to the Tourney Manor. Where would you like to place your luggage in the manor?" Percy asked.

I thought for a moment and replied, "Just inside the door should be sufficient. I do not wish to take everything to the room in which I will reside."

Percy nodded. The wagon continued to roll forward down the muddy road. The horses seemed to never tire of this pace. It seemed as if we could travel at this speed for miles. Though I knew that it would not take so long a time to arrive at the manor. Percy seemed to be content to be going to the manor but also seemed slightly on edge. He glanced at me quickly and then said, "It has been a long time since I have been to the manor. I am not sure what to think about the place anymore. The last day that I was there was the day after Caroline had passed. There was a darkness that seemed to fall over the property. I dare not alarm you about staying there, but I would be remiss if I did not warn you of what I had felt."

These words seemed to stand out the loudest in my mind of any conversation that Percy and I had had. I was stunned and surprised by these words. It was as if I almost did not wish to stay in the manor. Though I am firm that I do not believe in such things as hauntings or demons and ghosts. These, I believe, are the workings of a fantastical mind. Nothing, in reality, could account for such events in my mind. I simply dismissed Percy's words. Not only to not alarm myself to fears that had no tangible evidence but also to not close myself to the idea of staying in the manor by myself.

In a few short moments, we had arrived at the road that led to the Tourney Manor. Percy gently turned the wagon onto the drive and began leading the horses to the middle of the road. The horses began to trot at an increased pace and almost seemed to be approaching a full sprint. Percy pulled on the reins slightly and slowed the horses. Then he began to guide them right up to the front door of the manor. I glanced upward to take in the front of the home. There were two levels to the home with the upper level being marked by a balcony that stretched across the front of the home. The boards that made up the house had all been painted white, though now were faded to a slight off-gray color. There was a steep roof that marked the top of the home with two red brick chimneys jutting from the top of the home. At one time I could sense that there was smoke billowing forth from each chimney. Though now the smoke did not linger in the air.

There were no signs of warmth that could be shown from the manor. In some way, this gave me pause. To know that there was once life and warmth that flowed from the manor and now there was only a seeming death that hung over the home. The whole property, as I would come to realize, followed this same theme.

Percy turned to me and said, "Are you ready to unload the wagon?"

Upon hearing his words I was immediately brought back to reality. "Yes, sir. I am sorry. This home is as striking as I remember from my youth." I immediately sprang to action and began to collect my luggage and started toward the front doors of the manor.

Percy beckoned to me to pause for a moment. "I have the key with me to the home."

I stopped immediately. It seemed that my mind had forgotten that there was a key needed to open the door and gain access to the home.

It was not long before Percy had passed me and began unlocking the front door to the manor. He slid the key into the keyhole, and with a firm turn of the key in the hole, the door gave a loud click. Instantly he turned the doorknob and opened the door. Percy was almost graceful in these motions. A seeming fluidity dictated his movements. I could not quite place it, but I felt as if I were looking at a graceful dancer or someone that seemed to flow with life as in a wave. This compelled me to follow Percy into the home. As soon as I entered the building, I turned to the left and set my luggage onto the floor. When I turned back toward the door, Percy was staring back at me with his arm stretched out. I followed his arm down to his hand and saw that he was handing me the key to the manor.

Percy smiled and said, "I am sorry that I did not hand you the key earlier, but it honestly slipped my mind. I will drop you off here after we have had lunch. I do hope that you enjoy your stay in Hillsborough. I would also prefer if you call me Percy."

I nodded and replied, "Very well, Percy. I am thankful that you have been so willing to help me and welcome me to the town. This would have been much harder to undertake without someone that I knew here."

Percy nodded in acknowledgment. He then moved his hand in a motion that invited me back to the wagon.

"Right. Thank you," I said. I then walked back out of the home and took my place back on the seat of the wagon.

Percy followed and walked around the horses to sit in the driver's seat. He checked his horses as he went so as to make sure that their harnesses were still in place. I could see that he was straightening the harness of one horse and pulling a strap on another harness. He then moved to take his place on the driver's side of the wagon.

With a quick pop of the reins, we were off again. We moved down the entrance to the Tourney Manor and back into the muddy road. With a slow left turn, we were heading back in the direction of Percy's farmhouse. Once again I could feel the slight bumps as the wheels of the wagon wore on down the road. It was not long before we were turning left yet again, but this time into the drive to Percy's farmhouse. The entrance was a very small road. I could not imagine what sort of home Percy would live in, but I knew that it had to be well taken care of for a man such as Percy. He seemed a man that had learned the same strictness from my aunt. The road was lined with a few bushes and trees. I enjoyed seeing the different colors of flowers that grew into the bushes. A few of the trees had been wrapped in ivy and looked as if they were art pieces. Blues, reds, and purples made up the collage of beautiful colors along the road. I looked to my right with a delightful surprise as there had been a few sculptures mixed into the landscape. None of the sculptures were of fine craftsmanship but were as beautiful nonetheless.

"I'm a bit of an amateur sculptor, Benjamin."

I nodded and said with surprise, "You are the magnificent artist of these beautiful works of art, eh?"

He nodded and replied, "Most of 'em took a few weeks to make, but that one there of the woman with a fine robe took a month."

I smiled as I looked toward this particular sculpture. The details of the stone were amazing. The woman seemed to have a natural beauty and grace about her. I could not imagine how any farmer would find the time to work on such time-consuming things. I asked Percy about this, and he responded, "In this area, we only have so many months that we can grow crops. The rest of the time is spent preparing for the next growing season with the exception of the month just before the season begins. That is when I work on my sculptures. I am a hardworking man, Mr. Price. I do not waste time with anything that I don't enjoy."

Percy's words were like music. I had never imagined that a man could enjoy something so much as to put a special time of the year to work on such art. I looked at Percy with a smile and said, "I have always wanted to begin painting, but I have never found the time."

Percy laughed and responded, "You just have to place that as a priority, Benjamin. The things that you really love will always have time to be performed."

I understood exactly and took this advice to heart. It would be nice to try my hand at painting. Nothing seemed to be more attractive to me, and I would see to it that I could set aside time to practice.

Percy's home came into view as we rode further. The house was not immense, nor was it decorated lavishly. Percy's home was made of what appeared to be maple wood or oak. Though the wood did appear to have a darker color. A porch wrapped around the front and right side of the home. Where the porch ended, a row of ivy ran up the side of the house and covered part of the roof. The plants had blended well with the home so as to give the appearance that the house had become one with the forest. There was a window in the front of the home in which a beautiful young woman worked. She wore an intense focus on her face that few people possess. I was amazed that the woman worked near that particular window even with the only ray of sun shining intensely onto her face. Nothing seemed to prevent her from working diligently. The window in which she stood seemed to frame her face perfectly. I gazed at the woman as she worked until she looked out the window with excitement. She quickly left her position in front of the window to rush to the door to greet us.

The carriage bumped a few more times before we finally reached the front of the house. Percy brought the wagon to a smooth stop. I stepped down from the passenger's side of the carriage and waited patiently for Percy to invite me into his home. Percy swiftly stepped down from the driver's side of the wagon and quickly strolled around the front of the horses to greet his wife. As he moved closer to the porch on the front of the home, he beckoned to me to follow him. "Come in, Benjamin. Make yourself at home."

I smiled at Percy's wife and nodded slightly as to show respect. After this I moved toward the porch, trying to match Percy's speed. Percy's wife greeted me with, "Good day, sir."

I bowed graciously and said, "Hello, Mrs. Merivel. I am so honored to join your family for lunch this evening."

Mrs. Merivel looked at me with a sense of hospitality and said, "We are glad to have you for lunch, Mr. Price. Percy spoke highly of your visit, and I am sure that you will be pleased with the meal. Please come in and allow me to take your coat."

Percy turned to me and said, "Yes! Please come in, Benjamin. Have a seat anywhere that you like. You have had a long journey, and I am sure that you would like to relax for a moment."

I smiled with glee at the thought of resting somewhere besides a carriage or other mode of transportation.

"Would you like some water or a drink, Benjamin?" Percy's wife was standing just toward the kitchen, waiting for my response.

I thought for a moment and asked, "Could I have a glass of water please?" Percy's wife nodded and smiled, and I immediately followed this with, "Thank you, madam. I greatly appreciate the refreshment."

With this Percy's wife moved out of sight into the kitchen to bring me a glass of water. I sat for a moment on the bench just inside the door. I could feel the breeze coming in from the front door and wafting gently past me. There was a cool moisture hanging in each puff of wind, almost as if to let me know that the rain would begin momentarily.

Percy's home was clad in wood that had been hewn from the local trees. Everything had been placed neatly about the room. Each shelf held items that had been arranged in such a way as to appear as if no one had touched them for a long time. Everything seemed to have its place, and it stayed in that place. Especially the shelves of family heirlooms as well as the finer crockery that stay locked away in display cabinets. With the neatness of the room and cleanliness of everything in the room, it seemed as if everything had been staged. Almost as if this home was not lived in but occupied when Percy and his family needed to entertain guests. It was most unusual. Yet I welcomed the cleanliness of the home, the professional style of building, and the quality of the materials used to build the home. I could see that Percy's tidy personality was reflected in everything in this home. This was also enough for me to get the sense that Percy's wife was just as strict on cleanliness and tidiness. Though the most amazing aspect of the home was that everything seemed to follow a cozy country theme, almost as if to invite you to sit by the fire with a cup of coffee and talk about the day.

I felt a pleasant attraction to this home and felt completely comfortable. The final thing that I noticed was how the dining table had been set with precision. This was something that was a definite surprise. I did not expect to see such refinement in this home. It was the same style of setting that I would expect from a restaurant of the highest pedigree. This was a pleasant surprise. Upon viewing the room a second time, I was able to push my sight past the shock of the level of cleanliness. I noticed there were exquisite drawings and paintings on the walls. I could hardly believe that Percy or his wife would have created such fine art. Though some of the paintings, at least, seemed to be of family members that had passed on and other such ancestors. Even still, some of the drawings seemed to be of different properties or outlines of sculptures that had or had not been completed. I was completely fascinated even by this sight. One drawing, however, stood out to me. The drawing was of a bird sitting on a branch in what looked to be a pine tree. The detail of this drawing was amazing, and the colors were supremely vibrant.

Percy walked into the room and held the glass of water out to me. "Please have a seat at the table, Benjamin. We are almost ready to eat. Delilah is fetching the kids to come and eat."

I slowly moved to the table so as to not spill any water in my glass. Percy or his wife had filled the glass quite full. I sat in the middle seat of the side of the table closest to the door. Percy took his place in the seat across from me. I sipped on the water for a moment and felt instantly refreshed.

"Welcome to our home, Benjamin. I hope that you will enjoy your visit with us today."

I took another sip of water and replied, "Thank you, Percy. You have a beautiful home, and as I have told your wife, I am honored that you have invited me for lunch." Percy smiled.

"The honor is all ours, Benjamin. It is not every day that I get to have lunch with a member of Caroline's family. She often spoke of your mother, but she never told me anything about you."

I cleared my throat. "My aunt did not speak much of me. I fear that I did not have any time to visit her once I had come of age. After my mother passed away from consumption, I could not do anything but immerse myself in my studies and work. I tried to come see her for years, but my other responsibilities got in the way. I lost all contact with my aunt, but I regret to this day that I did not make more of an effort to visit her."

Percy leaned forward and looked me in the eyes. "Benjamin, your aunt loved you very much. She knew that you were busy. Do not regret that you could not make it here to see her before she passed. I know that she would not want that for you. Besides, you are getting everything that you deserve from your aunt. Surely you must realize that her home was the greatest gift that she possessed to give to anyone."

I looked into the glass of water that was now half empty for a moment. Percy picked up a pipe from the table beside him and began to pack it with tobacco. I subsequently looked up to meet Percy's eyes and said, "Thank you for your kind words. I appreciate them."

Percy smiled as he lit his pipe and breathed deeply. He exhaled and said, "You are most welcome, Benjamin."

At that moment, Mrs. Merivel emerged from the kitchen and said, "Lunch is ready. The kids should be in soon to sit. Do you have everything that you need, Benjamin?"

I nodded and said, "Thank you for the water, ma'am."

She smiled and said, "You're welcome, Mr. Price. I will bring out the food as soon as the children had sat for lunch."

Percy acknowledged her words with a quick "Thank you, dear."

Mrs. Merivel bowed slightly and returned to the kitchen.

I waited for Percy to stand from the table to help his wife, but he made no motion to move. He continued to puff away on his pipe. It was not long before the thudding of much smaller feet could be heard approaching from the bedrooms.

Mrs. Merivel emerged from the kitchen and sternly said, "Take your seats at the table! We have a guest with us today!"

Percy stood from his seat and greeted his son and daughter with a hug and a kiss. "Benjamin, this is my son, Jacob, and my daughter, Elizabeth. Say hello to Mr. Price, children."

Without hesitation, the children greeted me in a quite formal fashion. Then everyone took their seats at the table as we all heard, "Percy! Could you help me bring out the food to the table?" Percy stood from the table instantly and smiled. He then swiftly walked into the kitchen. It was not long before the food was being delivered to the table. Every dish was placed in a row down the middle of the table lengthwise. I was amazed that Percy's wife had prepared so much for me. I truly felt honored in their home.

It was not long before Percy and his wife took their seats at the table. Percy looked at each person sitting at the table before saying, "Let us say prayer." I bowed my head as I could hear Percy begin to pray. "Dear Lord, please bless this food, which you have gifted us. Thank you for the chance to gather with a new friend to share a meal on this blessed day. Please continue to bless our family and our guest with more days of happiness. Amen."

Mrs. Merivel looked at Percy and said, "That was lovely, dear." Percy nodded as if to say thank you, and everyone began to eat. The meal was laid out before everyone as if a chef had prepared the finest meal. I was about to partake in the sumptuous beef with stewed vegetables on the side. This was complimented with a glass of water, which tasted fresh as if from a local well. Each dish sat atop a lovely silk tablecloth that only the wealthiest would use for a simple lunch. I could see that I was indeed an important guest to the Merivels. The family seemed to have their discourse until I was abruptly brought into the conversation.

"Mr. Price, will you be attending the funeral tomorrow?"

I looked around somewhat puzzled. Everyone was looking at me as if waiting on bated breath to hear what I was about to say. I was shocked that a funeral for my aunt had not taken place sooner. I thought that she would have been placed in the ground much earlier. Yet I could understand if there was a preparation for the body that had to take place. I looked back to Mrs. Merivel and replied, "Yes, ma'am. I am going to the funeral tomorrow. I am unclear, however, as to what time the funeral will start."

Percy looked at me and said, "Don't worry about the funeral. I will come by the manor to take you to it."

I nodded and thanked Percy for his help. I once again looked at Mrs. Merivel and said, "Thank you for this meal. It's delicious."

She locked eyes with me, and I could see that she was pleasantly surprised. "Thank you, Mr. Price. I am glad that you are enjoying the meal. I must say that I was not sure that you would like such a simple meal compared to the food that you have eaten in New York."

I laughed graciously and, with all the passion I could muster, said,

"I have eaten many fine meals in New York, but none compare to this meal. Even in its simplicity."

Mrs. Merivel smiled and sheepishly accepted the compliment. We all ate our meal with vigor and slowly sipped our water as well.

After lunch, Percy and I went out onto the porch. I sat relaxed in a rocking chair toward the far edge of the porch. Percy sat closer to the door on my left. The rain had now begun to fall gently onto the roof of the house. Percy sat smoking his pipe, and we both sipped sweet tea while taking in the beauty of the world around us. The humidity didn't seem to be quite as strong now that the rain had begun to fall.

Percy and I began conversing about the recent developments in Hillsborough. Percy spoke on and on about the new routes that had sprung up to transport trees from the area toward the rest of the state. Percy told me about a project that had been devised to bring North Carolina to the forefront of modern advancement. Percy also told me about the social unrest that had started to flourish in the area because of the alienation that the federal government had brought about in the South. No one had wanted to be subjected to such a weakening of governance that North Carolina had over itself. There was even mention of "carpet baggers," people who had come to the area to take advantage of the farmers and try to sell goods. I got the sense that Northerners were not as welcome here as I had once thought.

We continued to converse for a while longer as Percy smoked the contents of his pipe. He had, indeed, smoked so long that the tobacco had turned to ash. Then Percy set his pipe on the table to his left and said, "Well, Benjamin, we must be on the road again if we are to reach the manor and get you settled before the rain becomes worse. I will also stay for a bit and help you to unpack your things and show you around the house."

"Thank you, Percy. I would greatly appreciate your help. Do you think that the rains will be even harsher tonight?"

Percy thought for a moment and looked toward the sky. "I reckon not, Mr. Price, but I can guarantee that the house will protect you from any amount of rainfall. That is one item of your aunt's things that was well taken care of with pride. Your aunt valued that house above anything else, but not through obsession that some might think."

I nodded to Percy and stood from the chair.

"Come, Benjamin, let us be on our way to the manor. Give me a moment to fetch the wagon from the barn. Wait here and I will return shortly."

I nodded again, and Percy left the porch and walked around the house. I stood there on the porch just outside the front door for a bit, looking at the pleasant yard decorations. I could also smell food being prepared in the kitchen. I could not imagine how many crops one would have to grow in order to amass such an air of wealth.

As I stood there viewing the yard, I could hear a slight rumbling noise as the wagon approached the porch. I watched as Percy drove the wagon closer and closer to the porch. It was not long before he had pulled the wagon up in front of me and was beckoning to me to get onto the seat. Briefly, I thought about my overcoat that had been packed into my luggage. I also wished that I had brought my hat. Still, I could not gain access to my luggage while it was in the manor and not in the wagon anymore. I assumed my place on the passenger's side of the seat. The horses that would pull the wagon bayed and shifted their stance as to prepare for the journey. Percy sat searching the sky for any darkened clouds that might suggest heavy rain. He looked back at me and then popped the reins against the horses. Instantly the horses began to slowly pull the wagon down the drive and back toward the road.

Percy leaned in my direction and said, "Hopefully with what little rainfall we have had, the roads will not be muddy. I don't relish the idea of getting stuck in the road with rain pouring down."

I pulled my watch and gazed into its face. The time read two hours past midday, and I hoped that I could make it to the manor house with enough time to settle in for the night. I did not have a terrible amount of things to do, but I did need to make sure that my clothes were put away and that the home was closed up for the inclement weather. Percy snapped tightly on the reins of the horse and drove it onto the main road. I watched as Percy's home and the property that held so many pleasant comforts faded into the forest and we were once again moving toward the manor. The sky looked like a fog that sat high above us and shrouded the sun from sight. I could see the trees waft in the wind ever slightly as we turned onto the main road. The wagon bumped and creaked a little as it drove over the ruts in the road. However, once we had completed our turn, the road smoothed and we rolled on toward the manor.

I did not envision what might occur once I got to the manor house, but I knew that the rest would be most welcomed. I had been traveling for two days without much pause at all. I just hoped that even if the rains fell, I would be able to get some much-needed rest. Percy had been right when he stated that my aunt cared the most for her home and above all else sought to keep the house in much the same condition as when she had the house built. Though the house stood vacant for a few days, I had come to expect it to be as spotless as when my aunt lived in the house. I would settle in for the night in the most relaxed manner possible and, upon my awakening in the morning, would prepare for the funeral. I did not know if anyone at the funeral would recognize me or if I would be a stranger at the gathering, but I had to see my aunt off one last time. I did, however, welcome the opportunity to meet everyone that was important to my aunt's life and those of my family that I had yet to meet.

I sat thinking about all that I might experience tomorrow as the wind whipped up and brushed swiftly over the wagon. I felt a chill pass through me, unlike any chill that I had previously felt. Percy looked again at the sky and exclaimed, "I think we will be able to beat this storm to the house!" I nodded. The wagon bumped and creaked a little as we passed over the small hill that was in between the manor and Percy's home. Percy seemed to notice the nervousness with which I embraced the thought of staying in the manor in such a storm tonight.

"Don't worry, Benjamin, you will be able to rest tonight peacefully and without any worries." Just as Percy had finished his statement, the wagon had begun to be turned onto the drive to the manor. It was not long before the wagon was approaching the manor. "Well, Benjamin, welcome back to Caroline's manor."

Once again I took in the beauty of the manor and the surrounding property. It was now that I could notice the colors of the home. The windows were all trimmed with black with the main wood paneling on the outside of the home white. Alabaster columns ran from the ground up to support the balcony above. Only what seemed like a thin layer of boards separated the tops of the columns from the black iron railing that ran along the front of the balcony. Beautiful rose bushes seemed to flank each side of the front of the manor. The reds of the roses seemed to stand out from and frame the front of the home. I could not believe that I had not noticed this before. I was rushing to drop my luggage in the foyer of the home and perhaps just didn't notice. Still, I felt confused as I noticed these details of the home.

Percy approached me from behind and instantly said, "Beautiful, isn't it?" I nodded, still keeping my gaze on the home itself so as to take in everything about the manor. I did feel, however, that it would be impossible to take it all in as the manor was immense. The home seemed to tower over the trees even. I could not imagine living in such an opulent and immense manor home.

Percy and I approached the home and stepped inside. I was amazed at the level of attention that was paid to keeping the home in mint condition. Immediately after entering the home, I was met with a large flowing staircase. The wood seemed to be pine that was well-finished. The sheen of the wood on the steps contrasted with the white posts and frame of the stairs perfectly. Each side of the stairs tapered off into other rooms. Though I could not see anything beyond that point, I could imagine how large these rooms were given the size of the house. The top of the stairs seemed to flow into an upper balcony that was just as lavish as the rest of the home. The walls were painted with a mild white color. Every so often there was a table or drawer set that broke up the room. As I walked around the home with Percy, each room seemed to follow the same theme of colors. It seemed as if my aunt had hired someone to decorate her home in such a professional manner. I felt almost as if I had been invited to stay in a hotel more than a home. I was pleasantly surprised. Yet I could not figure out how the home had stayed in such a beautiful state.

Moving from room to room, Percy explained about each room and for what it was used. I could not believe that there were this many rooms in a home, even one such as this. Every room seemed just as cozy as the last. Each one held an intimacy to them as if being designed for hotel guests. Eventually, Percy and I returned to the main floor and walked toward the back of the home. Just across from the kitchen, there was the main sitting room. I could not believe the size and opulence of the room. On the right side of the room set a fireplace. The opening was rather large and held an equally large basket for the wood to rest upon. The outside of the fireplace was all brick that had been framed with wood. It was as if the builder wished for this feature to be the focal point of the room, yet all the furniture was turned to face toward the door. The mantel of the fireplace was quite wide and seemed to have been polished and taken care of frequently. I could neither see a speck of dust nor see any wear and tear.

Percy caught me staring at the fireplace and assured me that this was the main heat source for the home as well as a second fireplace in the kitchen. I found this to be odd as there were many more rooms than it seemed two fireplaces could heat. On each side of the mantel, there set candle holders that still held their candles. Though it seemed that the candles themselves were replaced recently as they showed no signs of having been burned. If I had not known that my aunt had passed away, I would have sworn that she still inhabited the home. I had imagined the home to be rather dusty and unkempt. My aunt had been sick for years without relent, but her home looked as if she had never fallen ill.

I looked at Percy and said, "Percy, did anyone come to the house to take care of the property while my aunt was sick?"

Percy replied, "Yes, Benjamin. I came by weekly to clean and maintain the house and its property while your aunt was bedridden. I was amazed myself that the manor was in such spotless condition even when I started cleaning. Your aunt had an impressive talent for maintaining her home even when she was well enough to do so. Though I must admit, sometimes I pondered if there had been some sort of magic that had been keeping the home in such good repair."

I gave an expression of understanding but clearly did not have an explanation for the state of the home.

Percy continued, "I have not been to the home for a few months, though, so I am surprised just as you are that it is in such magnificent condition." Percy stepped into the sitting room and picked up a candle holder to light the candle held in its tray. "Follow me, Benjamin. We will place your things upstairs in the master bedroom."

I thought for a moment and decided against this. I did not wish to be too far from the sitting room and the kitchen if there were no other guests in the home. "If it is not too much trouble, Percy, I would like to stay in the bedroom just behind the sitting room."

Percy seemed relieved and replied, "Very well. I hope that every-thing will be comfortable for you in that room."

I nodded and we moved just down the hall and into the smaller bedroom. "This was one of the servant's rooms. I believe it was the kitchen maid. Ms. Helen was an amazing cook and stewardess of the manor. I loved her dearly, and she always had the kindest of words to say." With those words, Percy opened the curtains to the room and placed the candle holder on the desk just inside the door. We then moved hastily back to the foyer to collect my belongings.

With my luggage in hand, Percy and I made our way back to the small bedroom just behind the sitting room. We set the bags against the far wall of the room. I relayed to Percy that I appreciated his help with my luggage, and he sauntered back into the hallway. I had then moved to the doorway when Percy turned to me and said, "I will tell you that the room at the end of this hallway is locked. I am not sure where the key to the door is, and your aunt never would allow anyone to enter the room or even see the keys. I am not sure why this was. Even the servants weren't sure. So...I just wouldn't go near that room if I were you. There is no telling how to get the door open or what would be in there after all this time. I am just bringing this to your attention in case you were thinking to explore the home."

I acknowledged Percy's words with a nod and continued to move into the hallway. Percy then led me into the kitchen at which time he stated, "There is no food in the pantry anymore. I will bring you something by in the morning if that is all right with you?"

I nodded and replied, "Thank you, Percy. That shall be just fine. What about water?"

Percy looked stunned at this question and said, "You will have to bring some water in from the well. I am sorry, Benjamin. I completely forgot to bring any water in for you."

I held my hand up as a smile graced my face and replied, "That is quite all right, Percy. I am sure that I can manage. Thank you for all your help and your family's as well."

Percy nodded and then finished with, "I believe then that you are settled. It has been wonderful to meet you, Benjamin. I hope that you rest well tonight."

I thanked him once again as I followed him back toward the front door. Time seemed to pass quickly as Percy opened the front door to the manor and vanished into the world. I shut the door behind him and turned to take in the splendor of the manor. It was all that I could do to wonder how many people had stayed in this immaculate home. It would have been intriguing to know the sheer number of people that had come and gone from these walls over my aunt's lifetime. Though now it was only myself that would inhabit this home, even if for a short time. It was in this moment that I found my gaze had moved toward the room down the hall. Curiosity seemed to be getting the better of me, and I could not help but wonder what secrets could be held within that room. I had a strange feeling wash over me just then. I began to feel a strange pull to walk into the room. I felt as if I could not stop myself from approaching the door and opening it. Before I could come to my senses, I had walked down the hall and was now standing in front of the door. It was almost as if I knew that the door was not locked and the door would simply swing open if I just pushed. I began to reach my hand outward slowly toward the lock. All other sounds had flooded away from the home. There was only me now. Nothing else mattered. I felt as if my only purpose in life was to open this door and find out what was inside. No matter how much I tried to resist these actions, I could not. Like some other-worldly force had begun pulling me to the room and demanding that I open said door.

As soon as I had begun to catch on to what was happening, I heard a loud bang. *Bang! Bang! Bang!* Each bang was followed by a sound that could only be described as metal scraping against metal. I immediately snapped back into reality. The sound had startled me so that my heart was now racing. I backed away from the door and looked to my right where the sound had emanated. I could see that the screen door to the back porch was swinging wildly back and forth. Wind raged and howled outside, though with the actual door closed, it seemed quieter. I took one last look at the door and then moved to the back door at the end of the hallway. I then secured the screen door. I could see the well standing in the backyard. I knew that I had better bring in a bucket of water for the night as it had grown late and the storm was beginning.

I pulled the bucket up from the side of the well by its rope. I then held the bucket out over the opening for the well and began to crank the wheel. The bucket slowly lowered into the opening and was well on its way to being filled. As I turned the wheel again and again, I could feel the home behind me. It was the same feeling that one would get when someone walked up behind you. It was an intimidating feeling. almost as if some sinister person was waiting for me to turn around and be frightened by the sight of them. I couldn't shake the feeling. Each turn of the wheel brought the feeling into a state of increasing intensity. The feeling continued to grow until it consumed my senses. It was so strong, in fact, that I almost missed the sound of the bucket reaching the surface of the water below. Everything in me compelled me to turn and face whatever it was or whoever was giving out this feeling. I chose, however, to ignore it. I instead continued to crank the wheel in the opposite direction. Immediately I concentrated on the sound of the bucket returning to the surface. I did not wish to spill its contents. Yet I could still feel this sense of dread from behind me growing. One part of me wished to turn around, but the other feared anything that I might gaze upon. It was all that I could do to not entertain notions of some creature stalking me from behind or watching me from a window in the manor. My mind was racing with thoughts of what could be causing this. Even scarier still, I wondered what it was that I shared a space within this home. In either case, I decided to turn the wheel faster in order to finally reach a resolution. It was not long before the bucket poked out from over the side of the well. I could see my prize resting within. I quickly secured the crank arm of the wheel and pulled the bucket over to me. With all the grace and swiftness in me, I detached the rope from the handle of the bucket and turned to face the back of the home. Instantly the sense of dread and of being watched dissipated. I looked all over the back side of the home and could not see anyone or anything that could have caused such a feeling. I found myself paused there just beside the well as if waiting for anyone to show themselves. Though I indeed feared what else may reveal itself.

Once I had gained my composure, I began walking slowly back to the manor house. I still watched for any movement but hoped that I would find none. It was all that I could do to keep walking toward the home. My mind had now been relieved of the stress that I had just felt. I quickly but steadily moved into the home through the back door and down the hallway. I slowly rounded the doorway into the kitchen and placed the bucket on a table beside the fireplace. I then returned to secure the screen door and closed the back door to the home.

I immediately returned to the kitchen and began looking for a pitcher to pour some of the water into. Cupboard after cupboard, I searched the whole kitchen for a pitcher. Eventually, I settled on a slightly smaller carafe. I was amazed upon checking over the carafe. There was no dust of any kind. It seemed as if someone had just washed each dish in the cupboard. I wondered if this was one of the rooms most cleaned by Percy when he would visit the home. Everything here was spotless save for the soot that lingered inside the fireplace. I then noticed that every item was in its place, left to its place in time, frozen as if no one would ever disturb their final resting places. Even the pots were still lingering on the hangers in the fireplace. Even the iron of the pots and hangers had been wiped clean. If Percy had indeed cleaned this kitchen, he was extremely thorough. I was utterly amazed.

A crack of thunder rang out from outside the home and jolted my mind into refocusing on the task at hand. I placed the carafe beside the bucket of water and began to use the bucket to pour the water into the carafe. The water seemed so clear and pure. It had been a long time since I had had the pleasure of tasting the cool and refreshing water from the well.

Once I had returned to my room with the carafe, I knew the only thing left to do was to jar the window open. The room had now become unbearable because of the humidity. I knew there was no way that I would be able to sleep in such a room. I hoped that the storm raging outside would have stirred up the wind to cool the room. Though I also worried that the rain would flood through the window through the night and begin to rot the wood of the room. It was all that I could do to settle in after such a long journey. I could feel my will to do anything but rest begin to slip away. I used that time to prepare my room but ultimately found myself being drawn into the sitting room. I gently opened the window to allow for the breeze to enter the home in a different location. The last candle holder from the mantel had been lit, and I was enjoying my thoughts for a moment. I thought about everything that had occurred during my trip and how it seemed that something did not want me to arrive safely. It was almost as if a force had been pushing me to stay away from the home.

My mind drifted from thought to thought for a moment until I realized that I should simply forget all these events. I had traveled for a long time, and I was likely sleep deprived. That must be it! I thought. I must be so tired from my journey that my mind had been fabricating events to keep itself alert and functioning. After all, there was no possible way that these events could be real. I also realized that I had not slept well in a long while even before my journey. I chuckled about this for a moment and then decided that I had nothing to fear. I would go into my room and collect my book so that I could pass some time reading before I finally turned in for the night. Reading would help my mind settle and my imagination be satiated so that I could rest tonight. That is really what I needed. I walked into my room and retrieved my book. Subsequently, I returned to the sitting room and began reading. It was this moment that gave me the understanding to know that I would deal with anything. After all, ghosts and demons do not exist. I kept that thought in my mind as I continued to read.

Time seemed to pass quickly now as I noticed that the sun was beginning to fade. Though the storm completely covered the sun, now the world grew darker every minute. I closed my book and gently placed it on the table beside the chair that I had sat upon. I closed the window and slowly trudged toward the doorway. My mind could no longer process anything at this point. I rubbed my eyes to alleviate myself of the tired feeling in my eyes. As I rounded the frame of the doorway and entered the hallway, I could see that the room at the end of the hall was open. I immediately froze where I stood. I hadn't even heard the sound of the door opening. I thought about the possibility that Percy could have been mistaken about the door being locked. Though I had never tested this theory by trying the lock. I began to think that perhaps someone else could be in the manor. I walked a little closer until I was standing directly beside the door to my room. I gazed down the hallway at the now-opened door. I refused to move my gaze from the door. I immediately began looking around. I walked through the kitchen, checking for anywhere that someone could hide. I found nothing. Everywhere in the home that I looked yielded no answers as to who could have opened the door. I checked every corner of the downstairs of the manor. Nothing was out of place. There was no sign that someone had entered the home. Furthermore, I peered down the hallway and noticed that the door to the sitting room was in such a position that no one could have sneaked past without me noticing them.

The thought then occurred to me that I should enter the room and check for anyone that could have opened the door. Perhaps someone lived nearby and had returned for an item they had left. That is of course if they wished to brave the weather. I refused to believe that anyone would travel through a storm to simply retrieve something. It was then that I paused. I was apprehensive at the thought of no one else being in the home. I did not wish to take a step anywhere near that door. I moved quickly back to my original position outside the door to my room. I simply stood there studying the door, as if waiting for someone to close it.

Eventually, I decided to make my way into my room and close the door. I had no desire to be involved with the room or its door. I turned and walked into my room, shutting the door behind me. A crash of thunder boomed outside, and for a moment the room was illuminated. I was startled not only by the opened door but also by the thunder. The more disturbing notion that I did not wish to entertain was the thought that there still could be someone else in the manor. It was at this moment that I began to compose myself. Rational thought dictated that I simply bar the door and go to sleep. I slid the chair from the desk and propped it up just under the knob of the door. No one would be entering the room as I slept tonight. I approached my luggage and began pulling my clothes for the next day out. I searched through almost every pocket and opening in my luggage to pick the proper attire. After all, I did not wish to draw attention at a funeral. I focused myself solely on what I was doing and seemed to be easing my mind. I now felt as though I were safe here in this modest room. I placed my clothes in proper fashion on the desk in the room and then poured a cup of water. Silence crept back into the room as I sat on the bed and slowly sipped the water down. It seemed that peace would be prevalent tonight.

As I began to feel sleep beginning to take me, I heard the most dreadful sound, a sound that could only disturb the inner depths of a man. Even the most rational of people would cringe at the terror of it.

The gnawing feeling of dread rose in me. I heard the terrible creaking of the door to the room down the hall slowly closing. I thought of checking the hall for anyone who might be present in the hallway, but after checking my watch, I was deterred. The time was ten o'clock, and there was no chance that anyone would be out in a raging storm at ten o'clock. I sat listening for a moment, realizing that the creaking had stopped. I did not hear the door close. It was most disturbing to think that someone could be standing in the doorway to the room simply staring at my door. Waiting for the chance to terrify me. I quickly scrambled to gain control of my mind. I was running from all sanity. It simply could be that the door was opened by the wind. Perhaps it was a faulty doorjamb and Percy had been mistaken about the door being locked. Just as this thought had crossed my mind, the door slammed with unnatural force. The sound echoed through the home. It seemed that someone was indeed in the manor with me. I instantly jumped to my feet and gazed at the door in amazement. I could not know what course of action to take. I was simply waiting for my date to present itself.

I slinked back to the bed and began removing the outer portions of my suit. It seemed that I had now abandoned all reason. I was simply poking my clothes on the floor while staring intensively at the door. I tried to make all my motions undetectable by anyone that might be in the home. I quietly lifted the cover and the sheet and slid into the bed. I now lay in the bed, listening to the rain pour down outside the window. I waited for some time to hear the next sounds of life in the home. Everything in me screamed for me to simply go to sleep. Yet there was a small portion that begged to know what had made those sounds. Dark thoughts began to swirl in my mind. I tried as hard as anyone would to drown out my thoughts. Fear had now set into the night as the wind and rain pounded the manor, the sounds of lightning sporadically cracking in the background. In this moment it seemed the whole world was ending.

In the end, the rain calmed my nerves. I loved to hear the rain, and it seemed comforting given all the stress that I had experienced. I lay there for some time slowly drifting off to sleep. I heard the thunder crash and boom outside. I felt only comfort in this cozy bed, however. I thought only of happier times, my fondest memories of studying in New York City, and the friends that I had met. I chuckled at all the times that I had to stretch the money that I earned to pay for my coursework. All the interesting hijinks that I had partaken in to gain money. How I would work myself to the bone every day and try my best to be in the lecture hall on time. I had little money, but I managed to afford paper enough to form collections of my favorite stories—stories that I wrote down from periodicals and newspapers. Sometimes it was as simple as writing down a funny headline. I lay there thinking a little more and then turned in for the night amid the swelling winds and pounding rain.

4

MEETING AT A FUNERAL

The clock ticked away on the table beside my bed. I awoke and rolled over to look at the clock. I had awakened two hours before sunrise at which time Percy would be by to take me to the funeral. I rushed to get out of bed and prepare my clothing before leaving. I walked to the desk in my room and began to put on my clothes. I made sure that I was not unclean or had a foul odor as I dressed. Unfortunately, I did not have the time to bathe. I had prepared a suit just for today. I put my suit on with ease and quicker than I could have ever anticipated. The coat that I had chosen was not as high quality as I would wear to meet with clients, but was fine enough for Caroline's funeral. The shirt was as white as snow and would contrast the black of the pants. I also laid out a bolo tie. I smoothed out any creases that I could see in the fabric and straightened my tie.

The room was very dark, but there was a flood of moonlight that lit the room with a white haze. In any case, I was able to see what I needed to do. I walked cautiously to the other side of the table where I had placed the candle holder last night. I pulled a match from the box and lit it against the table. The candlelit vigorously as if it had waited all night to radiate its light.

Once I had lit the candle, I held it a little higher to radiate the light toward the door. Nothing seemed out of place save for the chair that braced the door shut, of course. I had worried that as I finally fell into my deep sleep, something might bother the door in the night. I was overjoyed to see that I was wrong. I walked to the door and gently unlocked the lock and pushed the door open. I held the candle out of the doorway and peered in both directions in the hallway. Once again nothing was out of place. The door to the room at the end of the hall now remained closed just as it should have in the night. I chuckled at the thought that I was unsettled enough to believe that it had opened last night and shut loudly. After all, who would have opened or closed the door? I gained a new confidence in my own sanity at the sight of nothing having changed while I was asleep.

I walked out into the hallway and started toward the kitchen. My mind was still focused on my surroundings. I had half expected to see something that I could not unsee. Even a sound that I could not place, but nothing. I continued into the kitchen and checked to make sure the water bucket still held its contents. It would be an unfortunate development if the bucket had been turned over. Though I would not be able to understand how this would happen. It was much too early for the sun to rise over the horizon, but the view from the kitchen window was otherworldly. The moon caused the trees to dance in shadow as though there were children playing in a never-ending playground. I could see, however, that everything was still drenched from the rains last night. The storm did not seem to topple trees or leave a lasting mark. I was relieved as I had entertained the notion that a tree might block the road. This would greatly delay our arrival to the funeral.

I left the window and walked farther into the kitchen. It was then that I remembered that I would need to stock the kitchen with what food I could. Yet I did not know how I would. Perhaps Percy would know of a market in the area. I knew that my issue was not money, just the ability or place to obtain the food that I needed. I walked back into the sitting room to watch the sunrise over the fields beside the home. I was feeling a slight pang of hunger but knew that Percy would bring something for me to eat before the funeral. As I sat there, I began wondering about the door down the hall. It seemed that nothing could tear my mind away from that awful door. It was as if the door itself haunted me. I worried that the door lock as well as the hinges might be failing and what it might cost to fix. Surely, with all the care that Caroline had put into the home, there would not be so much as a light draft. I didn't wish to lose money on a home that I did not even have any plans to reside in. No one would invest in a house that had such a terrible issue. My mind quickly considered the possibility that I might be here longer than two weeks. I did hope that selling the home would not turn into a massive headache, which I did not need.

The sun rose steadily above the horizon as I drifted in and out of thought. I knew that Percy would arrive at any time. I thought about how much stranger it was that the house seemed to have a darker side after the sun had begun to decline. During the day, however, the house seemed to not hold any darkness whatsoever. I could not understand how such a magnificent house seemed so gloomy. None of these thoughts mattered, however. This house was just that— simply a house. I would not allow myself to be bothered by the sinister thoughts of this house harboring a dark spirit or other evil things. After all, those were just stories that church ministers told to their attendees on Sunday mornings to keep them faithful. Campfires were made that much more interesting with such stories. Yet nothing such as this could or would exist in this home. I laughed to myself at the thought that something inhabited the house with me.

I stood from the chair and walked to the front door. I peered out just as the sun had slowly begun to break through the trees. Percy's timing was flawless as I could see him riding his wagon from the window. Percy's family all seemed dressed for the occasion as well. Everyone bounced with the wagon over a few humps in the road. Sunrays glinted onto the wagon and seemed to give Percy an angelic appearance. I retreated into the manor to retrieve my coat. I quickly placed the coat over my shoulders and raced out of the front door to greet Percy and his family. I closed and locked the door behind me then placed the key into my breast pocket. I checked my pocket watch to see that it was now 6:45 a.m. This was apparent by the chill that hung in the air.

As the sun continued to climb over the final tips of the trees, I could tell that this day would be clear and without such violent storms. The sky was clear and only a few small clouds dotted the beautiful Carolina sky. Everything seemed perfect for travel back into town, which I hoped would be uneventful. I could see that the wagon had reached the beginning of the drive and begun its turn toward the manor. I stood on the edge of the porch waiting. It was not long before the grinding of the wheels could be heard above all else.

Percy yelled out a greeting, and I returned it. "How are you this fine morning, Benjamin?"

I waved and replied, "I am fine, thank you. How are you and your family?"

The wagon was now grinding to a halt as Percy turned to look at his family. He chuckled and replied, "We are all just fine this morning. Are you ready to leave?"

I nodded and climbed into the passenger's seat on the wagon. I turned and greeted Percy's family with a smile and was met with many smiles. With a quick popping sound, the wagon was off again. I was fortunate to know someone such as Percy. It was nice to know that I would have a contact in the area that could help me to get around. Just then I saw a hand protrude from my left side holding a muffin. I turned to see Percy's daughter looking back at me. "Mother made this for ya. We hope you like it!"

I nodded and smiled and replied, "Thank you, miss. I am sure that it is delicious." I took the muffin and smiled again. I turned forward again and began to eat the muffin. It was sweet yet savory. I could tell that Percy's wife was an accomplished baker as well as a chef. The bread of the muffin was moist and still slightly warm. I could taste the poppy seeds amid the sweetness of the muffin itself. It was by far the most delicious thing that I had eaten in a long time. I was amazed but quite satisfied to eat something so delicious.

"I am sorry for your loss, Benjamin. I hope that you will be able to find peace with your aunt's death while you're here."

I looked toward the ground that was racing by underneath the wagon. "That is quite all right, Percy. My aunt lived a full life. I am just thankful that I was able to spend time with her when I was younger. It would have been harder if I had witnessed her decline in health."

Percy and his family seemed to all understand my words completely. It was as if they collectively sighed with melancholy. Percy drove the horses onward slowly over a bumpy turn in the road. "I would like to extend an offer of lunch and dinner at our house today if you feel up to it," Percy said sincerely.

I thought for a moment and happily answered, "I would like that. If it wouldn't be too much trouble."

Percy chuckled and added, "Not at all, Benjamin."

We rode back into the forest that separated Percy's home from town. I watched as the sun rose higher into the trees. Light flooded through the forest as the glow of greens and browns could be seen illuminating everything. In certain places you could see beautiful rays that illuminated each side of the rows of trees that stood thick in the forest. The light bounced to and fro as if playing in this endless sea of forest. I could see that the light was welcomed by a plethora of animals within the forest, mainly squirrels, but with a few deer and a rather large selection of birds. A slight mist veiled the forest floor. Leaves and bushes alike were slightly obscured by this hazy vapor. The forest seemed to be enchanted with magic rarely seen by humankind. Rain droplets would sometimes drip from one leaf to another leaf below. I could not imagine a more complete and peaceful sight.

As I sat there watching this most wonderful sight, Percy drove the wagon farther toward town. We all seemed to sit in anticipation of what the funeral might bring. The apprehension seemed to hang thick in the air. It was a dreadful feeling of not knowing what would happen upon arriving at the funeral. It was not long before the wagon had approached the connecting road into town. I was not much farther to town for the funeral. The farther we rode, the more tensions hung thick in the air.

I looked toward Percy and asked, "Do you know where my aunt will be buried after the funeral?"

Percy thought for a moment and replied, "She will be buried in the town cemetery. It isn't far from the funeral parlor."

I acknowledged Percy's words with a nod and continued, "Why is it that she did not wish to have her funeral in her home?"

Percy looked at me quickly with the strangest look on his face. "I am not sure. I have often asked that question myself. She seemed to have a fear of the idea when anyone would ask. She seemed to also be irritated about it when anyone would ask." I looked puzzled for a moment. Percy continued, "That is the same look that I had when I was told of the arrangements for her funeral. Though I do know that her plot in the cemetery is near to some of her family and friends." Percy's words comforted me if only for a moment. At least she had planned to be interred with others that she would have known in life. Though it was only a resting place. It was not as if she would be visiting these people and having parties. I chuckled for a moment at this thought.

Ahead I could see the back side of the building that Percy and I had passed when I had arrived yesterday. It was not much farther from the funeral parlor. I continued to think about my aunt and the life that she had lived. I could see why she settled in Hillsborough. The town was rustic and lacking in many amenities, but the surroundings more than made up for this fact. The forests and meadows were so captivating. Flowers grew everywhere. Trees stood tall and imposing against a sun-filled sky of azure. Animals were seeming to enjoy life, running as far as they wished, and the only sounds in the area were those of farm animals baying. Her life had been filled with peace and contentment. I just knew that these reasons were chief in her decision to settle where she did. I had longed for this as well—to escape the cities for some time and relax in a remote location, where my only company was wild animals and visitors were often hungry squirrels or birds. Life seemed to be so peaceful and relaxed. Though it wouldn't be a life that I would wish for forever. I did feel the pull of the hustle and bustle of New York City. Though now I would receive this gift of a vacation. Even if I had not planned for this getaway, I welcomed the chance for a change of scenery.

The wagon bumped along as we entered the town and turned to the right to enter the main street. The road seemed to be less rough now that some of the surfaces had washed out to the outer edges. I no longer felt as if I were riding an enraged bull through the streets of a forgotten wasteland town. Once we had entered the town completely and begun riding down the street, the townsfolk could be seen wandering about. At first glance, it seemed that everyone had come for the funeral, but that quickly changed. The townsfolk wandered about from one side of the street to the other. Though there were not great numbers of pedestrians as I have been used to in New York City. Still, there seemed to be a number of people gathering. I just had to wonder why people would be wandering about in what seemed like a lifeless town. Though I had to admit to myself that I had not seen the majority of the town. I welcomed the idea of seeing a vibrant selection of different markets and shops. This would be beneficial to know given that I was staying alone in a home with no food or supplies. Though I also wished for the non-necessary items such as clothing and other such items.

We continued to drive deeper into the town as smells of baked goods and roasting meats began to fill the air. I could instantly feel my mouth water. Surely this town contained an inn that would serve such delicious-smelling foods. There was also the occasional sound of pinging metal. I could clearly hear blacksmiths plying their trades as the sounds of hammers on metal began to grow louder and louder. These sounds and smells instantly transported me to a time long ago when I was a child. I could remember hearing the workers building things around the manor property. It was the smells that I seemed to remember most, the smell of bacon and sausages as well as delicious breads and stews. It was all that I could do as a child to not wish to try it all. The desserts were of utmost importance in my mind, however. I remember the cakes and delicious pastries that the chefs would make in the kitchen of the manor, especially a cake that was my favorite. A crunch cake was the most delicious. I had never and will never taste a dessert of such amazing decadence. The cake was chocolatey and creamy with a crunch at the bottom. It was delicious.

The cart rode over a large hole in the road, and my mind snapped back into reality. I was once again faced with the reality of the funeral. I was anxious to meet anyone that had been associated with my aunt. I did not know of any family besides her that would live in this area. Though I had not visited the area since my childhood. I just knew that I no longer had any family or relatives in the north. In all actuality, I have been alone for some time. This was not to say that I have been lonely or miserable in any way, but merely that life had chosen for me to not know or meet any extended family. Since my mother had grown terribly ill and passed, I had not had the ability to meet anyone from my family. Surely my aunt would have had children. Though I did not remember any other children in her home when I would visit. These thoughts still left me with questions about whom I would meet or if they would share the same optimism about meeting distant family as well. This all served to increase my anxiety about the funeral. It did not matter, however, as soon I would see my hypothesis proven right or wrong.

Percy stopped the wagon beside a building down from the funeral parlor. The building seemed to glow in the morning sunlight. The timbers that fashioned the siding of the funeral parlor also seemed to glow with a faint moisture that clung to the siding. It was an interesting sight to be sure, almost as of a sign from God himself. Percy and I stepped down from the seat of the wagon and began helping the rest of the family out of the wagon. As I had begun to move about, trying to collect the children and help them from the wagon, I could feel the mud squish under my feet. It seemed that the center of the road was still quite firm, but the mud had all gathered along the edges. This pained me greatly as I knew that the bottom of my shoes would be covered in this thick mud. In the end, it would not matter, however. Surely there would be others that would be in the same situation.

Percy and I walked briskly toward the funeral parlor. Percy's family followed us in the same swift manner. It was as if we were a procession of our own. This impressed me as I could feel that Percy and his family were all so close. They almost seemed to function as one. I had longed for such a family in my younger years but chose instead to further my own career above all else. We all walked up the steps and slowly entered the funeral building. The whole room was filled with people. There were beautiful flowers all around the room. Though much of the decorations were obscured by the people that seemed to obscure everything. Percy led his family to an open pew to the left of the coffin. I followed but would ultimately sit the farthest from the coffin in the middle of the room. The funeral hall was very nicely decorated otherwise as well. The walls seemed to be covered in scenes of heaven as well as God and Jesus. From where I had sat, I could not tell if these were paintings on the wall or had been painted onto the surface of the wall itself. I was impressed with the level of detail as well. The flowers also seemed to be placed around the room so as to flank each of these artworks.

The other side of the hall from me contained the coffin that was now covered in flowers. I could see flowers of all white adorning the casket, which was closed. I thought this to be very strange as I had thought that my aunt was well enough to be viewed. Though it had been several days since she had passed. Perhaps the mortician was not able to properly preserve the body. Whatever the case, Caroline's funeral was beautiful in every way. Even in the faces of the people that had arrived, I could tell that she was much loved within the community.

I turned to Percy and asked, "Are any of these people related to my aunt?"

Percy looked around the room slowly and then replied, "Some I am not sure about. But most are families of people that worked with Caroline. As I said before, she was a valued member of our community. Everyone loved Caroline like their own mother."

I let Percy's words sink in. Things are often said differently in words, but when seen with your own eyes, it is another matter entirely. I was in disbelief that this many people would have come to revere my aunt. Perhaps I was wrong in assuming that this town held few people and even fewer that would have cared about my aunt. I was touched in a lot of ways. Percy and his family began talking among themselves as I continued to take in my surroundings. It was not long before the minister had made his way into the room and had begun conversing with the others in the room. I could tell readily that this minister was from the only church in town. I had wondered if my aunt had been to church at all in her life. I always found it odd that we did not visit the church at any time when I visited Hillsborough as a child. The more that I sat in the pew thinking about my past, I felt regret begin to surge within myself. My regrets, however, did not matter at this point in time. I was more appropriate to see my aunt off into the ether of eternity without regret.

The minister had slowly begun to work his way to the front of the room, but it seemed inevitable that he would say hello to Percy and his family. Percy leaned over and spoke emphatically, "Benjamin. Would you be willing to say a few words?" I shook my head slightly so as to not accept his offer.

"I wouldn't feel right to say anything. I have not seen my aunt in a long time."

Percy smiled and nodded. I knew that he wouldn't push the issue, but I wondered if the minister would feel the same. Just as this thought passed from my mind, the minister tapped me on my shoulder and I turned to face him.

"Good morning, sir! I haven't seen you in town before. You are...?"

I smiled and shook his hand and replied, "My name is Benjamin, sir! I am the nephew of Caroline. I trave—"

The minister interrupted. "I am so glad to meet you! Any family of Caroline is welcome in Hillsborough. I hope that you are being cared for while you're 'ere!"

I nodded vigorously and replied, "My friend Percy and his family have been very welcoming since my arrival yesterday."

The minister instantly looked up and turned his attention to Percy and his family. "Mr. and Mrs. Merivel! How are you all?" It was then that I no longer tuned into the conversation. The minister had now moved halfway down the pew in front of us so as to talk to Percy directly. I was somewhat relieved. I had never been one to meet new people, especially people who were so full of energy. The minister seemed to wrap up his conversation with Percy rather quickly. He had now left his position in front of Percy and moved to the front of the room. "Excuse me! Excuse me! Would everyone please find a seat? If you don't have a seat, one may be provided to you." With these words, the room had gone from being filled with the sounds of mourners whispering among each other to the sounds of shuffling feet and people being settled into a seat. I could only anticipate what would come next.

"Thank y'all for coming! We are here on this fine morning to celebrate the life of Ms. Caroline. I will say a few words, and if anyone has anything to say, then you will have a chance to do so at such time." Everyone sat in their seats and waited patiently for the minister to settle himself. He gracefully moved directly in front of the casket in the middle of the front of the room. "I am glad that so many have come to be with Ms. Caroline today. Are there any family members of Ms. Caroline in the room?" With these words, I raised my hand. I looked around the room and noticed that I was the only family member in the room. How could this be? How was it that my aunt didn't have any other family members that had moved to the area with her? I was amazed by this revelation. "We are pleased to have you here, sir! I hope that your family will be honored by our service today." I half expected to be called to say something or to be brought to the front of the room, but this was not the case. With a simple nod of my head, the minister continued. "Ms. Caroline was a fine member of this community and often helped those around her. She even gave to the poor of our town. She was always more than willing to share any food that she had. Even her own farmhands and servants admired her. She was truly a woman to be remembered. I often think of all the times that I had been invited to share lunch with Ms. Caroline. She would always sit on her porch after a fine meal and share sweet tea with any servants or guests that had finished their work. Yes...she was a fine woman indeed. I am sure we all can speak to her loving nature and her willingness to help in any situation. In fact, I would often see Ms. Caroline speaking with any people less fortunate in our congregation after church service. It warmed my heart when she would bring in the leftover harvest at the end of each season to share with the poor."

I looked on with focus as if hanging on every word that the minister spoke. Most of the mourners had lowered their heads as if reflecting upon a burden from their past. It was almost as if they had transgressed against my aunt in the deepest way. I continued to listen to the pastor.

"Ms. Caroline may have passed on to be with the good Lord, but she will always hold a special place in our hearts. This community has been touched by her kindness and will never be the same without her loving nature. Thank you for allowing me to speak. At this time I would like to invite anyone who would like to say a few words to come forward and speak."

It was then that I could feel eyes peering at me from my left. I looked to my left and was met with Percy leaning over and gesturing for me to do the same. I leaned in toward Percy. "Would you feel right about me saying a few words for you?"

I smiled nervously and nodded. Before I could finish even one nod, Percy had already stood from the pew and was striding toward the front of the room. The minister looked to the right and exclaimed, "Mr. Merivel seems to have a few words! Please come down, sir!" Percy seemed to move with the speed and grace of an angel. I simply blinked, and he was already standing in front of the coffin.

"Thank you all for coming!" Percy exclaimed. "I am so glad to see so many of you here. It has been a long time since all of us were together. I remember, as many of you do as well, Ms. Caroline always took care of us as if we were her family. She was always so good to everyone that had the fortune to work with her. She would always be so happy when we would celebrate the end of the harvest season or finishing the work for the week. She was the only farmer that I had ever seen to allow her farmhands to be off on Sundays. I always admired her and know that she will be missed dearly. I would also like to bring it to everyone's attention that Mr. Benjamin Price is staying at the Tourney Manor. He is Caroline's nephew and will be visiting until such time that he can settle her estate. I will not embarrass him by asking him to speak, but any help or food would be appreciated." Percy then began to return to his seat.

I could not feel as if I were being watched. I looked around the room and could see that others had begun talking about my visit, every so often glancing over to see me. I felt as if the attention was that of reverence and not shame or to be outcast. I then noticed a group of people sitting toward the back of the far side of the room. They seemed to be unaffected by the sermon. It was as if they were here to revel in my aunt's demise, not mourn. I was confused by this and somewhat irritated. Eventually, however, I decided to overlook them. I returned my focus to the front of the room and awaited the pastor to close the ceremony. I could not understand how my aunt had meant so much to so many. I had never seen anything like it. I knew that there were many people who had worked on her farm, but I did not expect them to all be here to mourn.

I sat continuing to wait for the pastor to speak. It was then that I felt an overwhelming feeling. It was as if I were drowning in anxiety and fear, almost in a fashion that made me feel like I had been surrounded by water. I began to sweat and found it hard to breathe. I felt as if I were being watched from all sides. My skin began to crawl, and I felt as if a thousand bugs were crawling their way across my flesh. Suddenly I felt the urge to turn and look behind me. I could not explain these sudden feelings. Though the thought did occur to me that whatever had been following me to Hillsborough had once again caught up to me. With each passing moment, I could feel it stronger and stronger. It was such a disturbing feeling that I did not even have the ability to pay attention to the speakers in front of the room. Could it be that I had anxiety about being in such a large and densely packed crowd? I shifted in my seat slightly to try to regain the comfort that I once had. But to no avail. The feeling to turn around and see what was calling to me from behind grew stronger still. I could not shake this feeling. It had now become unbearable.

It was not long before I found myself slowly turning my head to see what it was that beckoned to me. As I turned my head, I could hear a low raspy voice whispering in my ears, like the whisper was coming from all around me. I knew nothing of what was happening and did not seem to have the time to understand. Could it be that I had begun to slowly slip into insanity? Did it even matter now? I was clearly hearing the whisper. As I turned my head, the sounds grew louder until they had completely occupied my thoughts. I could literally hear the words in my head. I cautiously turned my head until I was looking behind me.

At first, nothing was in view. Nothing seemed out of the ordinary. It was then that a form came into my peripheral sight. I began to move my eyes farther to the right as the shape of a head came into view. The face was that of a demonic being. The face was both human in ways but seemed dead at the same time. The cheeks were sunken, and the skin had grayed to an almost dead and leathery appearance. I had come face-to-face with something so terrifying that it left me speechless. I could not think or move at all. I could only stare in amazement at what I could not believe that I was seeing. The face had no eyes, and where the eyes should have been, the sockets and eyelids had been sewn shut. The stitching was a cross pattern that gave me the most unsettling feeling. It was as if someone wished to silence this horror forevermore. I was even more horrified at the fact that the mouth hung open as if the jaw had been completely shattered. This was the face of nightmares, the face seen upon one's demise if being sent to hell itself.

The face then began to smile without closing its mouth, and blood ran from the sewed-up eye sockets. I closed my eyes as tightly as I could manage. I dared not open them for fear that this horror had crept closer. I could feel myself regain control of my body and immediately turned my head forward. I opened my eyes and took a deep breath. I was now in control of myself. I was not sure what I had just witnessed, but my heart still reeled as if this thing were real. I felt the terror wash over me fully and begin to subside. Slowly I could feel relief, but it would not last long. I then began to feel breath circulating against the back of my neck. The sounds of deep and pained breathing could be heard in my right ear. It was almost a wheezing that was coming from behind me. I felt the terror slowly return. My heart once again began to beat faster. This went on for a moment before I heard it. A low, guttural utterance filled my ears. "WE ARE COMING FOR YOU!" the voice growled. My eyes widened and my mouth, no doubt, stood agape. I waited silently in my own personal hell for the next words to assault my ears. Yet nothing could be heard. The room fell silent. I now could not hear any words or coughing. Not even the sound of people shifting in their seats or children being scolded by parents. The room was completely devoid of sound. I was horrified but could do nothing. I now knew what the deaf felt. I was panicked that this being had taken the ability for my ears to absorb sound completely. I sat focused on the person that was speaking, focused on their lips. I could not make out any words and still no sounds.

Instantly all sounds came flooding back to me. The room had once again filled with all the sounds of life, especially the sounds of people growing ever more impatient at the length of this service. The speaker had now taken their seat and the minister had now moved to the front of the room. I was relieved at this sight. I could not be still any longer. Everything in me urged me to leave the room at once. The pastor spoke.

"Thank you everyone for your kind words. As stated before, if anyone would like to donate food or assistance to Mr. Price, please let Mr. Merivel know. We will now ask the pallbearers to come to the front and gather the coffin. We will start our procession to the cemetery shortly. Thank you all."

With the pastor's words, everyone began to stand and file out the door. Percy tapped me on the shoulder, and I turned to my left to see his family walking toward the other end of the pew. Percy had now moved to sit directly to my left side. "Would you like to help us and be a pallbearer as well?"

I replied, "Yes! I would love to help."

Percy stood and motioned for me to follow him. I moved as quickly as I could to catch up to Percy and the others. In a short amount of time, we had gathered around the casket and began hoisting it into the air. Despite my aunt's size when she was alive, she was now as heavy as if someone had filled the coffin with bricks. It was all that we could do to carry her out of the hall and down the steps outside. The walk to the graveyard seemed never-ending. We hefted the coffin as quickly as we all could and tried with everything in us to not cause the others to lose balance and drop the coffin. It seemed an impossible struggle at times as the road leading toward the graveyard had hardened and turned into an uneven mess. This was followed by thick, soupy mud that seemed to suck our shoes to the ground. We all seemed to struggle to simply walk. Eventually, we did reach the grass, and our forward movement became swifter. It was not far now to place my aunt in her final resting place.

Once we had reached her grace, we all set her coffin gently onto two ropes that cradled the coffin and began to lower it gently into place. Everyone had begun gathering around the gravesite with the exception of a few. I watched as my aunt was lowered ever deeper into the hole. I felt the burdens of regret lift away from me. Though I was still completely unsettled by the sight of that horror in the funeral hall. I tried with everything in me to forget the images that I had witnessed. Though at times it seemed that my thoughts wandered back to the horror. I was not supposed to be focused on anything other than assisting my aunt to pass into a peaceful rest for eternity. Instead, my head was filled with visions of horror and unrest. Eventually, I felt a hand being placed on my shoulder. Percy had come to comfort me in this time of reflection. "We will be waiting at the wagon, Benjamin. The children have become restless, and I do not wish to have them disrupt the ceremony."

I nodded and felt Percy move away from me. I stood in the same position until I could see that the coffin had rested against the bottom of the grave. My aunt could now be at peace. I turned back toward the funeral parlor to see glowing sunlight illuminating the building. The sun shone so brightly even out into the road. I began to return to the wagon as the feeling of missing my aunt grew stronger. It seemed that the farther I walked away from the gravesite, the more the feeling grew. It swelled up inside my throat until I felt as if I couldn't speak. I did not even notice what the other mourners were doing. I really didn't care. I simply continued on until I had reached the wagon once again. The walk saw my mind drifting to the worry that this estate sale would not go as planned. I felt that I would not be able to accomplish my goal of traveling to Hillsborough. The worry grew more prevalent.

As I approached the wagon, I could not see anyone waiting in the wagon. I looked around for a moment and noticed that Percy and his family were now conversing with the minister. I wasn't in the least bit annoyed by this but instead decided to wait patiently. I produced my pipe from my pocket and began to pack the bowl. One strike of the match against the rough exterior of the building and I began to puff. The taste of the tobacco for the first time in days was refreshing. I could tell that Percy and his family were now engrossed in a deep conversation with the minister. Each puff of my pipe seemed to calm me even more. Still, I wondered what could have been so important for Percy and his family to speak to the minister. Perhaps it was simple paranoia that caused me to wonder so intently. Something about the minister had seemed so unsettling, almost as if I had an intrinsic distrust of the man. It seemed to not be the way that he acted toward anyone, but just a feeling that gnawed at my mind. Something about the minister seemed withdrawn. Eventually, I decided that it was simply my mind seeing something that was not real, and I focused on my pipe once again. I drew ever deeper upon the tobacco and continued to settle in this place beside the wagon.

I stood there for what felt like an eternity. Just then I felt a soft touch upon my arm. The touch was startling enough to almost make me drop my pipe. I looked to my left where the touch had emanated. I slowly ran my eyes up the arm of a young woman. I met her beautiful hazel eyes with my eyes and stood in somewhat of a shock. The woman looked at me and said, "Hello. My name is Mary. I believe we met at my parents' farmhouse."

I looked deeper into the woman's eyes and was reminded of that embarrassing incident. I immediately recognized her. I could not fight back the embarrassment as my face changed to a deep shade of red. "I would like to apologize once again about kicking you, madam. I didn't mean to harm you in any way."

Mary looked at me with a sweet smile and said, "Everything is all right. I am fine, sir. I saw you standing here, and I wanted to talk to you and tell you that I am sorry for your loss."

Mary seemed to be a sweet girl. I longed to make a good impression given everything that had happened between us. "Thank you, Mary. It is good to see you again. How have you and your family been?"

Mary looked away shyly and stammered slightly when she said, "I am well, and my family too. I had overheard my family say that you might be traveling this way, and I had hoped to meet you here." Mary's face turned red, and she began to hide her face from me as if she was trying to retreat from my gaze. She was a young woman of about sixteen years of age. She was a small woman with accentuated curves. I had never seen such a beautiful woman in my life. I noticed that she was wearing an elegant black dress that fit her perfectly. She stood with her hair waving in the breeze and her beautiful doe eyes fixated on mine.

She seemed to be over her sudden embarrassment. I looked into her beautiful eyes and said, "How long will you be in town?"

She smiled at me and replied, "My family and I will be in town for a month. I am here helping my aunt and uncle on their farm."

I smiled at her until she finished talking then casually replied, "I don't have a way to get around very quickly, but I would like to see you again if that is acceptable to you."

She giggled a little under her breath. "I could talk to my parents to see if it would be all right with them to invite you to lunch Wednesday."

I teased Mary with a look of consideration to her proposal and said, "That sounds perfect. Where—"

Before I could finish my statement, she smiled and said, "That will be great! I will send my father to bring you to our home if they accept. You are staying in the Tourney Manor, correct?"

I nodded at her quickly with a large smile on my face. She seemed to melt with every smile that I gave her. Reality then flooded back as I could hear Mary's father calling to her. She never took her eyes off mine as she said, "I am sorry, but I have to go now. I hope to see you Wednesday." Her words felt like fire touching my heart. I could not control myself from being overwhelmed with excitement. She giggled again and then walked briskly to catch up to her father.

I stood there for a moment relighting my pipe. This simple action now seemed impossible. Nothing could be done. I seemed to have been overtaken with nervousness. Just then I heard Percy's voice beside me. "Well, it seems that you have made a friend, Benjamin."

I stood there in amazement and replied, "Yes. It seems that I have." I looked up from my pipe to see Mary climbing into her father's wagon. I turned to Percy and said, "I am sorry if I took too long."

Percy smiled and replied, "Nonsense. We have all just loaded into the wagon." Percy then took his place on the driver's side of the wagon, waiting for me along with his family in the back.

I took my place on the seat, and Percy snapped the reins of the wagon. My mind was still racing as we began to ride out of town. I was amazed at how forward Mary had been when she told me that she had wanted to follow me to Hillsborough. It was refreshing to see such honesty in a woman her age. It still left me wondering why such a beautiful young woman would want to follow a man she barely knew, a man who had kicked her a day earlier. It was baffling to me that I could have a woman who admired me and possibly desired my time. Who was I, however, to not accept a meeting with her again? If she truly wished to meet again, I would not wish to pass up on such a truly amazing woman. After all, she knew what had happened and still made the conscious choice to talk to me again.

After a moment my thoughts began to turn once again to my visit in Hillsborough. My true fear, however, was more to the point that I might not be able to sell the house or its property. After all, I could not simply leave the home in such a state and return to New York. The thought that expounded upon this issue was that I might have to return home without selling the house and having no idea when I might return. This fear gripped my mind in such a confusing quandary. After all, how would I be able to leave after not honoring my aunt's wishes of leaving someone to care for the manor? I did not wish this to be the case. The Tourney Manor was much too magnificent to be left to rot where it stood.

I looked toward the sky as we rode out into the forested area beyond the town. I could feel that the air was light and a gentle breeze stirred the air. I was refreshed to feel this breeze blowing all around me. It was the purest feeling of peace and tranquility that I had felt in a long time. I could not imagine a better day than this save for one strange occurrence. Even so, today had proven to be a beautiful and amazing day. Though I could not explain these strange events, I was determined to not let them destroy my peace. Nothing would hinder my enjoyment of the day. I still pondered slightly about all these odd happenings, but I knew that if I talked to Percy about the house, he might shed light on why such odd things were happening. I also hoped that if I had to repair the door in the hallway, Percy or his family would know someone that could accomplish such a task. I would need help if I were to be able to finish my business in North Carolina within two weeks.

I also had no clear path of how I would begin to sell the home in such a remote location. Though I could formulate my next course of action after I was sure that the house was in selling condition. Percy drove the wagon on, but it seemed that the distance traveled was much shorter. That or I had simply been too deep into thought to notice the passing trees. Before too much longer we were making the turn into Percy's drive. When we finally reached the porch of the home, Percy said, "Benjamin, would you help my wife out of the wagon and see them into the house while I unhitch the horses?"

I nodded and Percy thanked me. I quickly helped the children down from the wagon first, then Percy's wife. Once we were all on the porch, Percy guided the wagon into the barn. I did not wait for Percy to join us. I continued into the home with the rest of the family and removed my coat. Before placing my coat on the coat rack, I removed my pipe from the pocket and immediately moved back out onto the porch. As I relit my pipe, Percy emerged from the barn and began walking in my direction.

"I don't think we have to worry about rushing to get you back to the manor since the day has been so clear and beautiful."

I nodded and replied, "I agree." I began to stand from my seat when Percy stopped me.

"Don't get up on my account. I will go into the house and fetch my pipe."

I nodded again and sat back down in the rocking chair. Just then Percy's wife emerged from the home. Without a moment passing, I asked, "I am sorry, Mrs. Merivel. May I smoke my pipe here on the porch?" I had feared that the smoke had somehow agitated her senses.

Before she responded, Percy chimed in, "I am sorry, Benjamin. I seem to have forgotten my manners. I never properly introduced you to my family. This is my wife, Chloe. My son's name is Albert, and my daughter Catherine."

I looked at Chloe and said, "It is nice to meet you, Chloe."

Chloe seemed relieved that Percy had finally introduced her to me. She then turned to me and said, "I do not mind if you smoke here, Mr. Price."

I responded by saying, "You can call me Benjamin, ma'am."

Chloe smiled and then beckoned for Percy to come inside. I simply sat waiting for Percy to return and continued to puff on my pipe. I could not imagine that he would take too long to return. I continued to think about the tasks that I needed to complete before returning to New York. However, even the fears of failure could not drown out my thoughts and feelings toward meeting with Mary on Wednesday.

It was a short time before Percy returned with his pipe. He took his seat to my left on the porch. "I am sorry, Benjamin. I didn't mean to keep you waiting. Chloe is finishing up lunch with a servant of ours. It shouldn't be too much longer before we will eat. I also left my pipe on the table and had to retrieve it and some tobacco."

I nodded and replied, "That is quite all right, sir."

With a few strikes against the chair, Percy lit his pipe and began puffing away. "I do hope that you felt that the funeral honored your aunt. I understand that losing a family member can be hard even if they have not been well known. Indeed, in spite of not being well-known, sometimes that is the hardest loss."

I sat puffing on my pipe for a moment and then replied, "I thought it was nice. I think that she would have truly enjoyed the ceremony. It was simple but elegant. Just as she was in life."

Percy nodded and continued to smoke.

"I thank you deeply, Percy, for allowing me to spend time here. I am also very thankful for your wagon and the ability to get around. I had feared that I would have to walk everywhere."

"It isn't any problem, Benjamin. We are all happy to have you as a guest here. It would have been a tragedy for you to have to walk into town. It is much too far. Especially when you are staying in a manor that has no food."

I laughed and agreed with Percy.

"We have also been looking forward to meeting someone related to Caroline. I know that you do not understand what she has meant to this community. She has always been the one person here who has helped almost everyone. Even during times when other farms faced drought or dying livestock, she has been able to provide. It was odd to everyone at first, but we all came to accept her. She also had taken in people whose farms had failed and they were forced from their land. Even if they have all intentions of abandoning the town. She has always been seen as someone to turn to in your time of greatest need.

"She has also been instrumental in helping the farmers gain control over their farms when the politicians in Raleigh have tried to gain tax money from us. Our town may not look it, but we are an important farming town. We produce a lot of the food that goes to the rest of the state. Though it is not easy, politicians only see money that they do not yet possess." With that Percy trailed off.

We sat in silence for a moment, and I pondered his words as we continued to smoke. The sun continued to rise ever higher into the sky as the world around us warmed. We were now in the midst of one of the hottest days that I had felt. It had been a long time since I had felt the wretched humidity of the south. Percy didn't seem to mind as he had probably felt worse. I had come to understand from a young age that August was often one of the hottest months here in North Carolina. My aunt had often spoken of her crops being scorched by the sun during August. Though I didn't think that she would care much since it was the end of the growing season. That is if North Carolina even experienced autumn and winter. It was days like today that seemed to make me certain that there was only spring and summer in this place.

We continued to sit and talk for some time. I could only guess at the work that was being put into preparing lunch. Still, I was extremely fortunate for the assistance from people who had never met me. I was touched by the fact that I had been welcomed wholeheartedly. I could have never hoped for a better outcome.

It was a short time before Chloe emerged from the home and beckoned for us to take our places at the table. Percy and I tamped out our pipes and stood in unison to enter the home. The family was already seated comfortably around the table, and it seemed that the servants had also been invited to eat as there were now many more guests. I sat down for the meal of roast beef and fresh vegetable salad. The smell of the spread made my mouth instantly water. I could only guess at the taste of this delicious-looking meal. Before we ate, however, Percy was called upon to say grace. The time spent praying seemed to heighten my hunger, and I felt that each second passed painfully slower. After grace, we all tore into the food. It would have seemed to anyone that had just entered the home that we had never eaten a meal in our lives. No one cared for the neatness of the setting or the table surface. We had all devolved into a sloppy animalistic mess. The beef was tender and the salad was crisp. Everything complimented each other. The saltiness of the beef was offset by the sweet taste of deep, leafy greens. I had never tasted food as fresh as this. I had a glass of water to wash down the delicious meal we were partaking of in preparation to eat more. I saw the water as a chance to cleanse my palate so as to taste new combinations of flavor. I ate and spoke with everyone.

Eventually, I worked up the nerve to question Chloe and Percy about the source of this delicious meal. "I do wish to ask, from where did this delicious meal come?"

Percy and Chloe looked at each other and replied, "The beef is from our cattle and the vegetables from our garden." Chloe continued, "Though the seasonings are from our friends at the ranch over the hill."

I nodded and replied, "This is the freshest meal I think I have ever eaten." I looked at the servants and thanked them for their part in the meal. The conversation continued.

"So, Benjamin. What will you do with the Tourney Manor?"

I looked at Chloe and replied, "I wish to sell the manor." These words seemed to unsettle everyone at the table. "I cannot care for the home, and I do not wish to try. I would like to find someone to care for the home as my aunt had. I would also like to extend the offer to your family to purchase the home from me. At a discount, of course, due to your hospitality."

Percy and Chloe once again looked at each other. "You couldn't be serious, Benjamin," Percy replied.

I nodded in reply and said, "I am quite serious. I am not sure when I would be able to return here and care of the home. My work in New York is very demanding of my time. Banking is growing more and more needed." I could see that Percy was deep in thought.

"We would need to think about this for some time, Benjamin. We appreciate the offer but would still wish to give you a fair offer for the home."

I held out my hands and said, "I understand completely. If I am to sell the home, however, I would need to make sure that the memory of my aunt will be honored."

With this Percy seemed to be much more relieved. After all, whoever purchased the home would ultimately become Percy's neighbor. I did not wish to offend anyone here with my news, but I felt it only right to extend the offer. It was Percy, after all, who had cared for my aunt and her home until the end of her life.

After lunch Percy and I moved back outside, this time choosing to sit on the porch on the back of the home. The servants worked vigorously about the property as Percy and I began to smoke once again. "Percy. When you were caring for my aunt and her home, did you notice any strange occurrences within the manor?"

Percy sat in thought for a moment with a confused look on his face. He took a deep drag from his pipe and replied, "There were some odd things that happened from time to time, but I didn't pay them any mind."

This piqued my interest and I had to ask, "What kind of occurrences?"

Percy paused for a moment and conceptualized his next words carefully. "When your aunt began to fall into her sickness, I was at the home helping her servants care for the animals. Everyone witnessed her walking extremely quickly from window to window in the upstairs portion of the home. This was odd due to her having shut those rooms up. She no longer had enough servants or guests to warrant the use of these rooms. We simply cleaned them as normal but didn't have to make them a focus as they were never in use." I knew that I had a shocked look upon my face. "I do not wish to imply anything about your aunt, Benjamin. I do not believe the gossip that she had been possessed or any such nonsense."

This caught my attention. "What do you mean?"

Percy was taken aback by this question. "I simply mean to say that some of her servants had begun to spread rumors that she had been possessed. Some of them claimed to see her floating and such. I never put any stock in this as people simply spread rumors out of fear of the unknown. The stress of caring for a dying woman and her farm is too much for some to take. Perhaps they were also jealous."

I nodded at Percy's words and quickly changed the subject. "Could you tell me if there has been any damage to the home?"

Percy thought for a moment and replied, "Nothing more than the usual wear and tear a home experiences when in use by many people. Though, as you can see, this has all been repaired."

I agreed with Percy, and his nervousness seemed to subside. Percy seemed to be making his statements honestly, so I did not question him further. We sat there talking for some time about the state of the southern states with all the unrest. The northern states had seemed to reach for power over the southern states. We both agreed that this could lead to a dire situation but did not want to entertain the notion of war at this current moment. Eventually, Percy offered to look over the home with me. I welcomed his help in searching for any damage in the home. Two sets of eyes would be better in this case anyway. I also could not imagine that I would know enough about construction to be able to accurately judge the condition of the manor. After all, I was only a banker, not a tradesman.

Percy and I eventually ended our conversation and decided to use this perfect day to our advantage. We would travel back to the manor and begin assessing the condition of the home. I said goodbye to Chloe and Percy's children. Everyone wished me farewell for now. I was sure to return for dinner as offered originally. Chloe assured me that Percy would be sent with food for me for tomorrow. She also offered for me to visit the local church with them, but I regretfully declined. I thanked them once again and left with Percy for the manor. We rode steadily out of the drive to Percy's farmhouse and turned back into the road. I held on to my hopes that we would discover a reason for such strange sounds last night. If there was not anything that did need to be fixed, I surely would begin to think that I was losing my mind or that something strange was going on in the house. Either conclusion was an unsettling one. I could not imagine either that I might have to give into my previous conclusion that the house could be unsellable. All these fears culminated in my mind, and I was ready to face the fact, whatever that might be.

In this moment I cared nothing about the forest around me, nor the day that was bright and beautiful. I was only focused on one thing, and that was to fix any problem that was found. I had to move on with my life, and I certainly couldn't do that in North Carolina. As my mind whirled with thoughts of the possibilities that I could have taken on more than I could handle, I then began to think of Mary. I was still taken aback by her words and actions. I also knew that I would have to take the responsibility upon myself to be kind and caring to the girl even with all my fears. She was so cute and sweet. Her innocence was refreshing to me, and I did not wish to taint that in any way. She was pure as the snow that falls on a winter's day. How could I or any man wish to destroy that portion of her? Still, I knew little of the girl or her family, but I had a deep-set feeling that I would not find anything that I didn't like.

Percy and I concluded our very silent wagon right back to the manor. I had thought that Percy, too, seemed to feel some kind of pressure from my questions or the thought that the home could be damaged. After all, Percy seemed to regard the manor as a shrine, and who was I to tell the man otherwise? We both would have seemed very cold and distant to any passerby if there had ever been one. I did hope as well that Percy was not furious with me over the announcement of my plans to sell the manor. I did not wish to make enemies of anyone from his family. Especially since they had done so much to lend aid in my time of need. I did not, however, anticipate that I would upset him so by this announcement. He truly had regarded my aunt with the utmost respect. I also believed that his dreams of modeling himself after my aunt made him feel that if he could not have the home, he would have failed in his endeavor. If this was true, then it would surely devastate Percy's psyche to a level of being irreparable. This was something that I would not be able to forgive myself for, but the fact remained that I could not keep the home in my possession. I did fervently hope that Percy would be able to purchase the home. This would allow me to not have to put time into finding anyone else to buy the home.

By the time I had completed this thought, we had arrived at the fence that flanked the entrance to the drive of the manor. The tension of what we could find out about the state of the home rose to an optimum level. We both stepped off the seat of the wagon and walked to the door of the home. I unlocked the door, and we entered the home. I walked into the foyer and began to explain to Percy what I had witnessed.

"The room at the far end of the hall here is not locked."

Percy gave me the most perplexed look.

"Last night the door opened by itself and swung out into the hallway."

Percy continued to stare in amazement at my words. It was as if he waited for me to perform magic of some kind.

I continued, "I did not hear the door open, but it was after I had returned from gathering water from the well. I did not approach the door as I had no idea what I might find. I continued on with settling in for the night. This was the strange event that I had asked about earlier."

Percy gathered his wit and replied, "Are you sure, Benjamin?"

I nodded.

"No one has ever been able to open this door in all the years that I have worked here. Your aunt also would shoo people away from this door before she fell sick." Percy paused for a moment. Eventually, he said, "Let's look at the door then."

I motioned for him to lead the way and then followed him down the hall. We both approached the door with caution as if we expected the door to be thrown open. Percy began feeling around the door-frame for any looseness in the lock or the hinges. He found nothing. He looked at me with fear in his eyes and reached for the door handle. I watched with bated breath for the result of Percy trying the doorknob. He quickly and sternly twisted the doorknob back and forth. Nothing happened.

"The door is locked, Benjamin."

I looked puzzled. "The door cannot be locked. How would it have opened last night and then slammed without anyone touching it?"

Percy paused. "You said slammed?"

I nodded. "The door was open until I had begun to settle into bed. As I was laying out my suit for this morning, I heard the door suddenly slam shut. I admit that I had braced the door to the bedroom as I feared that someone had broken into the home for some unknown reason. Though nothing added up in my mind."

Percy was most puzzled by these words. He kept looking from me to the doorknob and back again. "How can this be, Benjamin? This door is still locked."

Though I knew that Percy was not accusing me of anything, I instantly became defensive. "Are you telling me that I am lying to you, sir?"

Percy shook his head.

"I can tell you that I witnessed these events as I have told them to you. I did not invite you here to not be believed."

Percy held out his hands. "Benjamin! I am not saying that I do not believe you. I am simply confused as you are. Now...given that the storm raged for a while last night, did you have any windows opened?"

I instantly replied, "Yes, I did. But they were not opened in the sitting room when I settled into bed. The door to my room was also shut and braced. There was no draft otherwise."

Percy turned to look at the back door. He began to pull on the doorknob and check to make sure the door was secure. "This door was also closed?"

I nodded and replied, "I had secured it after setting the bucket of water in the bathroom. I know that there was no draft from the door as it would have opened as well."

Percy now had the look of being puzzled deeply. I was sure that he didn't know what to think about our conversation or the events of the previous night. No matter how Percy tried to open the door, the lock would not budge. This perplexed him deeply. I could feel his frustration with the issue as it was the same frustration that I had had last night. In either case, my suspicions had now been confirmed. There was truly no explanation. If the wind had blown the door open, then the lock would have failed and allowed the door to swing open when Percy pulled on the door. The way the door was positioned, it would have taken more force than the wind or Percy and I could exert to open it. If the doorjamb itself were to fail, then we would have simply pulled the door right open. This could only mean that an act of God would have opened the door.

Percy thought for a moment and said, "What if the storm had something to do with the door opening on its own? Could it be that the air had caused the doorframe to contract and allow the door to open?"

These were both great questions that I did not have an answer to. I thought for a moment. "How would we be able to test this? The only thing that could change the doorframe so dramatically would be bad weather."

Percy nodded and finished, "We will just have to wait and see if the door opens on its own again."

I then added, "How was it that it slammed on its own as well?"

Percy still had a puzzled look. "I could not begin to understand that aspect of this issue."

I also nodded. "Perhaps time will tell us more," I said.

Percy agreed. We continued from there to look about the rest of the home. We checked the rest of the downstairs area but found nothing. We then began to climb the stairs to the second level, when Percy stopped dead in his tracks. He turned suddenly and said, "Did you look inside of the room when it opened last night?"

I shook my head and replied, "I was more startled than anything. I could not find the courage to enter the room and look about."

Percy simply looked at me with reserve and said, "That's too bad."

Percy instantly turned and walked onward up the stairs. As we reached the landing, Percy broke off from me and moved toward the right wing of the home. I instinctively took the left wing. As I started to turn to my right and enter the hallway, I looked back to see Percy moving into the master bedroom. I continued down the hallway to the farthest points and began looking about the rooms. I started with the left room and began looking from top to bottom. I found nothing out of place. I then crossed the hall to a small storage room. Still, nothing was damaged or out of place. I continued to do this for each room in the hallway until I had reached the stairs again. I stood there waiting for Percy. I had half expected to meet with him at the same time. It took some time, but he eventually walked up to me.

"Have you been in the upper rooms here?"

I shook my head and replied, "No, why?"

Percy looked over his shoulder. He seemed to be glancing toward the middle room to the right of the stairs. "The bedroom just behind me has been opened recently," he said.

I gave a very intrigued look and started toward the door before Percy stopped me. "We will go in together. There is a hatch to the attic in the closet, and the door to the closet is open. We go in together and block the closet. I'll climb up into the attic with the candle in the room and look around."

I nodded, and we immediately moved into position within the room. My heart was racing. I could no longer focus on anything save for the operation in which Percy and I were now invested.

We entered the room cautiously. Percy made his way through the door and to the doorway of the closet in a fashion and grace that only a dancer possesses. I was amazed by the speed at which he moved. I was soon to follow, albeit much less graceful. In a moment Percy had moved a ladder from the room underneath the hatch to the attic and had begun to lift the hatch upward. I handed him the lit candle and soon was watching him disappear into the attic. I could see nothing in the way of detail as I attempted to peer through the darkness of the attic. It was all that I could do to wait at the bottom of the ladder as silence reigned over the area. I continued to strain my eyes to see into the pitch-black abyss of the attic. It was then when I had begun to give up hope of peering into the hatch that Percy emerged. He climbed down into the room swiftly and stood beside me. Sweat dripped from his face and nose.

"Did you find anything?" I asked.

He shook his head as he was hunched over, trying to gather his breath. "There was nothing but darkness. Could you reach into the attic and bring the candle down?"

I nodded and immediately climbed the ladder and poked my head through the hatch. I could see the flame of the candle flickering some half a foot away from my face. I had just enough space to reach through the hatch and into the attic. With one swift movement, I removed the candle from the attic and placed it on the top of the ladder. My quick actions had put the flame out, and I was no longer in fear of setting myself or the home ablaze. It was then that I looked up into the darkness and could see deep red, glowing eyes looking back at me. It seemed that whatever these eyes belonged to was huge, an imposing being that towered over any height that I could have achieved. I was horrified and could feel the numb sting of fear as it consumed my body. I moved my foot quickly into position to begin my descent and alert Percy to what I was seeing. Just as I placed my foot back onto the ladder, this thing rushed toward the hole. I yelled out with a savage roar as I lost my footing and swiftly descended to the ground. As I fell, I perceived the world passing at a slower rate. It almost felt as if I were going to fall forever. I could no longer see the red eyes as I stared upward but now wondered if this fall would be my undoing. Then as if time resumed instantly, I fell to the floor below and lay halfway in the closet and halfway out. I continued to yell out as I used my legs and arms to scoot backward on my back and get away from the thing in the attic.

When I came to my senses, Percy was perched over me, saying, "What? What! Benjamin, is everything all right?"

I continued to try to speak but ultimately continued to point into the hatch of the attic, saying, "Uh! Uh!" My mind had now devolved into guttural speak that was not discernible.

Percy continued his line of questioning as I yelled out, "THAT!" Percy instantly turned to face what I was pointing toward, and for a moment, I expected him to ask me what again. Instead, Percy stood frozen. I could see that fear gripped his mind as he stood gawking at whatever he was now witnessing in the attic. I knew now that Percy had witnessed the being that had rushed toward me out of the darkness of the attic as if to pull me into the void that had once concealed its home. I felt just like the rat as the snake begins to pounce and I make my narrow escape. I had dodged my own demise and felt nothing but fear still yet. I yelled out again, "Percy!"

He turned to look at me and then came to his senses. He sprang into action and climbed the ladder so swiftly that I thought he had become a monkey. With one graceful motion, Percy closed the hatch and jumped back down the ladder. He was now standing between myself and the now-closed attic hatch. We both stayed just as we were. Motionless. Waiting now for a demise that we could not understand or a realization that what we had just witnessed was not real. There would, however, never come an answer. As we began to realize the gravity of our situation, we rushed out of the room and down the stairs.

Percy and I now waited at the bottom of the stairs, looking upward as if this beast would come down the stairs and greet us. Eventually, Percy broke the silence. "What was that thing!"

I looked him in the eyes and replied, "I have no earthly idea. It was terror itself." We continued to try to gather our wits and breathe. Percy was still drenched in sweat. It was another moment or two before we got a hold of ourselves and retreated toward the kitchen. I now stood with my back against the counter while Percy paced back and forth.

"I cannot believe what I have witnessed, Benjamin. Was that...?" He trailed off then added, "It couldn't be."

I just shook my head and awaited another sentence from Percy's mouth. Finally Percy uttered, "I don't know if it is safe for us to stay here."

I agreed within my mind but responded with, "Where shall I stay if not here?"

Percy turned to me with an almost regretful look. "I do not know, my friend. I am sorry that this is happening."

I nodded in acknowledgment but knew that I had nowhere else to stay. I quickly added, "I am sure that I will be fine as long as I am not approaching the attic at night."

Percy looked into my eyes as if I had gone mad. "Are you certain, Benjamin?" he asked. "I would not curse anyone with a stay in a home like this. If I had known then, I would have made arrangements for you to stay somewhere else."

I nodded once again and replied, "I know, Percy. But I truly have no place to stay if not here. I will just have to take precautions when I am here alone." Now the only thing that entered my mind was the fact that Percy had seen something strange as well. I was no longer alone in thinking that I was insane. Perhaps I could now believe in my mind that the door in the hallway opened and closed by itself. That, or the thing in the attic had emerged from its lair and decided to open and close a door. This thought being fully realized made me feel ashamed to think it. I dared not proclaim a thought such as this to Percy.

Percy's words then broke the silence. "Have you seen this creature before?"

I shook my head.

"Even last night around the door?"

I shook my head again but still did not speak. Percy had now reached the same thought pattern that I had been so rushed to push from my mind. We both paused for a moment before Percy stormed out of the kitchen with great speed.

"Where are you going?" I received no response. I followed Percy out of the home and out to a shed that stood just beside the well. Before I could ask another question, Percy had retrieved a black-smith's hammer and started toward the house again. "What are you doing?" I tried to catch up to Percy and block his path, but he was almost at a full run now. Percy moved back into the home with me right behind. In one smooth motion, he came down as hard as he could with the hammer. I could hear a loud pinging noise but could see nothing as Percy's shoulder had now moved to block my view.

The doorknob fell to the floor with a loud thud against the wood flooring. I could hear the weight of the doorknob as if slowly rolled to a stop. Percy paused now and did not make any further sounds. The door itself didn't move at first but then, with a click, creaked open. Percy stood blocking the door from opening the rest of the way. I stood in shock. I could not believe that Percy would resort to such quick action. Percy then reached around the door and pulled it the rest of the way open. I quickly ran into the room in which I was staying and retrieved the candle holder. In an instant, I was back at Percy's side and began lighting the candles. The room became dimly lit but showed nothing. There was just an empty room. We looked around the room several times before we looked at each other with the deepest of puzzled looks. Nothing could explain, now, why the door had been locked. The even more troubling idea was why have a room locked that contains nothing? Even more to the point, why keep others away from the room so strongly? We both began to look around the room closer. We scanned every nook and cranny for any sign that this room contained anything at one time. Nothing seemed to indicate anyone had ever used the room. Nothing could explain any of the events that had happened recently.

Percy and I moved back outside the door and stood puzzled by all this. I looked at Percy and said, "Perhaps there was something that was once in this room. Otherwise, why would my aunt wish to ward off anyone that wished to open the door?"

Percy stood in silence. I could understand how Percy felt completely. I too was second-guessing my thoughts. We both shrugged our shoulders with extremely confused looks on our faces. I turned to leave the doorway as Percy took one last look around the room. Nothing could be explained at all. It was very frustrating for us. We both had invested in the idea that this room would hold answers about what was happening within the manor. Eventually, we stood in the sitting room looking out the door, waiting to hear the sounds of something marching down the stairs toward us.

After a few moments, we realized that nothing should happen and sat down. We both produced our pipes and began smoking. Percy sat in silence looking toward the fireplace.

"What would you say could be causing these strange events?

Could it be the creature causing everything, or is it the home itself?" I could safely admit to myself now that I did not know anything that was happening. It all seemed so maddening. All rational thought now had to be suspended when dealing with the issues in the Tourney Manor.

Percy shook his head and looked down at his pipe and replied, "I haven't the slightest clue, but surely there is an explanation for everything that we have witnessed. Perhaps it is simply we are both deprived in some way as to allow us to see these things." We both puzzled over this quandary for some time as we watched the sky change its color with the setting sun.

"Whatever the reasoning, Benjamin, I assure you that you have no dangers living in this house."

I nodded in acceptance of what Percy was trying to do. I just hoped that I would be able to deal with this situation long enough to solve it. I also would make sure that I received adequate sleep tonight so that I could eliminate lack of sleep as a possible cause of my hallucinations. Percy and I sat there discoursing about how to go about investigating these occurrences. Eventually, after a few bowls of tobacco, Percy stood and said, "I am sorry to leave you in such a frightful manner, but I really must get home before it is too late."

I stood and shook Percy's hand and thanked him for all his assistance. "Tomorrow I shall be by to gather you for breakfast. Would that be acceptable to you?"

I nodded and replied, "That will be great, Percy. Thank you."

Percy nodded in reply and left the manor.

5

A FRIGHTFUL NIGHT

I watched Percy as he rode out of sight on the wagon. I decided that if I had to stay in the house even with all the eerie issues that I had been facing, I was going to need to quickly figure out what needed to be done. I needed to eliminate this issue before I had to sell the house. I did not know anything about the supernatural or whatever force seemed to be at work in the manor. I now was not discounting the notion that the supernatural was the dominating force in all these occurrences. Neither Percy nor I could explain anything that was happening in the house, and I was not going to be hindered by something as trivial as this. I had no choice but to reinforce my courage and face whatever might happen. This conclusion unsettled me to the core. Once again I felt the fear that I might not be able to sell this home and continue with my life in New York City.

I sat down on the porch trying to decide how I could test what was going on in the home. I tried to imagine a more thorough method of testing the integrity of the supernatural forces within the home. I had to know for sure that nothing ordinary was going on in the house. I did not want to be involved in a lengthy and expensive restoration project, but if that was needed, then I would simply have to do whatever it took to restore the home. I sat there for a moment looking off toward the forest across the manor. I couldn't help but think that maybe all this was a little silly. I mean, what would Mary say if she knew that I was dealing with something so extraordinary? I had simply not discovered how this had all been possible.

It didn't take me long to finally see the sky grow too dim to sit out on the porch. I moved into the sitting room and locked the door behind me. I prepared my candle quickly and lit it with a simple flick of the match lying on the mantel. I carried the candle over to the table near the window and set the candle on the table. I sat down in the chair directly beside the table and began to read my book that I had left the night before. I imagined that it might help to read to help ease my mind. In no way did I wish to allow whatever could be in the house to gain a place in my fears. That would be a true loss in this situation. No matter what happened, I had to control the situation. I would still need to live and sleep in the house, which meant dealing with whatever was going on. I would not allow myself to be terrified of anything, especially that which, until now, had been manifested in cheap tricks and vivid dreams. If nothing else, I had to prove to myself that I was sane and hold on to that sanity no matter what.

As I sat there reading, I could distinctly hear the door to the other bedrooms creaking. I knew that it was happening again, and no matter how much I heard, I would not let it interrupt me. I sat there and continued to read as the creaking continued. The doors were only moving slightly back and forth. The sounds reverberated throughout the home. The doors seemed like they were moving back and forth at a snail's pace. I began to feel the presence that I had felt before in the funeral parlor, but this time it was like something was standing at the top of the stairs. Like it was peering down to look for me. I did not even give this feeling a reaction, which seemed to be a mistake. A few moments after I began feeling this, I heard the door upstairs slam. With that, something ran across the floor above. Each footstep was heavy but not so much as to move the floorboards. The sound was thud after thud, a muffled shuffling as of something that only carried what weight it wanted to carry in this world. As if the rules didn't apply to this thing. The sound also seemed as if whatever it was had claws as they clacked and clicked with each step. The steps started about where the door would be and ran down the hall until this thing had taken position at the top of the stairs. Back and forth it ran. Then it stopped as suddenly as it had begun. I imagined that the creature was sitting hunched over, gazing out of the darkness toward the light that emanated from the sitting room. Even with these sounds I didn't make a move at all. Nothing on my face said that I was even the slightest bit fearful. It took all the courage I had in order to hide the fear that was quickly growing inside of me.

The creature sat there for a prolonged time. It seemed like hours had gone by before the feeling finally dissipated. There was no other sound in the house for a moment. I sat there reading in silence and basking in the fact that I seemed to have won against this being. Yet I did not know what was to come. As I sat there reading and enjoying the silence, I began to feel a sense of dread. Nothing could shake it. It was as if a very heavy weight had been placed on my shoulders. I could imagine the creature wanted to terrify me in any way possible, and this new tactic seemed to be working. I heard a rumbling noise upstairs as if all the furniture were being shoved back and forth. The creature was making as much effort as possible to unsettle me further. I resolved to fight against my fear as much as possible. I would not give in to such a horrid beast. The creature began making hideous scraping noises against the floor before it completely threw the door open and rushed out of the bedroom and down the hall. The stairs creaked and cracked with each step as the creature rushed toward my position within the house. I held myself in place in the chair but had abandoned covering for my fear. I was now prepared to face whatever this thing might want of me. It charged to the sitting room and stood outside the door. It paced back and forth as if waiting for me to open the door. With all the power that this thing had, I could hardly believe that a wooden door could stop it. I awaited the door to be ripped off of its hinges or simply disintegrated. The creature then began to pace back and forth and growl from the hallway.

I opened my book once more and began to read aloud. The being's growling continued to grow louder and louder. Eventually, I could barely even hear the words that I was now yelling. This continued until I had stopped reading and began to hold my ears. The growling literally had begun to sound as if it were coming from all around me. My ears were burning as if someone had lit a match deep within my ear. Just as I had begun to writhe in pain, I heard laughter as if the creature were gaining pleasure from my suffering. What creature gains pleasure from the suffering of others? I put my book aside and said forcefully, "I will not be shaken by you, beast! Try as you will, I will not leave this home!" Every bit of my body seemed bathed in fear now, but I could not feel that because of my courage being bolstered from deep within me. I paused a moment after I had said that, only to hear the sound of silence. I looked to the window where the breeze was wafting into the room. This creature was powerful indeed. It seemed as if I had come face-to-face with Satan himself, but I still would not relent. I came here to achieve a goal, and that goal would be met. I forced laughter out of myself and pointed toward the door.

"Is this all you have, beast? A cheap magician should conjure such magic!"

This response seemed to get an entirely different effect than I had come to expect. In that moment I heard the creature move back from the door. I was puzzled by this but decided that my taunt had worked. This is until I looked to my left. My sleeve had sparked into a fire that burned through the fabric with ease. I tore off my jacket and threw it to the ground. I stomped the sleeve vigorously, trying to extinguish the fire. The creature bellowed another round of laughter and said, "I will be your end! You fight with the host of the devil himself!"

At these words, the creature fled. I could hear its rapid footsteps as it ran down the hall and climbed the stairs once again. Once it reached the landing at the top, the sounds dissipated. I stood in the sitting room, appalled at all that I had witnessed. This was the creature that had visited me on the train, and I would venture to say this was the creature that had been behind all the other events as well. I had to deal with this, but how could this creature be conquered? I stood there reclaiming what I could of my composure and picking up my charred jacket from the floor. It was useless to try to hide my fear from this creature. It knew all too well how much I feared its return. I did, however, have an overwhelming desire to rid the house and my life of this thing once and for all. How to accomplish this was another matter entirely. I didn't even know from where this creature came or who had called it here. I had to find out if I was to be able to sell the house. Nothing could be more clear than my need to sell the house and return to my normal life in New York.

I wondered if my aunt had known that this creature existed. Surely, she would have mentioned it, or she would have, at least, let someone know that the creature was in the house. I wondered if there was some clue that could have been left by my aunt for me to better understand what was happening—that is if she herself had known. I could not trust anyone else with this matter save for Percy. I was sure that he was also hiding something from me. Nothing could be done now except to investigate what could be happening in the house. There was something odd about all this besides the usual sinister explanation. It seemed that the creature wanted me specifically to leave and never return. I had no other option but to lead my own investigation into this evil and how to vanquish it. I could only trust what I could find out for myself. I gazed around the room in amazement that the creature had actually fled back into the darkness. I had reservations about going into the next room and going to sleep. Traveling into the next room would leave me exposed should the creature wish to return.

The more that I regained my composure, the more that I saw that I was truly frozen in fear. No matter how hard I tried to overcome that fear, I could not. Nothing could make this horror relent. I took one more look around the area and decided to try to walk into the next room. Even with all this fear and blood coursing through my veins, I still had a desire to sleep. I had been drained all day. I walked briskly toward the door to the sitting room, candle in hand. I opened the door slowly and kept my eyes moving back and forth as I looked into the hallway. I could not allow the creature to gain the upper hand and surprise me. I crept through the door and looked to my left then to my right. I couldn't make out anything in the candlelight that could harm me. The darkness of the hallway seemed to consume everything. I could barely see anything. There was no light even filtering into the home from the night sky. It was as if someone had stolen the moon from the sky. This made the hallway all the more eerie. I walked quickly to the door of my bedroom. I placed my hand on the doorknob and turned it. With one graceful and speedy move, I opened the door and slipped into the room. I shut the door firmly behind me and locked it. This gave me comfort as I could now feel safer and blocked off from this thing. The floors creaked under my feet, which seemed to fill the room with an almost human groan.

I felt the bed give in as I slowly sat down on the edge of the frame. I slowly began to remove my suit and lay it on the table across the bed. The fear that I had once held now began to subside. I also could feel an overall sense of relief. I had never been as terrified as I was in the sitting room in my life. I continued to place my clothing on the table. I wondered how I would be able to sleep tonight with such a terror in the house. It felt uncomfortable for me to think about. I could not imagine a more terrifying scenario than the creature doing harm to me as I slept tonight. I could not imagine simply sleeping in the bed. I thought of sleeping directly in front of the door in case the creature returned. It seemed real in my mind that the creature had to open the door to enter the room. This would cause the door to hit me as I slept, waking me from my sleep and enabling me to defend myself in the night. I was determined to not allow this house to defeat me, nor that beast. I could not give up against such odds. I feared the creature, but I had to find a way to defeat it so that I could conclude my business in North Carolina. There seemed to be more to this situation than I could understand.

I sat thinking in the dimly lit room. I thought of possible solutions, but one thing remained. I could never truly understand the situation or a solution without more information. I could not even begin to fathom how to vanquish this creature without research. I needed to search the property tomorrow and see if there was anything else out of the ordinary. Perhaps the answer to my issues lies somewhere on the property. If not, perhaps Percy could point me to anyone that might know about such a thing.

Surely there would be some sign as to how this creature was made that could tell me how to send the thing back from whence it came. I sat there in the dark, staring toward the door. Silence once again had taken over the room. I had now become engrossed in watching the door for any sounds from the hallway. I had the desire to sleep, but there was a stubborn rejection of putting myself in such a helpless mode. I had the desire to wipe all fear from my mind and deeply rest. My stubbornness grew in me until I had decided that it was better to investigate the upper floor of the home. I had to know what was going on and if I could be in danger of losing my life. Call it foolishness or stupidity, but I had to know. I had to investigate anything that could help me in my struggles against evil. I did, however, still hold on to the fear that going to the upper level would be the end of me. I did not wish to attract the creature's attention, but I found that with each thought, I was drawing closer to the conclusion that I must investigate.

I began to prepare my mind for what would come next. I knew that if I even ventured near the upper level and even farther, the creature would accept this as an invitation to torment me. I could not allow that. I finished my thoughts and began to work up my courage once again. With a dreadful heart, I gathered my overcoat and tied it around my waist. I then stood and slowly worked my way across the room to the door. As I walked closer to the door, I could only imagine what could happen next. Would the creature be waiting for me? I took a deep breath and choked my fear down as well as I could. I didn't want to give the creature any fuel to be able to torment me. I slipped my hand onto the doorknob and gently turned the knob to unlatch it. With my other hand, I slowly reached out and grasped the deadbolt. I followed this with a delicate turning of the lock. As I turned the lock lever to the right, my heart sank. I would re-enter the hallway of the manor and make my way to the foot of the stairs. This was only worse because of my knowledge that this was where the creature had originated within the home. I could only imagine this horrid thing ambushing me as I continued.

I cracked the door open and looked out into the hallway. My eyes slowly followed the edge of the door as I opened it further. Eventually, my eyes were pointed toward the stairs at the front of the home. With a swift turn, I entered my bedroom again and retrieved the candle holder that was on the table. Its dim light shone brightly in the pitch-black manor. I slowly worked up my nerve as I rounded the edge of the door and began to move down the hallway. Nothing could be seen as I moved farther and farther toward my goal. I felt a slight rush of relief as I moved onward. This relief was soon crushed under the weight of knowing that I would soon journey to the upper portion of the home.

My heart raced as I approached the stairs. I could barely see the stairs, however, because of the dim light of the candle. I carefully crept forward to the door of the sitting room and closed it. I moved forward to the base of the stairs and looked upward. Even with the candle held out in front of me, I still could barely make out anything in this large open space. I crept up the stairs as I continued to stare into the second level. It seemed that everything had returned to the way it was before the creature had shown itself. I held out the candle to try to see as best as I could, but the light was still too dim. I now stood on the landing at the top of the stairs and began surveying my surroundings. I could see nothing else was out of place. I could not know if the creature hid, waiting for me. The fear rose in my throat as I looked around on the landing. I could barely make out doors and openings to rooms. I wanted to leave no chance that I would be easy prey for this thing. I also still had no clear idea of its capabilities. All this aside, I still felt as if I were only being toyed with currently.

My heart pounded as I considered taking a step forward, each moment only further solidifying my worry and fear. If there were any time that this being would be attracted to my fear, it would be now. With effort, I picked up my left foot and moved it forward. My whole leg felt as if it were made of lead. I found it harder and harder to move forward quickly. Whether it was out of fear or caution, I did not know. I moved toward the right of the stairs and began to venture toward the room with the hatch to the attic. The door was now open again, and I could see darkness hanging in the air. I slowly reached out my hand and grasped the doorknob. As slowly as I could, I pulled the door shut. I twisted the knob to the right and pulled firmly against the door. I then slowly released the knob. I did not know if the creature would wish to attack me further, but I could at least know that it would have to open the door to do so. This, in my mind, gave me an advantage. I would clearly be able to hear the door opening as each door in the manor creaked distinctively. Sweat now began to run down my face and I could feel the anxiety well up inside me. Even with a failsafe such as listening for the door, I could not settle myself properly.

I turned and slowly began working my way down the hallway. With my candle held higher to illuminate further down the hallway, I checked my surroundings as thoroughly as I could as I moved forward. No matter where I looked, it seemed that the house was back to normal. I knew this could not be possible, however, because I could still feel that pressure in my chest. I walked as quietly and slowly as I could. I occasionally turned around to check behind me to make sure I was as alert as possible. I reached the end of the hall and turned to my left to look into a door that had been opened earlier. I began to step toward the door when I felt something like a hand grab my left ankle. With a firm tug, I was dragged down the hall and thrown down the stairs. It seemed like I would never reach the end of the fall. I could feel nothing but fear as I flew through the air and began to collide with several steps on the way to the bottom. At last, I knew that I had reached the bottom when I came down painfully on my right side. The floor seemed to give slightly as I collided with the wood in the floor.

For a moment I thought that I had injured myself as I lay there feeling shooting pain up and down my right side and my arm. The front door of the manor opened itself before my very eyes. I could feel a sense of dread again as I once again felt something grab my ankle and begin to pull me toward the front door. With a firm tug, I was wrenched out of the home and dragged all the way to the fence at the very front of the property. As I regained my footing and stood up, I could see the front door swing shut with a loud bang. I was horrified at the thought that I might be locked out of the manor completely. Just then the pain of landing at the base of the stairs and being dragged outside caught up with me. I stood in the dark of the night hunched over and grasping at my right side. I could not understand what it was that gave this being so much power, but I was still determined to eliminate this demon from the manor.

I now looked toward the house with a deep frustration. I charged the front of the home with as much spirit as I could muster. I reached the door and began to try to open the door. I could not, however, because the door seemed to be barred from the inside. It was most unusual since the door would not open, but I could turn the knob completely as if the door was not locked. This didn't sit well with me. I beat my fists on the door as if demanding that the demon open it. I feared entering the home, but sleeping outside was not an option. I did not wish to be exposed to the weather, and beyond all else, I had no desire to lose my foothold against this being. I continued beating on the door more furiously than the last. I could not allow myself to give up against this thing.

At that moment I stopped, for I heard a strange sound coming from inside the home. The sound came like a low rumbling followed by a shuffling sound just beyond the door. The sound gave me pause unlike any other. It made me think of some large man dragging one of his feet back and forth across the floor. I struggled to hear the rumbling noise for it was far too quiet to be completely audible. I leaned against the door and listened for whatever was causing this sound. As I put a slight pressure against the wood of the door, I heard a creaking sound as the door was partially supporting my weight. I stood leaning against the door listening, but the sounds had stopped. I listened for a moment, and after some minutes I heard the shuffling again but it was coming toward the door. The sounds were so strange that I could not help but lean there and listen. The sounds grew louder, and the rumbling began to shake the door. These sounds grew so loud that I could have sworn that someone was approaching the door. I listened until the sound had reached its peak and dissipated just beyond the door. I continued to listen for any other sounds.

As I stood there in complete silence now, I felt a chilled air as if someone was breathing through the door. The air gushed from the inside of the home against my face until I heard, "Benjamin! Help me! I am burning!" This voice spoke in a soft and gentle way but grew faint as the statement was finished. The voice gave me chills that ran down my body. It was almost as if I had gone completely numb. The fear grew inside of me until I heard creaking noises just behind me. I stopped and stood straight. My eyes were open-wide in their sockets. I was in terror to turn and face the creaking noise until I could feel that cold breath against the back of my neck.

I turned suddenly so as to catch the thing off guard. This was not successful in any way. As I turned, I could see a woman dressed in black with her long black hair floating. The hair was stretched outward from the back of her head. Her face was ghostly pale and was missing the right side of her face. She had her long, spindly fingers stretched out in front of her as if she were trying to grasp me. She had a creepy smile on her face and just floated closer and closer to me. I fell back against the door and then through the doorway as the door opened under my weight. I fell into the foyer of the manor and looked upward toward this woman. I scrambled backward as I let out a guttural scream. I rushed to my feet and turned with all my might to enter the home and close the door. I grasped the edge of the door and with all haste slammed it in the spirit's face. I took a few steps back from the door and waited for the being to attempt to open the door. I did not know what I would have done if the spirit burst through the door, but I was ready for anything. I had been met with good fortune, however, for the apparition seemed to make no moves to open the door.

I exhaled slowly and rubbed my hand across the back of my head. I did not realize that I had been holding my breath the whole time that I was being tormented by this floating woman. I regained my composure and moved toward the door to lock it. I skillfully turned the latch into the locked position. I hoped that nothing else was coming my way. As I stood there in front of the door, I realized that I was engulfed in darkness. I did not know how I would be able to defend myself if I could not see. This caused me to wonder what had happened to the candle that I held in my right hand when I was being dragged down the hallway. I turned and peered into the darkness. I could not see any illumination to indicate that the candle still burned. I decided that the only course of action would be to walk up the stairs and retrieve the candle and its holder.

I took one step forward and felt something soft squish under my foot. It seemed malleable but firm once it had been crushed against the floors. I bent down and picked it up. I could feel the porous material of wax. This was the candle that I had meant to retrieve. I reformed the candle as best I could in my hand and produced a match from my right pocket. With a strike against the ground, I was able to get the candle relit. I looked around me in the foyer and could not find any trace of the candle holder. I retreated back to the bedroom and shut and locked the door behind me. It didn't take long to set the candle back on the table in an empty holder that set on the table. I stepped gently back and sat on the edge of the bed. I was also cautiously listening for signs that I was being pursued, but there was nothing. I felt nothing, in this second, but a cold fear that ran through my veins like water. I could not dream of from where such creatures emerge, but wherever these things were from, it must be a dreadful place.

My heart pounded in my chest but was now calming. I could feel a slight sweat running down my cheeks. I thought for a moment that it could be blood, but with further investigation, it was not blood. I continued to sit as if waiting for the spirit to enter the home and then my bedroom. I feared what might happen to my sanity if I stayed here. I was exposed to such strenuous supernatural forces. I feared that I might lose the last shred of myself that lingered in my mind.

I sat listening for a moment before I decided to get a drink of water. I could at least drink from the pitcher that was still half full on the end table beside the bed. It was also nice to have the door to the room shut and locked so as to keep anything that I couldn't trust away. Though I feared the creature, there was nothing that it could do without me noticing it now. At least this was my hope. I did not know what power the creature really possessed, but as long as it could not enter rooms through walls, then I would be safe. I stood from the side of the bed and slowly moved over to the end table. I picked up the glass that I had drank from last night and the water pitcher. It didn't take long for me to pour a glass of refreshing water. I set the pitcher down and took a deep sip of water.

The water was still cool even after sitting in the room all day. Each sip gave me the feeling of being refreshed almost as if I had gained a new energy. I was not sure what I would do about sleep, but if I could lie with a period of quiet, then I might be able to rest. If I could not simply destroy the creature, then I would outsmart it in any way that I could. This meant being set when I was in my room at night and making sure that the door was locked tight. I drank deeper into the cup of water as I thought about how I would prepare myself each night until I could deal with this dark being.

The light from the candle glimmered off the walls and shone ever brighter off the pitcher. Each flicker of the candle caused my shadow to dance across the walls as I had the glass tilted to drink from it. The shadow's movement looked somewhat eerie in the room. I stood beside the bed watching my shadow as I finished off the glass of water. Upon further inspection of the pitcher, I knew that I had at least two more glasses worth of water for the rest of the night. I then turned my attention back to my shadow, which seemed eerier now in the dim candlelight. I waited in horror for the shadow to move of its own volition. I did not want to think in such negative and horrific terms, but with all that had happened tonight, I could not be too careful. The shadow danced to and fro but did not act in a suspicious way at all.

I moved closer to the bed and sat back down. I watched the candle flicker in the dimly lit room. The flame danced around the central core of the candle itself. The wick seemed to be its guide and its source of life. It seemed as if the flame had now begun to dance with a rhythm that only the flame would understand. I could not imagine the depth that these supernatural events would devastate anyone that wanted to move into the home. Even as I knew about the creature and the other horrors that it seemed to command, I still had had a strenuous time staying in the manor. I lay back in the bed and gave one final look toward the door. I felt my eyes growing heavier and heavier until they had closed. I gently laid my head on my pillow and fell into a deep sleep.

I fell into the darkness that surrounded me. It was deep and never ending on any side. I had reached the deepest sleep that I could and began to feel my mind slipping into a dream state. My mind whirred with thoughts and feelings. I could feel fear riddled with doubt as I awoke in a bed on the second level. The bed was so soft and comfortable. I did not know how I had arrived in this bed last night. The last thing that I felt was falling asleep with the door to my room locked tightly in my bed. I looked around the room, but it was different than it usually had been. The room was filled with a strange mist that was almost thick enough to obscure my vision. I could still see the walls on each side of the room. The room was, of course, not ablaze with any fire that I could see. I could not tell from where the mist had come. The door on the other side of the room was closed and looked as if it had been firmly latched. I was startled at the thought that the house could be on fire and I was not able to see or feel the flame. I rushed out of the bed and toward the door. I still did not feel any heat. Upon further investigation, I also could not smell smoke and the mist did not seem to act like smoke from a fire. There was not a dampness to the air either. It was as if the mist were simply an illusion. I could not feel the mist, nor could I see any effects of the mist if indeed it was water hanging in the air.

I came to the door and swiftly unlatched it. The door creaked rather loudly as it opened. I peered out into the hallway, but the hallway did not seem to have the same light filtering into it as the bedroom had. Upon looking back into the bedroom, I could see what looked like sunlight filtering in, but not the hallway. It was darkness that reigned in the hallway. This caught me off guard as I could not explain any reason for this to happen. I looked back into the bedroom one last time, and it still held an extreme amount of light shining into the room. I had perfect vision save for the mist that was hanging in the air. I turned back to the hallway, and the darkness was still thick and seemed to block nearly all vision. I shut the door and turned back to the bed. I walked to the bedside table and grasped the candle to light it. I looked down at the candle, and before I could do anything, the candle lit itself. I was startled by this but was far more intrigued by the deep candle holder firmly and walked to the door. I stood in the doorway and held the candle out to see through the darkness. I looked toward the stairs but was astonished when I could not see that the stairs were in their place. I knew that this could not be possible. I thought for a moment, pausing in the hallway. I could not believe that this was real. The information that I had observed led me to the conclusion that I was still asleep and this was a dream.

I had only a moment to think about this before I heard a loud creaking just behind me. I turned my head and held out the candle in the opposite direction. I peered deeply toward the guest room door that was now swinging open and smacked against the wall. I tried to look into the room but could not see anything. I could not even see the window that I had observed when I had investigated this room earlier. I ultimately began to creep toward the door. I felt the bold fear hanging in the air around me. My stomach now felt upset by this strong fear. I crept ever closer to the door and peered around the corner and into the room. There was no furniture in the room, and the darkness seemed at its thickest in the far corner. I began to see a shifting within the corner that seemed to be the darkness itself moving.

The fear that I was feeling had now jumped into my throat. I felt as if I could not swallow or breathe. I stood there for a moment, watching this shifting in the darkness. I began to turn and run for the other bedroom, but before I could, the door slammed behind me, blocking my escape. I stood in horror as all that I could do was watch this happen before my eyes. The darkness continued to shift, and what looked like a creature began to emerge. It was very large and had giant red eyes. I could see a small portion of its face, but not enough to get any detail. Its eyes gazed into mine with a fire that seemed to almost burn my eyes. There was no sound that the creature usually made. It simply looked at me. I was frozen in fear and could barely think. My mind was empty as I stared at the being that was so intent on destroying me or at least chasing me away.

I could feel the creature's gaze fixated on me as I tried to squelch my fear. The darkness grew thicker until I could barely see anything around those piercing red eyes. I felt chills running up and down my spine. My head was spinning with fear, and the only desire that took me over was to try to break through the door. I turned and began hitting the door as hard as I could with my hand and rammed the door with my shoulder. Nothing that I tried even moved the door at all. I continued to beat on the door and try to escape as I heard very heavy and forceful steps behind me. It sounded as if the thing was slowly walking toward me. I turned to look toward the footsteps and was only horrified at what I saw. I stood there looking upon the creature for a second and was horrified at its appearance. It was twisted with hatred and malice. I could feel evil coming off the creature.

This sight made me turn toward the door again and continue beating on the door, but harder now. I used all the strength that I could muster until I felt hands around my ankles and began to fall toward the ground. When I had become prone on the floor, I could feel myself being dragged backward toward the corner. I could not stop this from happening no matter what I did. I tried to get to my feet and run toward the door again, but nothing could release me from this grip. I felt my feet slide from under me again, and I watched as the floor rushed up to meet my face. My head slammed against the floor, and I lost my bearing. The shock was too much for my head to take, and I was nearly knocked unconscious. I lay there for a moment and tried to regain my focus as I turned to look up toward whatever was behind me.

As I opened my eyes and allowed them to focus on what was in front of me, the creature's face was mere inches from my face. The horror was insurmountable as I began to be dragged farther into the corner. I screamed out as I entered the darkness, only to see the creature's clawed feet firmly planted on the floor. I felt darkness take me, and in an instant, I awoke in my bedroom downstairs. I could see nothing but darkness. The candle that flickered within the room had now drowned in a pool of wax. My face was somewhat numb from being pressed into the pillow firmly. I looked toward the window in the bedroom and saw nothing but darkness outside save for some scant rays of moonlight. My impression was that I had awoken only hours after I had fallen asleep, but the lack of even a sliver of sunlight disturbed me. I had no idea if I was awake or if I was still stuck in a dream state. I questioned all possibilities in my mind but could not be sure without further investigation.

I stood from the bed and walked even closer to the window. Without hesitation, I looked out of the window and toward the sky. I could see the moon's outline through the clouds that thinly covered the moon. I looked around the room for any further signs that I was not asleep. Nothing seemed out of place. I looked toward the door that was directly behind me, but it was shut and did not seem strange in any way. I looked to the left of me to the table, but it was just as it had been when I had fallen asleep. My investigation of the room did not reveal anything that was not where it should be. I wanted to investigate the rest of the house, but I could still feel that fear of the unknown. I felt compelled to investigate, however, as if I was being pulled toward the door. I could not stop myself. I tried to will my body to lie back down in the bed but to no avail. I could not force myself to stop approaching the door.

I reached out and put my hand on the doorknob, and without voluntary action, my hand twisted the knob. I felt the door begin to open and felt called to look forward and could not turn my head or close my eyes. I was forced to look forward toward the other wall. I could see there was a dimly lit area in the wall with ghostly shadows dancing around. I could also hear what sounded like laughter or a loud conversation. I was now compelled by simple curiosity to investigate the hole in the wall that had now formed. As I approached, the laughter grew louder and the air in the room became more warm and more humid.

My mind raced with possibilities of what I would discover. I rounded the corner of the hole and peeked into the space. The light was very bright as it gleamed throughout the room from a fire. I had a strange feeling that something was very, very wrong within the space. I leaned further into the hole and squinted my eyes to see better in the area. I could make out several people dancing around a bonfire and chanting. I could not make out their words, but it sounded as if they were performing a ritual or ancient rite. I observed that some of the people looked very familiar. I looked closer at the faces of two of the women that were mixed into the others. I could make out very distinct details and could see my mother and my aunt dancing around the fire and chanting. I was amazed at the fact that my mother and aunt were in the group. Was this a real event in time or simply something that I wanted to see?

Everyone that was dancing in the formation was almost naked. I leaned further into the opening, and in the corner, I could see that there was a young man sitting with fear covering his face. This was the boy from my dream. If this was to play out like in my previous dream, then this was the period when this man was sacrificed. The whole assembly seemed sinister in every way. I did not really want to be there but felt as if I was supposed to see this vision. The worshipers stopped dancing and chanting around the fire and began to prepare the boy. I did not know what terrible ritual they had in mind. I watched as they cut the ropes that held the boy to the chair while others of the group prepared some sort of concoction in a bowl. I could not tell what was in the mixture, but I was sure that it was a preparation for this intrinsically evil gathering. The boy gurgled out what seemed to be a cry for help. His mouth was filled with a cloth that was held in his mouth by another cloth tied around his head. This made it impossible for his cries to be understood.

I looked toward the others that were still preparing the mixture and noticed that they had begun placing strange plants in the bowl. I couldn't tell what the plant was or what it might do if ingested. The solution was poured from the bowl into a very finely crafted goblet. The goblet was ebony and held rubies around the middle banding of gold around the goblet. I was amazed at such craftsmanship and was certain that no one in this collection of worshipers could have crafted the goblet.

The mixture was stirred within the goblet and presented to the boy. My mother reached out and grasped the boy's mouth and gently opened it. She caressed his face gracefully as if to comfort the boy. My aunt grasped the goblet and placed the rim on the boy's lips. With a gradual tilting of the goblet, my aunt poured the mixture into the boy's mouth. I screamed out to stop this torture of the young man, but no one heard me or even reacted to my reaching into the hole. It was as if I was not even there, or if I was, then I was some sort of spirit to the worshipers. I even reached out and tried to take the cup from my aunt, but I could not. I simply phased through the object. The boy drank the elixir and seemed to wince with distaste for the flavor of the mixture. My mother released the boy's mouth and looked toward my aunt. At that moment, my mother's eyes caught mine. I could not tell if she was looking through me or if she could actually see me. Her mouth moved into a rather sinister smile. It was wide and creepy. This caught me completely off guard. I had no idea what to do in this instance. I felt as if I should run but also seemed to understand that I was not really there at all.

Both stood without clothing, rubbing a chalky substance just above their breasts. They now were both staring deeply into my eyes with an aroused smile. It was as if they were taunting me to stop them from their evil actions. They painted a symbol that was a circle with what looked like a roughly drawn goat's head in the center. I was shocked at this symbol. It was unlike anything that I had ever seen. It seemed that the goat-like creature that had tried to attack me on my journey here was somehow worshiped by these people. The boy looked on in fright as my mother and aunt grasped each of his arms and forced him to walk toward the fire. I could not believe that this was occurring, for it was not unlike the dream that I had witnessed earlier. The rest played out like a repeat in time. Though if that were the case, then how did it seem that my mother and aunt knew that I was present?

The worshipers gathered behind the boy, my mother, and my aunt and began chanting again. I once again tried to stop them, but I could not. My aunt pulled a dagger from the cloth that was wrapped around her leg and held it high over her head as she chanted and showed it to the others. My mother stood just beside her, still holding the boy so that he didn't run.

With a swift and sure slice at the boy's throat, the dagger cut open the flesh as blood began to pour out into the same bowl that held the mixture. The boy was simply held up by my mother and aunt as he passed from life and his blood poured into the bowl. I witnessed this event yet again with horror and disdain for these people's actions. The boy was laid to the side while my aunt performed an incantation over the bowl and began to drink the boy's blood. The others soon lined up in front of my aunt and began to follow her actions. One by one they all drank from the bowl.

I had thought before that the boy was a worker for my aunt, but I did not recognize him at all now. I was certain of this now as I could see the details of his face vividly. I looked upon his face as he lay dead on the ground. I studied his face and did not know who he was or what relationship he had to the manor or my aunt. The boy lay motionless on the ground until I began to study him further and the carvings that his skin held. The carvings were made of individual cuts that formed symbols. I looked at his cuts in more detail until he opened his eyes and with a twisted face grinned at me. I fled the scene in terror and ran back into the bedroom. As soon as I had passed the doorway, I fell forward into a brightly lit pit, which had fire springing up from within. I tried to stop my fall but could not and plummeted into the fire. I watched from outside my body as I burned to nothing. My skin blackened and I slipped beneath the fire and out of sight.

6

SECRETS

I awoke with a jolt at the horror of watching myself burn to death. I checked myself to make sure that it was only a dream. Everything seemed to be just the way it had been when I had fallen asleep. I looked toward the window and noticed that the sun had begun to shine through the trees as it rose over the horizon. I stood from the bed and took the pitcher of water back into the kitchen and fetched another pitcher of water from the bucket. I looked out the window as I poured the pitcher full of water. I could feel a sense of peace and joy that the night had passed. It seemed to be a distant memory that I was once fighting for my life against this horrid creature. I had hoped that today would be an uneventful one as I would meet with Mary's family. Though I had not forgotten that Percy would arrive soon to gather me for breakfast. I put the pitcher on the counter and walked to the front door. Even with the sun shining into the home, I was still apprehensive. I looked over my shoulder several times after I had passed the stairs in the foyer. I felt as if I could not become complacent and allow this being to get the better of me.

I looked out of the window to see if Percy had arrived. I hoped that I would be able to leave this evil behind and enjoy my day without torment. I imagined that this day would be perfect in every way. Though tonight, I was sure that I would have to be on my guard. I moved back to the bedroom since I still had time to dress myself before Percy arrived. I quickly slipped on my suit and straightened my tie as I had become accustomed. In all my years as a banker, I had learned to dress myself in a rather swift fashion. I then grabbed my glass of water and moved back into the kitchen to pour a glass of water. I had worried that I would not be able to rest enough given my eventful night. I drank the glass of water vigorously as if I had never had water before.

As I moved back into the foyer to check the window again, I realized that I could not feel any danger or fear. It was as if this demon didn't even inhabit the home. I had felt this before, but it had never been more apparent given all that I had faced in the past several days. I reached the window and checked for Percy to arrive. I could see that he was now coming this way. I walked out onto the porch and sat down on the chair that sat to the right of the entranceway. The air was refreshing as I sat there feeling the breeze. I could hear the trees wafting about in the wind. I had never felt so comfortable in the manor until this moment. I had hoped that the dark occurrences were over. The fact still remained that I would have to deal with this demonic creature if, in fact, it still remained within the home. Perhaps today would yield the answers that I sought to fight this thing. Somehow I knew that Percy would know how to get the answers I needed. I did not wish to pull Percy into this situation any more than I already had, but it would be his choice to help me or not. I suspected that he might know more about this evil than even he knew, anything that he could remember about my aunt or her actions here on the manor property.

I watched the wagon moving closer to the home. Percy was now guiding the horses through the turn onto the drive of the home. He seemed to have a concerned look on his face as his eyes met mine. I suspected that he knew that I had had a rough night in the home. Though this was only my guess. I waved to Percy, and he responded as he approached the porch.

Percy smirked slightly and called out, "How are you this morning, Benjamin?"

I stood from my chair and replied, "I am a bit exhausted but still in good health!"

Percy pulled the wagon up beside me and stopped. "I had hoped that you would be able to rest last night, but I see that I was wrong."

I rubbed my eyes and replied, "I did not think that my lack of sleep was that noticeable."

Percy smiled with amusement at these words. "It is not only your eyes that gave it away. I could see and hear some of the difficulties that you were having."

It was then that I remembered that Percy was relatively close to the Tourney Manor. His farmhouse was in a line of sight from the manor, after all. "What did you observe?"

Percy climbed down from the seat of the wagon and walked around the horses, patting the horses as he went. Percy strolled onto the porch and produced his pipe from his pocket. "I could see that you were having issues staying inside the home. I am glad that no one else can see into the front yard of this house. You were dragged by nothing out to the road there. I then saw you run toward the door and begin yelling to be let in. I knew what was happening, but I am sure that no one else would know. I do have to ask, did you see it again?" Percy looked at me with an intense gaze. It was almost as if he relished the idea that I had seen the demon again. This was odd at first as I could not understand why Percy would be excited about seeing a demon.

I smiled and sat back in the rocking chair. "I did see the beast again, but it was in a dream."

Percy seemed intrigued at this admittance. Percy began cleaning the bowl of his pipe. "I am sorry to bring all of this up, but I feel that we need to know all that we can about what this thing could be. Would you be willing to speak with the minister about it?"

I thought for a moment and replied, "I would be accepting, but I am indisposed today as I am going to meet with Mary and her family."

Percy smiled suavely and asked, "Oh! You are going to Mary's home today?" He finished this question with a suspicious smile I felt I should not trust.

I looked to the right and said, "Yes, I am."

Percy began to chuckle in the most amused way as he packed the bowl of his pipe and lit it with a match. I felt as if Percy was not supportive of my meeting Mary today. "I am sorry, Benjamin. I just did not think that you would be willing to entertain a relationship with someone so young and completely tied to Hillsborough. It is also so sweet."

I gave Percy a most annoyed look. I could agree with his first points. I had not wished to be tied to Hillsborough in the way of staying here. After all, I still had to return to New York and continue my work at the bank. I did, however, have a good feeling about Mary and my meeting with her today. I wondered if she would be willing to correspond with me from so long a distance or possibly come with me to see the city. This would break every social norm for anyone, but I felt that I must at least trust myself enough to try. "I appreciate your guidance, Percy. I understand what you mean, but I am still going to try to have the best time that I can today. I do not know if I will survive another night in this home, after all."

Percy nodded as he began to puff on his pipe. "I am glad that you are not allowing yourself to get carried away. I know that things could change, but you do not know that either. Best to take it all in store today." I agreed and Percy added, "I will go to arrange a meeting with the minister for tomorrow if you are able to go."

I considered what I needed to do tomorrow and replied, "I would appreciate that. Perhaps a man of the cloth could shed light on how to deal with this terrifying creature."

At my words, Percy sat looking into the distance. I could see that his mind had wandered back to yesterday's meeting with the demon. I broke the silence by saying, "Am I still able to enjoy breakfast with your family this morning?"

Percy snapped back into reality and replied, "Yes! I am sorry,

Benjamin. I had a hard time forgetting that devil. Now it seems that it is all that I can think about. Let us be off."

I could sense Percy's unease. I too wished to be far away from this manor even in the daylight. Though I was curious as to whether the demon would haunt the home during the day should I remain. I thought it best to not explore that idea and quickly loaded into the wagon.

Percy wasted no time in driving the wagon back onto the road. It seemed that Percy was pushing the horses much harder to pull the wagon faster than I had ever traveled along this road. We sat in silence as Percy concentrated intently on the road. I could tell Percy had no desire to be anywhere near the manor. We arrived at Percy's farmhouse in record time, it seemed.

I looked at Percy as he brought the wagon to a complete stop. "Are you all right, Percy?" I asked.

Percy did not answer at first. He simply leaped off the wagon seat and looked up at me. "I am fine, but I had a bad feeling about lingering near the manor. Besides, we wanted to eat breakfast, right?"

I nodded and accepted his response. I could not fault Percy for wanting to stay away from the manor. This was the same thing that I had wished for last night. I could not wish a terror upon anyone, let alone someone like Percy, who had assisted me when no one else seemed to care. I stepped down from the other side of the seat and assisted Percy with leading the horses into the pasture and unhitching the wagon.

"I am sorry that I dragged you into this, Percy."

Percy did not seem to hear my words as he kept working to close the gate to the pasture. Eventually, he did turn to look at me and responded with, "It's all right, Benjamin. It wasn't as if you knew that we would see such a horrible thing. I have come to terms with what is happening in Caroline's home. I just cannot understand how to defeat this thing. I am also wondering how I have not seen this all before. I was her caretaker for years and before that a worker at her farm. I have no recollection of anything relating to this creature!"

I looked away from Percy for a moment. I thought about whether

I should venture to tell Percy about the vision that I had witnessed in the hallway. Percy began to walk away with a seeming anger welling up in him.

"I saw something in the hallway last night! It was a vision of people dancing and chanting. They sacrificed this young man and drank his blood. My aunt and my mother were both present."

With this outburst, Percy stopped dead in his tracks. He made no motion for a moment and then turned to me and said, "How many people did you see?"

I thought back to the vision. "I don't know. There were a lot of people. Maybe twenty or thirty people?"

Percy walked intently back over to me and said, "What you have seen cannot be true! I refuse to believe that Caroline would have called something like that into her home!" Percy had all the fury of a spurned lover in his voice. It seemed that he was almost accusing me of lying. Though I could understand. If anyone had told me something like that about my own mother, I don't know what I would have done. I suppose that I would have told them they were lying as well.

"I am sorry, Percy. I know that was hard to hear, but I think that you have suspected something like that had to have happened. Ever since—"

Percy interrupted me, "Ever since what? That thing tried to kill us in the manor?"

I stood silent and eventually nodded.

"I know that you have not seen your aunt in many years and this is all lost on you, but I knew her like my own mother! Caroline did not seem of the sort to do such a thing!"

I paused and waited for Percy to walk away. "You mean to tell me that you didn't know about anything?"

Percy stopped once again but did not return. "I knew nothing of this. In all the time that I stayed with Caroline, the manor was quiet. There was nothing strange going on. If anything like this had happened, then I would have never been around her. This was all before I arrived in Hillsborough."

I stood there feeling like a fool for even mentioning the vision.

After all, I had had time to deal with what I had seen. Percy didn't have time for anything now. Foolishly I asked, "So what do we do now, Percy? Are we to allow such a sick perversion to remain in the home that we both have come to bond over? Do you feel that this is the proper way to deal with Caroline's legacy?"

Percy stood there looking at me for a moment. I could feel his heart tearing in two. One part of him wished to defeat this being at all costs, but this was being hidden by the portion that could not process all this information.

"I don't like this any more than you do. My own mother was taking part in this practice. This perversion of all that God has placed here. I will not allow their memories to be sullied with such evil!"

Percy said nothing. He simply looked into my eyes and nodded. "Then there is only one course of action. We must meet with the reverend tomorrow. I will talk to some of the other servants that Caroline employed and see what they know." With that Percy turned and began to walk away.

I yelled out, "Thank you, Percy!"

He didn't stop moving away from me. He didn't even act as if he had heard anything that I had just said. I stood there for a moment and processed what had just happened. Surely Percy would not hold any contempt for me at the words that had started this quarrel. I knew that he was right. In a way, I still did not know how to accept any of this information. My aunt and my own mother were worshiping satanic forces on the property, calling dark horrors into this world and into their lives. Could it have been that this was the reason for my visits when I was a child? Did my own father know about all this? I shuddered at the thought that both my parents had been involved. I could not come to understand in any way why anyone would wish to do something so terrible. Of course, nothing about this mattered now. Now it was our job to put an end to this evil and conclude the business that I had traveled to do.

Eventually, I followed Percy into his home. I had to compose myself as I entered the home. I did not wish to alert anyone in Percy's family as to what was going on in the manor. I also had hoped that

Percy had not informed his wife of anything either. I would prefer to not share any of this development with anyone but Percy. I sat down at the table and began to eat breakfast. No grace was said on this morning. I think that Percy and I sat in shock of all that had happened since last night. That or we were both simply focused on what we had to do with this demon. I did hope that Percy would not have too much of an interruption to his life by helping me. The conversations with Percy's family were short and pained. We both struggled to answer any questions. We simply sat in quiet as if we knew the other would betray our secret. It also had dawned on me that Percy probably did not wish to talk about any of this also because of the fact that he seemed to be in denial of it all.

After breakfast, Percy and I loaded some supplies into his wagon and fetched the horses from the pasture. It seemed as if time flew by as we had already hitched the horses to the wagon and began to drive away from Percy's farmhouse. I could tell that Chloe and Percy's children suspected something was happening but did not wish to say anything. This gave me comfort as it would have been harder to answer questions with half-truths and lies. Percy once again drove the horses hard to get to the manor. It seemed like an instant before we were pulling up to the porch in front of the home. I then helped Percy unhitch the horses again and place them in the holding pasture while we walked to the back of the home. Percy and I had now come to stand facing the well.

"I believe that I remember seeing a circle burned in the grass of the yard here. Perhaps that is where these ceremonies had taken place."

I nodded but stood in silent reserve. We both began to walk through the backyard, looking for any signs that dark rituals had taken place. I had hoped that the grass had not grown to obscure the sight, but I knew that I could not be that lucky. I followed Percy's lead, and we both began to move farther away from the home in our search to find out evidence. After some time, we walked to the back of an old hayloft and could see that the back of the building contained soot. It seemed caked on the outer wall of this building. I could not understand why soot would be on this building. I did not see any structure in the vision in the place where the ritual was being performed. Percy and I wasted no time examining the wood and grass beneath for any signs of a fire being burned in this spot. Finally, we uncovered this whole spot had soil that was still blackened. Though no rituals had been performed here in some time. The grass was not grown back and verdant. I could not believe it. Percy and I looked at each other with shock and surprise. We both had now confirmed that the vision, at least in part, had been real at one time. Though if we could confirm this, then the rest had to be true in our minds.

"This is not good, Benjamin. We have evidence that I will show to the minister if that is acceptable to you."

I replied, "I am fine with that. We need anyone that can help us. Perhaps the servants and the minister know more than they act like they do."

Percy nodded. We both stood there for a moment as the sun began to dramatically warm the world around us. I could tell that the thought of what we had discovered now began to set in. We both looked like men who were haunted by a past that was filled with sorrow and regret. Though I now felt certain that this was the reason that my mother would travel to North Carolina. For what purpose? What were they trying to accomplish? There seemed to be more questions now than answers. It was then that Percy punched the side of my arm with the back of his hand and said, "Follow me." He then rounded the side of the building and moved back toward the front of the home. "Benjamin, there is not much time, but I think there is something we need to see closer."

I did not reply to Percy's words. I simply followed his lead. I followed him to a small path that led deeper into the woods. We walked deeper into the forest for a bit and then turned onto another footpath that ran to the back of the property.

We came through the trees and out into a clearing that made it possible to see the footpath curve to the left around a small field and down to a circular clearing that seemed to have some objects made of stone. We continued to walk until we reached this clearing. I could now see that the objects were statues that sat against an embankment. On the other side of the circular clearing sat two benches that were also made of stone. Both the statues and the benches were ornately carved and had fine craftsmanship. We stood in the circle for a moment and then sat on the benches. Percy looked toward the statue in front of himself and said, "I do remember something that may be worthy of mention. I remember Caroline carrying something in her hand as she walked through the home one afternoon. I was leaving the farm by way of the road that entered the property and could see her through the windows. She looked as if she were carrying a book of some sort. She held it in her hands with great care as if she were holding a child. She walked from the kitchen up the stairs and then into the guest room, but that was all that I could see. After that, I never saw her carry anything like that again."

I nodded and looked forward to the statue that stood in front of me. I wondered if that book had the answers that we sought. I also wondered if the book would still be located on the property. Surely something so important had been kept safe and far away from anyone else that could not be trusted. Perhaps there was a secret storage space within the room that had been locked. It was still odd that there was nothing in the room at all.

We sat for only a moment longer until Percy stood and walked toward the statue in front of me and seemed to look intently at the details of the face. He rubbed some of the dirt from the top of the statue. "Benjamin! Look for any signs of something being burned in the field just behind you." I gave Percy a puzzled look, and he exclaimed, "Go!"

With that, I stood excitedly from the bench and walked out into the field. I looked on the ground for any signs that something had been burned there. Percy swiftly moved into the field and began to do the same. We walked around in a large circular area examining the ground. We each moved the grass around with our feet and peered deeply into the grass so as to see what was lying on the soil. I continued to look for a few more moments until Percy exclaimed, "Benjamin! Over here!" I ran to where he was standing with all haste as he pointed excitedly at the ground. When I had reached him, I stopped and scraped my foot across the ground to reveal what was under the grass. There were small pieces of charcoal that covered the ground in a large circular radius. Upon further investigation, it was clear that the area where we stood had been dug out just slightly so that it made a shallow bowl in the earth.

I looked at Percy, and he looked back at me. Now we both had evidence that my aunt was involved in something that was directly related to my dreams. I was curious, however, how Percy knew to look here.

"When your aunt had asked me to carve those statues, she had me engrave a symbol on the top of one of the statues. I remembered that it was the statue in front of you and realized what it had to mean. Caroline had asked me to carve a symbol that looked like a circle with a goat's head inside.

"When I removed the dirt that had built up on top of the statue, I noticed that the symbol also formed a point that was aimed toward this field." Percy seemed filled with intrigue and excitement. Percy almost seemed to dance with all this excitement. With that, we continued to move farther along the path.

Next, we came to a pasture that sat just behind the home. There seemed to be nothing out of the ordinary here, but I was able to see the layout of the other pastures from this point. We walked a little farther, and I looked at Percy and asked, "Do you think that the book you had seen my aunt carry is somewhere still on the property?"

Percy paused and replied, "I believe that we could find the book, but it all depends on if there was anyone else who would have wished to possess the book. It is possible that Caroline would have given such an important book to someone else within the book, especially if she wished them to continue her work after her passing."

I agreed wholeheartedly with this assessment. Nothing as important as a book of rituals would have been left behind to be discovered. Though it was only a guess that the book held any rituals or anything special at all within it. I continued to follow Percy down another footpath and added, "Do you think that the empty room would hold a secret storage area of any kind?"

Percy looked at me as if I had lost my mind and then smiled. "That is a possibility." He then motioned for me to follow him and began to walk toward the home with more vigor. We once again entered the home but through the back door now. Percy tore open the door to the room, and I followed him inside. The light that shone into the room seemed too dim. At Percy's suggestion, I moved into the sitting room and grabbed a fresh candle and another candle holder. With the grace of an angel, I lit the candle while quickly shuffling through the hallway and into the room. It was difficult at first to feel about the wall for any openings that could be a door or false wall with the candle in my hand. I did not wish to burn the wall in any way or to place soot on the nice, clean walls.

It was odd, however, that the room was so clean. No dust or dirt had gathered in the creases of the wall or near the floorboards. I was confused by this. "Percy! How has this room stayed so clean?"

Percy stopped what he was doing immediately and looked about the walls. He seemed to have come to the same realization that I had. "I am not sure. It has been several years since anyone has been in this room to my knowledge."

We both resumed our work but with more haste. It was apparent that we had both felt the same thing. The demon maintained this room for his own. In our minds, no other explanation could exist. There was no other rational explanation. No one had entered this room in some time. This was evidenced by the fact that Percy had felt the door locked the whole time that he had come to clean the home in my aunt's last days. That is unless Percy was lying and he truly held a key to the door the whole time. I knew this to not be true, however. Percy reacted with the same fear that I had seen and felt in myself. I had witnessed his distress at opening the door and seeing that nothing was contained within. If Percy had any involvement in this, then his face told no secrets, and I found that impossible to believe.

I began searching in new areas, but this time bringing the light closer to the wall at times to see if there were any cracks. Whatever importance this room held to the demon was not clear. Just as I had begun to ponder what could be contained in the room, I came across what looked like a seam in the wall. It was well hidden, but the shiny aspect of the metal betrayed the seam. "Percy, I found something!"

Percy now moved to where I stood and saw the seam for himself. He instantly began looking about for another seam. It took some time, but we were able to locate another seam. The two seams perfectly outlined two sides of a door. It was an incredible discovery. Though now Percy and I stood gazing at the door and looking for any further seams. We had to be sure that there was no trick to this room.

With no other seams being discovered, we now began searching for a way to open the door. My thoughts began to turn toward breaking through the door, though we still did not know if the door was made of metal. This would present a problem. It also remained to be seen whether the demon would allow such damage to take place in this room. That is if it was the beast's lair.

Eventually, Percy was able to locate another seam. This one looked like a box that had been turned on its side. It did not take long before I was able to locate the handhold. With one firm pull, I could feel the latch to the door disengage. I pulled ever harder at the door as it slowly gave way. It took all the strength I could muster to pull the door open. The hinges felt as though they had stuck in the shut position. That or the door was made of metal and was extremely heavy.

Percy stood back from the door in amazement as we saw it slowly swing into the open position. We both held a curiosity about what this room would reveal. Once the door stopped, it was all the way against the wall that held its hinges. I stood back from the door and looked into the newly found room. It was not deep like any normal room, but was instead like a shallow closet, though I still couldn't see what it contained. Percy quickly grasped the candle holder from my hands and held it out in the doorway. I walked into the closet and beheld what looked like a lectern with an impression on it. It was in the shape of a book. This must have been where the book that Percy remembered was held. In some ways, I felt relief at the knowledge that I would not have to behold such a wretched thing. In other ways,

I felt sorrow that we were not able to secure an idea of what was happening within the manor. Though there was one thing that was contained within the room. It was a smaller book wrapped in cloth. The cloth seemed to have a wax property over it. I opened the book and beheld what seemed like a journal. The journal had a symbol of the goat with a circle around it. Though this time it was not just the head of the goat, but the whole being. It was a twisted and horrible image that seemed to be carved into the page. The page itself, however, seemed to be made of something other than paper. It was thick and oily like leather, but not any leather that I have seen.

My mind instantly turned to the boy. Could it be that this was his flesh that the leather was comprised of? I shuddered at this thought. I didn't wish to consider this as the answer to my question. I turned to show Percy what I had found. He looked on with horror as he realized what this was.

"Is that...?" I did not confirm; I simply gave the look of not wishing to know. Percy seemed to shy away from the possibility as well.

"Have you seen this before, Percy?" He did not respond right away. His eyes were still fixated on the book itself. "Percy?"

He then looked up at me and replied, "I have not." He opened the journal and began flipping the pages back and forth. "This is Caroline's handwriting though. I would recognize it anywhere."

I gave Percy an unsurprised look. I had now become so comfortable with the idea that my aunt was heading a coven of satanic worshipers. Had it really become so commonplace for me to understand the reality of demons and occult worship? I did not wish to consider the possibility that I was comfortable in any way with this idea. Though the truth would be that I had started to become numb to the thought of my aunt sacrificing people to Satan.

Percy and I closed the door to the secret room and allowed the latch to sink back into its place. I was amazed to watch the door simply disappear back into the wall as if it had never existed. Whoever had been hired by my aunt to construct this door and conceal it was a master of construction. I left the room with candle in hand as Percy closed the door as best as he could. We had now taken to bracing the door closed by wedging a piece of wood into the bottom of the door. I had every intention of replacing the knob and lock mechanism at some point in the future, just not now.

Percy and I moved into the kitchen of the home and placed the journal on a preparation table to one side of the room. I placed the candle down beside the journal and began to open the cover and first page. Percy paced behind me and seemed to be protecting me. He was a watchful person, but even more so now. I could tell that he didn't wish for there to be any interruptions. I could have agreed, but I was not sure what he thought he would do in order to protect me. Unless Percy had the power of demonic forces and I did not realize it. I continued to peruse the journal for any clues or entries about the rituals that took place on the property. Most of the entries were about knowledge of the occult and how my aunt had come to find out all this information. Apparently, she had been groomed from a young age by my grandfather. She wrote about deviant acts that would be carried out on her and my mother from a young age. She would describe how my grandfather would force my aunt and mother to take part in rituals of lust in order to attract other followers, spells and rituals all designed to make his coven stronger. Some were simple and others too obscene to think about. Some of the entries I could not understand as I had no basis for anything to which it pertained, knowledge of alchemical formulae that would attract a demon's attention. It was, in fact, these writings that would serve as a basis for me to understand how this demon came to be. I could see now that the ritual was simply a conduit. The true power was given by the user. As it was written in the journal: "A practitioner is the agent of power. Through sheer will and emotion, the practitioner must focus all the energy and will into one point of power. To concentrate one's self on the being that you wish to bring about is to achieve success in the summoning. It was my will that attracted Incarnum. It was my emotion that gave him life."

I could understand now that my aunt and mother were not willing pawns in all this. It was likely that my grandfather had poisoned their minds early on in their lives. Perhaps the abuse that had been described here made them perform such evil actions. The only question that remained was why. Why continue the work of a man who abused you? No matter where I searched within the journal, I did not find an answer to this question. It seemed that my aunt now no longer cared about the reason, just that it was done. Most of the people on this earth have human motives to perform wicked actions. My aunt and mother, however, seemed to not have any motives. That is if I believed their words in the journal at all. No matter how much any of the words made sense, I still resisted seeing this journal as being truth. The skeptic in me wouldn't allow it. Though I could see that the rituals had clearly worked.

The demon controlled the home and more importantly had controlled my aunt and her life. Though I did wonder if it was my aunt that would suffer for her dark dealings while my mother was allowed a quick death. It has always been understood that those who perform such abominable actions in the name of Satan are often rewarded with a miserable existence.

I looked through the rest of the journal and could find no reason to believe that this demon could be vanquished. Though if there was a way, why would it be written about by supporters of evil? After all, it would be the demon's ability to remain in this world that would ensure evil will reign in the future.

I could feel Percy's anxiousness toward the journal still. I had done well enough to fight through this overwhelming sense that Percy was emanating. "What does it say?" Percy asked while pacing back and forth.

"It doesn't give a reason why any of this was necessary, but it does say how this was all accomplished." I stood from the table and moved out of the way for Percy to read it for himself. He sat down in a hurry and began to look through the journal. I was amazed at the hunger that he had for this journal, almost as if he expected it to vindicate my aunt from her actions. I had known that Percy idolized my aunt in some ways, but now it was more apparent than ever. Percy looked like a man that would be released from some prison with the words of the journal being the key to his cage. I could tell that Percy was absorbing the words each page held. He was a man that hungered to be vindicated in his beliefs. I felt sorry for Percy that he had put this much intent into following Caroline's example. Now his idol was sullied. Sorrow filled my heart for him.

I continued to wait patiently as Percy pored over the journal as best as he could. The only thing left that I could do was to pour a glass of water and watch over Percy as he had done for me. I had the feeling, however, that Percy would need to take this journal as evidence for the minister to be involved in assisting Percy and me. Even if he could only offer information, it would be enough. I did wonder how any other information could be collected beyond even the journal, but that was something that would become clear tomorrow. The only thing I could concentrate on now was of dinner with Mary and her family. In my mind, I imagined that dinner would be the only release that I would be able to have from this horrible evil. Though I did fear that this being would follow me to their farm.

After what seemed to be hours, Percy looked up from the journal as he turned the page to the back of the journal. "I am sorry, Benjamin. I know that these words were hard to read. I am finding it hard to understand myself."

I replied, "That is all right, Percy. No one could have prepared me for this. I suppose that nothing can truly prepare anyone for life, but I have been even less prepared for something like this."

Percy hung his head in shame.

I could tell that he felt responsible for all that had happened. I approached him and patted him on the shoulder. "Nothing could be your fault in this, Percy. Did you know that any of this had taken place?"

Percy leaned back in the chair we had placed and said, "I did not. I know that I wish that I had so that I could have tried to stop it, but I did not."

I nodded slowly as he realized that there was nothing that he could have done.

"The one answer that we have now is the reason there are at least two circles on the property."

I agreed and added, "I suspect that the first circle was used before your farm had been built. Late at night, there would be no one to see any rituals from the road and your property had not been marked yet. However, once you had begun to purchase the property is when they began to practice their rituals in the far field."

Percy considered my words. I could tell that he agreed with my assumption and did not wish to deal with this matter further. "I just wish that your aunt had outlined a goal in inviting this demon into our realm. What would possess someone to bring dark entities into the world?"

I shook my head and simply replied, "I do not know." I had no answers for Percy more than what he had already read within the journal. Though I knew that he wished that I did have the answers.

Percy eventually stood from the table and stretched for a moment.

"I now know that the only action that I can take today is to visit with the minister in the evening and ask for answers from him. I never told you that the minister would often visit your aunt and speak with her in the days before her death. Perhaps she confessed to something about this with him. I only hope that he was not involved in some way."

Percy's words horrified my mind. To think that the minister would be worshiping Satan was a thought that I did not wish to begin to entertain. With this conversation concluded, I picked up the journal and handed it to Percy.

"Take this with you. Maybe the minister will know what the symbol is on the inside page. Promise me something, Percy." I looked deeply into Percy's eyes. "Please do not share with anyone about the abuse that my mother and aunt had undergone in their lives. I would like to keep that aspect a secret."

Percy nodded and replied, "I would not wish to betray your trust, Benjamin. I will not mention or allow anyone to read such things."

I thanked Percy and accompanied him back to the front porch. We both sat down in the rocking chairs outside and began to smoke.

. . .

The rest of the time that Percy and I spent together was quiet and uneventful. I believed that we both had to absorb the information that we had now been given. I could not believe that we would need to speak on this matter further as it would not show any new information. We simply puffed away on our pipes and listened to the world move around us. The birds singing and the breeze wafting through the trees gave us a reminder that there was more in this world than evil. The earth and the nature that it held were sacred and seemed to not be sullied by the actions of such sycophants. No amount of darkness could take this world and engulf it in hatred and malice on a satanic level. This was the belief that was now apparent, and I wished that this would never change. The beauty of the world around us made Percy and me understand what was at stake. Even if evil could not infest this world and take it over, there must be someone to stand and protect it. Currently, the home had settled enough to give no impression that there was ever a being residing within the home. I almost wished to bask in the serenity that now resided in the space. Nothing gave the impression that there was a darker feeling within the home.

Eventually, Percy piped up and said, "I fear for your night tonight. I hope with everything in me that you are not going to return to the manor tonight."

I could understand Percy's sentiment. I did not wish to return to the home and face another night of torment. Though I did not understand how I could stay with Mary and her family tonight. It was not appropriate in any way, but I did not know how far I would travel to visit her. Perhaps it would be too far for them to bring me back tonight. Even with my ability to sleep in their home, where would I? All the guest rooms would be filled with Mary and her family. Though I wondered if sleeping in a barn loft would be more comfortable than sleeping with a demon roaming the home. "My wish is that you are able to find something that would help us to defeat this being once and for all tonight. Dinner with the minister should reveal something, and if that is the case, please retrieve me from Mary's aunt and uncle's home. I will not wish to be kept from being present to assist you."

Percy nodded and replied, "I promise that I will not keep you out of any efforts made to rid the home of this demon."

I thanked Percy for honoring my wishes as we continued to smoke.

I could not understand, at first, why Percy would wish to be a part of this nightmare that I had been mired within, but now I was glad that he had decided to assist me. Going alone into an unknown world at this stage in my life seemed completely idiotic. I did not understand any of this and save for the few scenarios that I had already faced, I did not understand what the meaning of all had been. I had feared that I would be the one to shoulder this burden. I did not wish to be seen as crazy or misguided. I also did not wish to be the one to allow anyone else to know what evil resided within Hillsborough. Nothing could have been enough to cover such a stain upon my family and Caroline's name. Though should I still consider my mother and aunt a beneficial aspect of my life? Could I myself be an innocent party in all this? Though I did not know how that I could be blamed as I had no recollection that anything like this could or was happening. I could not have known either. My theory still remained that I could not have known about anything. I believed that my aunt and mother had stopped practicing dark magic sometime before I was of age to remember anything. The only idea in my head that gave me relief was that my mother and aunt had not groomed me from a young age to be like them and to take part in summoning such dark entities within this world. This, at least, could be the saving grace to my family's name.

Percy and I continued to sit in silence as we smoked. There seemed to be nothing to say now. Our course of action was clear. The only desire that I had was that I would be able to help Percy tonight, but I couldn't change my mind now.

7

DINNER WITH MARY

The sun began to sink into the trees as we heard Percy's horses baying in the distance. Percy instantly sprang to action, and I followed. We dashed back to the side of the home to check on the horses. Luckily there was nothing bothering them. It was simply Mary and her father arriving to pick me up. I waved to them and then turned to Percy. "I thank you for all of your help, Percy. Please let me know what you discover. I should return here after dinner tonight. Will you be able to share the information with me then?"

Percy nodded and replied, "I shall come up with a solution to this while you are gone. Just don't let this ruin your good time with Mary and her family."

I nodded and then moved swiftly to get into the wagon with Mary and her father. I looked back at Percy as we rode away from the manor. I could tell that Percy was in a hurry to hitch his horses to the wagon and return to the farmhouse. I did hope that he was not tormented by the entity as we had been the day before. I would have regretted not helping him hitch his horses before I left him with the manor. It had become painfully obvious that neither Percy nor I would wish to remain at the manor any longer than we needed.

I did not have long with my thoughts as Mary spoke, "It is good to see you again, Benjamin."

I nodded and smiled. "It is good to see you again as well, Mary."

Mary smiled in response in the most flirtatious way. Mary's father sat in silence as Mary and I exchanged glances for a moment. Eventually, I chimed in with, "I thank you, sir, for picking me up! My name is Benjamin Price, and you are?"

Mary's father seemed to be a beast of a man. He was broad-shouldered with large arms. He resembled a boxer of some sort but looked as if he had been tearing trees from the ground with his bare hands. I did not think that a life of farming would give anyone such a bear-like appearance. Mary's father snapped the reins to the horses once again. He sat with an amused smile on his face. I could see that his rather long, bushy beard did not hide his expressions completely.

"My name is Robert! It is good to finally meet you, sir." I reached out and shook his hand firmly. "I understand that you have taken a liking to my daughter, eh?"

I nodded and replied, "Yes, sir! Mary is a beautiful woman and very sweet as well. Though I do apologize for not meeting you sooner."

Mary's father chuckled heartily and added, "I will be honest with you, Mr. Price, I don't like any man who has taken an interest in my daughter! Especially not a man that has such soft hands!" His voice boomed out and through the trees of the forest around us.

I felt almost ashamed to have presented myself for such scrutiny. Though I did not shy away from this man. "I am sorry that you have an issue with my appearance, but I am the way that I am, and that will not change, sir!"

Her father laughed heartily once more, and I feared that he might teeter off the edge of the wagon seat. I began to laugh as well but in a more sheepish manner. "It is good to finally meet you, Benjamin! I'm just pulling your leg! Though I am curious about your profession. What does a man do in a city as large as New York? Is it an honest day's work?" I thought about how that I would answer his question. "I feel that it is an honest day's work. I am a banker in the city, and it has brought me much satisfaction."

Robert nodded and seemed to understand what my profession meant. "So what does a banker do all day?"

I smiled and replied, "I mainly greet clients and help them with any investments that need to be made with the bank. I used to deal with small-time clients when I was an apprentice, but since I am the head banker, I usually only deal with more wealthy clients. I have assisted people from railroad owners to oil tycoons. I really enjoy the work and the people that I have had the chance to meet."

Mary's father gave me a rather peculiar look. "You're a head banker?"

I nodded.

"How long does that take to become a head banker?"

I replied, "Usually it takes years, but I had the fortune of meeting a rather wealthy new client who invested quite a large sum of money with our bank."

Mary's father seemed quite impressed with my profession. I could tell that he was beginning to warm up to me. Mary then added, "So how do people in the city live?"

I smiled and gave her a rather daring look. "I live in an apartment within the city. It is really more of a condominium, but I enjoy it. Though I never get much time in the house to myself. I am always working."

Mary seemed confused, along with her father. "What is an apartment or condominium?"

I looked at Robert and then Mary with a confused look now. "It is like a home but a little smaller and inside of a larger building. I have neighbors but no yard or pastures."

This seemed to amaze both of them. Mary asked, "How do you get food?"

I chuckled and replied, "I go to the market and purchase the food. There is nowhere for me to grow food at all, so I simply purchase what I want to eat and store it. Though currently, I eat at restaurants a lot due to my time being limited."

They both nodded in acknowledgment that they could understand what I was saying.

After these words, the conversation seemed to die off, though I was certain that Robert wished to concentrate as we neared the town. We rode on into the town and then down the main street. I could see the familiar sites that I had seen so many times before, though now we were traveling even further. We took a left turn off the main road through town. I could see the baker's on my left and the inn on my right. The inn was much larger than I had thought that it would be for such a small town. Seeing the inn gave me the idea to stay here should things become unbearable during my time within the manor. I did not wish to spend any more money than I had to, but it was a good secondary plan.

I looked at Robert and asked, "Do you know if there is a vacancy at the inn here in town?"

Robert thought for a moment and peered around me to the front of the inn. "Oh, you mean the Room and Board?"

I looked to my right and could see the sign now saying "Welcome to the Room and Board!" I was thrilled at this name. It was witty and quite humorous to me. "Yes! The Room and Board."

Robert thought for a moment and stopped the wagon in front of the building. "I'll wait if you wish to ask."

I nodded in surprise and leaped off the wagon seat. It didn't take me long to stroll across the porch and into the inn. I could see the innkeeper standing behind a desk as I entered. No one seemed to be staying here as there was no one at the entrance of the inn. I walked over to the desk and inquired of the innkeeper. "Excuse me, sir!"

The man moved directly in front of me and replied, "Yes, sir! How may I help you?"

I looked toward the key box hanging on the wall and asked, "Do you have any vacancies here?"

The man nodded and replied, "I do, sir! Are you interested in staying here for the night?"

I shook my head and replied, "No, sir. I am interested in a week and three days."

The man walked away from me and over to his check-in book. "I do have a vacancy for that amount of time, but it would cost you."

I then asked, "How much would that be, sir?"

The man gave me an odd look and replied, "That would be forty-two dollars."

I smiled and replied, "Thank you. I will return if I decide to stay here, sir." The man once again looked at me in the most suspicious way. I could tell that he was wondering where else I would stay. Though I didn't wish to identify myself or let on to the fact that I was staying in the Tourney Manor. I simply didn't wish anyone else to know my business in this way. I simply strolled back out the door and across the porch again. I swiftly took my place on the seat again as Robert snapped the reins. We began to ride off quickly from the front of the inn.

"Thank you for allowing me to ask, sir."

Robert nodded and asked, "What? Did he want your life in exchange for a couple nights?" We all laughed heartily.

"No, sir. He wanted forty-two dollars for a week and three days."

Her father instantly took a serious tone and replied, "You're going to pay that price?"

I also became rather serious and replied, "I may, but I will have to see what happens. I am trying to sell the Tourney Manor and its property. I just wonder if I will have to stay at the inn while I attempt to sell the manor."

Robert replied, "The Tourney Manor is up for sale?"

I nodded and added, "My aunt owned the manor, and she left it to me in her will. I cannot hold on to the house as I am not able to care for it from New York. I simply wish to sell it to a family that will care for it and operate the property as a farm."

Robert seemed amazed at my words but didn't ask anything further. In fact, the wagon ride was silent from then on.

We followed the road as it began to bear right. Time seemed to pass much more slowly now. I could see that the sun was slowly diminishing in the distance as it approached the horizon. I was not sure that I would return to the manor tonight, but I did hope that I would be able to early in the morning and speak with Percy. I had the deepest hopes that he would be able to discover the answer to all our questions. I also hoped that the minister would know how to eliminate this demon. I could not help but think about the ramifications of letting anyone else in this town know anything about the manor. I also didn't wish to alarm Mary in any way. The only consideration at this point was what to say for a reason that I would leave with Percy should he arrive to bring me back to the manor. I didn't think this would happen, but I was not a man to allow myself to be caught off guard about something as this demon.

It wasn't long until we had emerged from the last strip of forest. The farmhouse now began to shine in the distance as there were lanterns lit all over the backyard. I couldn't see the yard straight on but in a profile of the property. The light seemed to wreathe the farmhouse in holy light. It was almost as if I had arrived at my destiny. I could instantly feel the emotion of the moment and prepared myself to celebrate as it seemed that Mary's family had prepared for a grand event. I had not imagined that dinner would be so glamorous. I could see that Robert had noticed my astonishment as he said, "It is amazing from here, isn't it? We have prepared for this get-together for a rather long time."

I gave a rather agreeable expression and replied, "I can see that, sir! It is a very welcoming sight."

Robert seemed amused at my expressions and amazement. The wagon continued to lurch forward as we crossed over two roads to reach the entrance to the property. I could instantly see that the farmhouse had exquisite craftsmanship. We rode past the main house and underneath a wooden banner that was supported on each side by two pens. The left pen held hogs that were rather large, and the right held chickens that seemed to be rather curious about our arrival as they all clucked and strutted toward us. I was amazed at the size of the farm as well. There were so many pens and pastures with all sorts of animals all around. Mary's aunt and uncle seemed to have every farm animal known to man represented on the farm.

The wagon approached the hitching shed and came to a slow

stop. Robert relaxed the reins and wrapped them around the front peg. "I hope that you will feel welcome here, Benjamin. We have been preparing a lot of food and drink for tonight. Please make yourself at home." With those words, he reached out his hand and shook my hand.

I could tell that I had made a good impression upon Mary's father. I had hoped that I would be able to gain his support and trust. I had never had the time to pursue any woman due to my work, but I had hoped to change that now. There was simply something special about Mary. She was a rather sweet girl and a beautiful one at that. I helped her down from the wagon and guided her toward the other side of the road. I looked into her eyes and said, "I am going to help your father unhitch the horses. I'll be along soon."

Mary nodded sheepishly and smiled. I could tell that she was happy with my gesture and turned toward the home. I did not waste time watching her go as I did not wish for her father to think that he would do all this work alone. I turned to Robert and said, "Here. Let me assist you with the horses." I could see in his eyes that my words had caught him off guard. I knew that he wanted to say that I didn't have to help, but I moved closer and began helping him before he could say anything else.

We both seemed to work as one person. We unlatched each horse in tandem and pulled them out of the guides. It didn't take long to guide the horses into their pasture and remove their blinds. Each horse seemed to thank us for releasing them from the burden of the wagon as they galloped off together. They stopped some distance away and looked back at us. Robert and I turned our attention back to the wagon and began rolling it backward into the shed. The wagon rolled rather easily now as the port in front of the wagon shed was on a slight incline. I asked Robert, "If there is an incline here, how do you remove the wagon? Wouldn't it be too heavy to move up the incline?"

Robert chuckled and pointed to the front of the shed. "You see the hooks on the front of each side of the stall?" I nodded. "These hooks allow us to hitch the horses to the front of the building and guide them back into the guides of the wagon. It is still some work but not as much as pulling the wagon out by hand. Once we get them into the guides, we tie them to the wagon and use them to pull the wagon out. My brother has even done this with a load on the wagon."

I was amazed at the ingenuity of this idea. "Have you patented this idea?"

Robert laughed and replied, "I don't think my brother cares to do that. We are just simple farmers. Though the idea has now caught on with the other farmers in the area."

I didn't continue with any more questioning.

Robert and I walked back to the farmhouse and entered through the front door. I was met by another rather large man, but it seemed that he was less broad than Mary's father. Still, he was a very large man. "Welcome to our home!"

I shook the man's hand and said, "Thank you, sir and madam. My name is Benjamin Price. It is a pleasure to be invited to dinner."

The man with his wife beside him added, "My name is Bud, and this is my wife, Clara. We are happy to have you for dinner. Make yourself at home. Would you like something to drink?"

I nodded and replied, "I would, and thank you. It is a pleasure to meet both of you." With that, I took a drink from Clara's hands and began to take a sip. I could taste the bouquet of the wine. I wondered if Mary's aunt and uncle had grown the grapes used to make this wine and produced the wine on this very farm. I didn't get the chance to ask this question at this time as they had walked away to talk to other family members and helped set the table outside.

Mary approached me and said, "What do you think about the farm?"

I took another sip of the wine and replied, "It is amazing. I am very glad that you asked me to come for dinner. I must admit, though, I didn't expect for dinner to be such a grand event."

Mary giggled and said, "We didn't do this just for a normal dinner. Tonight is our family dinner. Every summer we get together to cele-brate our family. We all gather and catch up on what has been happening over the past year. It is the only time that we have to do this since harvest season is coming up in the next month or so."

I nodded and said, "Interesting. I am glad that I could be a part of this gathering then."

Mary smiled with a rather pleased look.

"Is there a specific place where I could partake of my pipe?"

Mary waved for me to follow her as she turned away. She showed me across the room and out onto the back porch of the home. I followed Mary to the far end of the backyard to a seat that had been placed underneath a rather large tree. The branches and leaves hung down from the top of the tree like an umbrella. It was a rather nice sight to behold. I wasted no time in sitting beside Mary and lighting my pipe. I took a relaxed position on the seat and asked, "Do you sometimes come into town to help your aunt and uncle?"

Mary nodded and replied, "Sometimes. This year they hired more farmhands. They have been doing well for themselves here. My father and mother have been helping them to establish a winery nearby where they can sell their wine. They have earned a lot of notoriety in the area for their wine. It has taken time to produce the wine, but they have had wealthy people travel from Raleigh here to taste their wine and purchase their own stock of wine."

I knew that my face gave away my amazement at these words. I was tasting such a fragrant and supple wine that had been made by Mary's aunt and uncle. I could think of no better place to visit and live. It was like a paradise here. Good wine, beautiful sights, and a simple life that gave great rewards. It was all surreal.

"I am amazed by the quality of this wine. I have never tasted such a fresh and flavorful wine in my life."

Mary giggled and added, "That is what everyone says. My aunt has been working very hard to gain interest in the cities for my uncle. He is the man behind the wine. He has grown grapes for years and made the wine as well. Though the grapes aren't normal grapes. They are wild grapes that we call muscadines. That is the strong flavor that you are tasting."

I was highly interested in Mary's words. I had always been interested in growing my own grapes and maintaining a farm for producing wine. I supposed that this fact was why I had been so ready to accept this as a paradise.

I noticed that Mary didn't hold a glass of wine in her hand. In fact, she didn't carry anything. I puffed on my pipe and began to notice Mary in a whole new way. She wore a simple but beautiful rose-colored dress. The fabric seemed to contour to her body in a very alluring way. She was a curvy woman that seemed to understand how to dress to impress. Her clothing had always seemed to accentuate her beautiful features without being too much. She was modest yet lovely. I almost couldn't take my eyes off her. She had a light complexion with a slight tan. I could see that she enjoyed working out in the sun as she held a very tan color to her skin. The light in the yard now seemed to give her beautiful tan skin a glow that I had never seen before. She was a goddess whom I wished for vigorously. Her beauty captivated me as I began to smile at her.

"What?" she asked with an equally flirty smile.

"I don't know if you know this or not, but you are so beautiful. I cannot take my eyes off you." Mary blushed and tried to look away. I took a deep drag from my pipe and added, "It is amazing that you have accepted my advances. I am rather captivated by you."

Mary giggled nervously and replied, "Stop, Benjamin. You're making me blush."

I smiled even more now. I could see the curls in her hair dangling down across her face. She reminded me of the sculptures of Aphrodite that I had seen before in New York. I didn't want this moment to end. Though I feared that I would have to miss the rest of the party in order to gain what I had dreamed of. It was a treat to spend time with Mary here. She didn't seem to mind at all that I smoked near her. I had known many women of her caliber that seemed offended by a man that smoked a pipe. Whether it was the scent of the tobacco or the thickness of the smoke, I had never met any woman that didn't seem bothered by this habit. I couldn't understand how Mary seemed to be so perfect for me. That is until I witnessed her father doing the same. He held a much smaller pipe, however. I could see that he had carved it himself.

"How long will you all be in town, Mary?"

She focused on my eyes and replied, "We will return to our farm by the end of this next week."

I gave Mary an odd look. "That is quite the coincidence as I am supposed to return to New York around the same time. Though my travel is not set in stone with the distance that I have to travel."

Mary nodded and replied, "That is interesting. How long will it take for you to return to New York?"

I thought for a moment about the journey to North Carolina. "I would say about the same that it took me to arrive here. That was about two and a half days."

Mary seemed amazed by this and asked, "You traveled by coach that quickly?"

I laughed and replied, "No. Not at all, dear. I traveled by train to Raleigh and then employed a coach to bring me to Hillsborough."

She seemed relieved by my answer. "That makes a lot of sense. I wouldn't want to travel that far in a coach."

I agreed with a nod and said, "You and I are alike in that respect. I think you would like the train. It is quite comfortable when you are traveling so far. Though I will say that I took a special train here. One of my clients owns the railroad and the trains that run to North Carolina. He graciously allowed me to use his sleeping car to come to Raleigh."

She seemed amazed and said, "You have clients that own trains?"

I replied, "Yes, ma'am. I helped him with a rather lucrative investment in my bank."

Mary's face had now turned from amazement to clearly giving an impressed look. I was pleased with myself at her reaction. I could feel that my anxiety had now turned to feeling empowered. I was happy that Mary seemed so supportive of my life in New York. My hope now was that I would be able to continue to have contact with Mary. That I would be able to convince her to travel with me. The latter was a hope that I doubted would come true in such a short time together. The custom of the day was to know someone for a period of time exceeding a year and then to be married. The other option would be in case of an arranged marriage, which I didn't think would be the case as I had nothing to offer this family. Though I also didn't think that money would motivate them at all. Mary herself didn't seem to value money above anything and, instead, seemed to want someone's time and attention. I felt this quality to be the main desire that I held in a mate. I did feel that I was becoming rather attached to Mary on this night and didn't want to leave her side, even in the face of work and progress in my life. I cherished any contact that I had with her. Mary was a prize to any man that she wished to have and I hoped that I would have a chance to be that man.

After a few more moments of smoking, Mary and I could hear her aunt Clara calling everyone to sit at the table outside. I could even see from where Mary and I sat that the table had been prepared for a banquet. The family didn't waste any time in gathering at the table as we approached the table ourselves. In the spirit of the evening, everyone had saved seats for us to sit beside each other. Mary and I were embarrassed by this a little but sat in the seats anyway. It was always interesting to me that we had felt such embarrassment even as we knew that the rest of her family knew what was really going on. After all, they had faced similar events in their lives as well.

As I helped Mary into her chair and pushed her under the table, Mary's uncle stood from his position at the table and announced, "Thank you all for coming on such short notice this year! I am glad that we are all able to gather here once again and share time with each other. It is a gift, in life, to share special events and gatherings with family. We have all seen the touch of death recently in our family and hope that this will be a better year. We have tonight a special guest with us, Mr. Benjamin Price! He has come all the way from New York to be here for his aunt's funeral, *and* to take a liking in our young Mary!" He said this in a jesting manner.

"It gives me great pleasure to welcome him to this gathering of family as I am sure that we all know he will be here for future gatherings." Mary blushed. "Let's enjoy this food, and may God bless us all as a family! Feast, everyone!"

With the last words her uncle spoke, we all began passing food around the table. The family placed food on their plates with such voraciousness that I wasn't sure there would be enough. I sat in silence, at first, and waited for my chance to grab food myself. Mary stood from her seat and said, "In our family, it is customary for me to get your plate of food. You are our guest and I invited you. Is that okay with you, dear?" Mary blushed as she realized the word had slipped out.

I sat in my chair smiling and nodded as I could no longer find words to speak. Mary didn't even wait for my response. She simply grabbed my plate and moved down the table to bring food back for me. I could see roast chicken, goose, deer stew, green beans, cabbage, potatoes and sweet potatoes, and various other dishes that I couldn't identify from this distance. The whole of the meal was inviting. The servants were bringing everyone wine and placing it at the tables before they took their seats. Everything smelled delicious and fresh. I could tell that the goose and the deer were lovingly prepared as only a hunter would know to do. It was amazing that I could see such a spread and still partake in all the sumptuous food. Mary soon returned with my plate and set it down in front of me. She then leaned over and kissed my cheek. I could feel myself blush and simply tried to act like nothing was happening.

Everyone roared with laughter and conversation as they continued to celebrate. It was only now that I could see how close Mary's family was to each other. Even the servants were welcomed as family. I had often heard that people in the South owned and operated slave labor to achieve their goal of farming, but couldn't understand why there was nothing like that here. Though it didn't really matter as everyone was having such a delightful time. It was refreshing to know that Mary's family didn't wish to continue such practices.

As I ate my dinner, I could tell that everyone was truly included in the conversation as I heard, "Benjamin! What do you think about having a winery and a farm?"

I could hear Mary's uncle at the head of the table. Everyone now seemed to be hanging on every word of my response. "I believe that it is a novel idea! I would love to own such a property myself!" Ben laughed along with a few others. I could feel that it was not a laugh that was meant to harm me in any way but rather a laughter or joyous agreement. I laughed with everyone else and added, "If anyone wishes to have a property of their own—"

Ben interrupted, "We cannot hear you, son! Stand up. Stand up!"

I stood with a panicked feeling in my chest. I did not relish the idea of speaking in front of a crowd. This was even more so as this was the family of a woman that I had so longed to share my time with. "I am sorry. I was saying that anyone that wished to have such a fine property for themselves should look at the Tourney Manor. I am selling the property as I do not wish for it to fall into disrepair. I would like my aunt's memory honored."

Everyone ceased their laughter as Ben added, "I would wish to talk to you after dinner, Benjamin. Please, if you have time!"

I nodded and sat back down. Mary rubbed my back as I continued to eat. Everyone once again returned to partying and raucous laughter. Once again, I would not describe any of the other family member's behaviors as hurtful or even in any way intentional. I could simply see a family that had become close enough to not have any judgment between each other or those that they chose to visit with them.

We all finished our meals and then sat around the table drinking wine. It was this time that the table seemed to empty as we all had more space to move more closely together in an intimate setting for banter. We all continued to drink wine bottle after wine bottle. It had been a long time since I had imbibed a drink such as this wine. I did not feel as though I was drinking too much but felt the need to slow down a bit on my drinking. I didn't wish to disgrace myself to Mary's family after all. We all continued our conversations that we had tried to have before but were too far apart.

"Benjamin! What is it that you do?"

I smiled and replied, "I am the head banker at the Northeast Bank."

Mary's uncle didn't miss a beat. "Oooo! That sounds important. What is it that you do at the bank?"

I didn't know how to respond except to say, "I maintain and calculate important accounts at our bank. If someone wishes to invest with us, I am the man they usually will talk with. Though I do not accept any accounts that are under ten thousand dollars." Silence fell over the table.

"That is an exceptionally large sum of money."

I nodded and said, "It is also a great responsibility."

Ben and everyone else seemed to wish to hear more, but I did not wish to share client information. I felt that it would be unprofessional. Mary also sat beside me with a look that she was amazed that I was able to perform such a job.

"I have met a lot of interesting people in the time that I have spent at the bank, but sometimes I do find that it is a demanding job. Most days I arrive to open the bank and then do not leave the bank until long after it has closed."

Mary's uncle asked, "Do you feel safe in the city at night?"

I thought for a moment and replied, "I don't feel unsafe. I also carry a revolver. It is not out of paranoia but more of a security measure."

Mary's uncle seemed interested at my words. "It is interesting that you would carry a gun. I thought that there were supposed to be police officers within the city to stop crime."

I thought about my next response carefully. "There are police, but they are often busy monitoring the city for other crimes. I also do not wish to place my trust in anyone else. I feel that it is my own personal responsibility to protect myself. Though I have never had to use my gun. I have made sure that it is always with me in case someone takes the wrong interest in me. I also never know if there might be someone to try to rob the bank. It hasn't happened, but I would hate to not have my gun if there should be something like that to happen. I care for my employees, and I don't wish for anything to happen to them."

Ben stared at me for a moment and then asked, "How would you feel should war be like?"

I thought for a moment and replied, "I wouldn't feel anything about it. War is a terrible cost of human lives and money. I wouldn't want a war, and I am hoping that the tensions that are being felt will dissipate. I also wouldn't shy away if war does come down as I would join the fight. I just do not wish for a war that no one wants and that can be prevented."

Ben nodded and then asked, "So how do you feel about the country wanting to form a larger governmental body?"

I thought about this now and replied, "I feel that a larger governing body could do some good to simply smooth out tensions between states. I do feel, however, that the states should never be asked to give up their own governing powers to a more expansive government. I feel this would open our country up for abuse and our ability for the people to have oversight over each ruling body would greatly diminish."

Mary's uncle sat in silence now with a large smile on his face. He eventually ended our conversation with, "Thank you for your input, Benjamin. It is interesting that two people from so far away have the same views. I would like to extend the offer of staying here tonight if you wish. Of course, Mary would have to sleep in a separate room, but the offer is open to you."

I thanked Ben and replied, "I would like that. I have had a long day, and I didn't rest well last night. I am not used to staying in such a large and imposing home."

Mary's uncle chuckled as he wagged his finger back and forth so as to say that I was jesting with him. He then stood from the table and added, "I thank you all once again for coming. I am now going to retire to my room. Have a good night everyone!" He then turned to leave the table then said, "Oh! And, Benjamin! I would like to speak with you about the manor in the morning. Please do not leave until I have had a chance to talk to you."

I nodded in acceptance of his offer and wished him a good night. Mary then stood from the table and grasped my hand. She led me into the home and showed me down the hall a bit and into a side room. It was small but held a bed and an end table. There didn't even seem to be a candle in this room, but there was a window that faced toward the rising sun. "You can sleep here tonight. Thank you so much for coming tonight, Benjamin. I really feel so close to you, and tonight has proven to me that I am more interested in you than I had thought. I would say that I am falling in love with you. Please have a good night's rest, my love. I will see you in the morning."

I nodded and added, "I feel the same about you, Mary. Sleep well, dear." With those words, Mary left the room and shut the door. I could hear her drag a chair in front of the door and brace it closed. I knew that this was a traditional practice and felt that I would comply. After all, I didn't want her family to suspect that I was trying to disgrace their daughter or myself. It didn't take long for me to settle into bed. I lay there looking out the window to the stars and thought about what a wonderful day this had been. I was delighted that I had met a family that was so agreeable with myself and my lifestyle. I felt accepted in every way and really knew that tomorrow would be a much better day. That and I wouldn't have to sleep in a haunted manor house for the night. I could rest well.

The next morning seemed to come quickly. I awoke feeling refreshed and completely rested. The sun shone brightly through the window. I could also hear birds chirping in the warmth of the sun. It was all so enchanting. I then realized where I had been sleeping. I felt fortunate to have slept so well in a comfortable setting. I looked toward the door, wondering if Mary's aunt had known that Mary blocked me inside the room. I could not imagine that she or Mary would leave me stuck in this space much longer as it sounded that breakfast was almost ready. I stood at the door for a moment until I realized that I should knock. Perhaps her aunt would have to be reminded of my presence in the room.

I walked up to the door and leaned slightly so that I could hear what was going on outside the door. I knocked lightly at first and then gave a second series of knocks that grew louder with each abrasive knock. I paused for a moment and just listened as I heard someone approach the door. I could now hear the knob on the door moving. The sounds had then turned to a scooting noise as someone had removed the chair from in front of the door. I then turned the knob and opened the door cautiously. I didn't wish to hit anyone. I could feel a deep pang of fear as I left the safety of the room. I could not be certain in any way that I was not dreaming again.

Eventually, I poked my head out of the doorway and took a look around. Everything seemed to be normal. I couldn't see anything that gave me cause for alarm. I walked out of the doorway and turned to my left. I could see that the table had been set. There seemed to be just enough room for the family to be seated. I could see Mary's aunt working with the servants still to make sure the table was ready. I could see frantic movement as it seemed that this table wasn't the only one to be set. I could see that the other servants were relaying the other food items to the larger table outside.

There was quite a lot of food to be provided for one breakfast. I could see that Mary's aunt and the servants had worked hard all morning to make sure that everything was ready for the family to eat. I walked into the kitchen and said, "Good morning, everyone!"

Mary's aunt looked back at me with surprise, as did all the servants currently assisting her. I could not tell if it was a surprise that anyone else should be awake or that the tables had not been properly set for the breakfast feast. The other servants turned and did a small bow to me as Mary's aunt did the same. She eventually responded with "Good morning!"

I could tell that she was only greeting me in order to be courteous to her guests. Her real focus was on making sure everything was prepared for the other guests as well. After our greeting, I simply moved out onto the front porch and sat on a bench closer to the pens. I produced my pipe from my pocket and began smoking. I decided it was best to stay out of the way of the work that was happening in the house. I didn't wish to be a pest this morning, especially not after the incredible night that I had experienced. Though the same thing remained that this farm property seemed magical. I was intrigued that someone had already fed and cared for the animals outside. I was sure that the servants had done this as it was too much work for any one person to do. This, I must say, was proven wrong as Ben rounded the corner and approached me.

"Good morning, Benjamin! How did you sleep last night?"

I waved back at Ben and replied, "I slept rather well last night. It almost felt as if I had never fallen asleep, but I am rested, and that is all that matters."

Ben chuckled and said, "You're right there! I was certain that you found it difficult to the barricaded in a room all night."

I laughed and replied, "It was not. I simply put it out of my mind and decided to rest. No use in thinking about it, after all."

Ben responded to my words with hearty laughter. "I suppose so. Have you seen if they are ready for us to all eat?"

I nodded and took a deep pull off my pipe. The smoke seemed to waft through the air and just past Ben.

"That is some nice pipe you have there, Benjamin. I didn't know that you smoked a pipe."

I nodded once again as I took another pull.

"Wait here! I'll retrieve my pipe and join you."

Before I could respond, Ben had moved into the home. I was not sure if I would hear any words of hassle coming from inside, but I heard only silence. It seemed like Ben had just walked into the main door when he poked his head outside and said, "Everyone is waking up. Breakfast will be served in thirty minutes."

I replied, "Thank you, sir!"

Ben then pulled his head out of sight and into the home. It once again hadn't seemed like Ben would have enough time to do anything before he emerged from the door. This time, however, he was carrying his pipe and didn't simply have an update for me. He walked over to the bench and sat down beside me. "Lovely morning, isn't it?"

I nodded and remained silent. "Are you sure that everything is all right this morning?"

I took another drag from my pipe and replied, "Yes, sir. I am just enjoying the morning. Have you been feeding all of these animals today?"

Ben smiled and said, "Yes, sir! I do it every morning. Our servants sometimes help, but they are not here to care for the farm unless something happens. Their main job is to care for my orchards and maintenance on the winery. I have to have a lot of help. It is cheaper than slaves as well."

With these words, I turned my head sharply. "What do you mean?"

Ben thought for a moment and replied, "Slaves are too much cost. I have to purchase them, which isn't cheap. Then I have to employ people to watch them and keep them in line. I also have to make sure that none run away. It is too costly. I also agree with Clara that no one deserves that kind of treatment. I am sure that there are a lot of farmers that would disagree, but every farm in this area is too small to warrant such a labor force. So I employ ten servants with the money from the winery."

I nodded and then replied, "Then you should be commended for not falling into such temptations. I also agree that slavery is not an idea that I enjoy. To control another person and their future is not what I seek in life. I also am not in favor of having to oppress a people just to maintain property or wealth. Though I had heard the South was rife with slavery."

Ben laughed and added, "Not in this area, you don't. Though I think North Carolina as a whole doesn't have a lot of slavery. Perhaps toward the coast with the bigger cotton and peanut farms, but not anywhere else. Farmers here are much too poor and the farms too small to need slaves."

I agreed and then asked, "So then how are there so many farms with servants?"

Ben took a puff from his pipe and replied, "The servants at a lot of these farms work for food and shelter. At times they are provided with money if the harvest is good, but not all the time. It is easier to provide food and shelter for someone than to enslave them. I can grow crops and slaughter animals. I can also assist with building a home for people, but I cannot pay farmhands to beat and maintain a slave population. I have known some families that undertook such things years ago. They are all in poverty now as their farms couldn't sustain enough money to pay the people to watch over the slaves. It just isn't the way to do business. The hardest thing about servants is that they have the ability to move on. I am different in that way. Many farmers would try to stop their servants from leaving with contracts of employ and such. I don't. If a servant wishes to move on somewhere else and work, then that is their choice. Even the Negroes that I have as servants are treated the same way. Though it is rare for me to employ someone that is a Negro. Sometimes the state sends out people to survey my land, and it is not as simple as hiding someone. Though when I have had black servants, the others will usually hide these servants so as to protect them."

I was amazed by the level of care that Mary's uncle had toward the people that helped him on the farm. "So I suppose that you are not of the conservative mentality?"

Ben puffed on his pipe again and replied, "I am conservative in my ideals. Though I don't see any way that I can make a change. No, I believe that there will be conflict before any of this unrest can be changed between the southern states and the North. Some would say that I am a fool, but tensions are growing, not relaxing. The only thing that will happen is the right set of circumstances and we will be in a full-blown war. The northern states cannot understand that the South just wants to govern itself. They only see that we are poor and cruel slave owners, but if they thought about it for a moment, they would see that this isn't the case."

I nodded again and sat in silence. It was a lot to process. Mary's uncle was right about a great many things. Though this was my opinion. I was glad, however, that we had been able to bond over politics. Often, people have been more divided over their beliefs in political matters than have ever come together. It takes a special mindset to simply discuss one's beliefs on the subject without making another come to your side. I found it refreshing to be able to have that sort of interaction with Mary's uncle this morning as it set the tone for the day.

Eventually, Ben and I were called for breakfast. We both moved into the house and put out our pipes. As I entered the home, I could see Mary waiting for me to follow her outside and have breakfast by her side. I could not resist embracing her in a loving and nurturing manner. I sought to kiss her as I had done last night but decided a more proper approach would be better. I could see now that the rest of her family had awoken and were waiting to partake in the breakfast. It was curious that everyone sat outside and not inside the home. I knew that the inner table had been set this morning with bowl after bowl of delicious breakfast foods. With that thought, I turned to the table inside the home as Mary and I passed and could not see any food. Everything here was seasonings and sauces. I was confused by this and decided to ask Mary on my next chance.

Mary and I walked side by side out to the table that we had eaten at last night. Here was a spread that was fit for a king. Some of the foods I had never seen, especially a brown substance that seemed to sit thick in the bowl that held it. I was not sure what it was but decided that it must be delicious. Though I was slightly alarmed that there seemed to be black specs suspended within it. Mary led me to the left side of the table and signaled where she would sit. As was customary, I pulled the chair back for her and assisted her with being seated. I then walked to the other side of the table and sat across from her. I feared that she had intended for me to sit beside her, but I did not wish to spoil the morning without looking at her beautiful face. I took my seat only to be greeted by Mary's uncle Ben.

"Welcome to the table, Benjamin. I feel like that I have seen you recently." Ben held a wide smile on his face and gave a slight chuckle. I could tell that he rather enjoyed playing with people. It seemed that I had only just sat down when the food started being passed around the table. I did not waste time filling my plate. Everything seemed to be delicious, and the smells all served to make my mouth water. I also was served coffee by Mary's aunt herself. I found it odd that the servants were all seated and being served by Mary's aunt as well. I was not hostile to this change, but interested. I was pleasantly surprised by this effort to allow the servants to relax in the morning.

This sumptuous breakfast brought back memories of my favorite café in New York. I had become accustomed to being served a rather large breakfast with coffee. I could simply leave my apartment and walk just down the street to the morning café. I felt that it was always easy to gain access to a plethora of food just as I was being served now. Also just in the same vein of the café I was being served the best food and coffee that anyone could buy. I did relish living in more rural areas but felt that it would be much more difficult to have the amenities that I was accustomed to in the city. I did, however, wish to have a breakfast such as this in the most beautiful setting that I had ever seen. The fragrance of the flowers that grew around the backyard gave all the smells of the food a sweeter smell. Though this was something that would be missed upon my return to New York City.

I sat there taking one sip of coffee after another. I had also begun to devour the tender bacon and delicious sausage. There was sweet bread that tasted like cake with what looked like a heavy cream with butter covering the top. I was amazed at the level of care and intricacy that had been given toward this breakfast. There seemed to be something for anyone represented here. Even with the brown liquid that I had been suspicious, I found it to be rather tasty on top of a biscuit. It was a rather earthy taste that seemed to be complimented by a taste of sausage fat. I wasn't sure what had inspired this dish, but I welcomed the flavor wholeheartedly.

I noticed that everyone around me didn't seem to be talking very much. We all were tasting such delicious foods and seemed to be occupied with the food itself. I found this odd at first and somewhat pressured to not say anything. Now I simply understood the reason for the quiet table. The food was simply too delicious to deny. I felt that it would be a crime to waste a moment of being able to partake in this fine meal. Just as I was finishing my meal, I wondered if Percy had been able to gain help from the minister. My mind had been released from the prison of my current situation, but I felt that it was only a matter of time before I was called back into the fray. I just hoped in this moment that Percy would hold off on picking me up from Mary's uncle's home until I had had time to visit with Mary. I worried that she would get the wrong impression of my leaving before our time here had been concluded. I also wished to be selfish on this day of spending time with Mary. I had a limited amount of time in North Carolina and didn't wish to waste it.

I could feel myself being pulled closer to Mary at every turn. No matter what I did to distance myself from the idea of bringing her back to New York with me, I still held high hopes that I would be able to achieve this goal. I wondered if Mary felt the same. I had thought that I had left Mary and her family with a good impression of me, but there was a small fear that we just weren't compatible. This fear, however, subsided when she looked at me and smiled as she whispered, "I love you!" I could feel the love that emanated from her. Instantly my fears were drowned in confidence. I had a knowing that I was looked upon favorably by Mary, and I hoped that this would be the case with her family as well.

Once everyone had had the chance to sit and eat, Mary's uncle stood from the table and announced, "Thank you to everyone for the delicious breakfast! I would like to ask any servants that have been assigned to the winery to please move toward the orchards now. I hope that we can all have a productive day today. I will feed the animals here and join you all soon. Thank you for all the hard work that you have all provided and would like to extend a bonus for this weekend. As you all know, this week had been the most profitable. So in return, you are all going to be off from all duties tomorrow and through the weekend. Please do not report to work until Monday. Thank you." With these words, Ben sat down in his seat and spoke with Mary's aunt for a moment as all the servants stood from the table and walked happily toward the winery.

I was intrigued by Ben's announcement. It was interesting that he would allow the servants to be released from work because of performance. This was a very modern idea that I would not have expected here of all places. The only thing that seemed to not shock me about it was the words that Ben had spoken this morning before breakfast. I could also see that Mary's aunt had just now taken her seat and begun to eat her breakfast. I also found this interesting but relegated this to a custom held by Mary's family. Though I had wondered if this also meant that her immediate family also practiced these customs.

After breakfast, I left the house and moved back out onto the front porch. The chilled morning air seemed to affect me more in the front of the home rather than the back of the home. There was now a mist that wafted in the air. The mist lay across the fields and roads that ran around the property. This gave a mystified or enchanted look to the land. It was almost as if magic had been at work in giving the land this mysterious appearance. I sat comfortably on the end of the porch on the swinging bench, enjoying the air that circulated around me. I was comfortable now being bathed in the warm sunlight but was kept cool from the breeze. Breakfast now seemed to have been a short memory. It seemed as if I had not only been away from the table for a while but also didn't seem to last very long at all. This was all in contrast to the fact that I now felt weighted down and sluggish. The food consumed could not be felt heavy in my stomach. My one and only desire now was to linger here and relax as my food was being consumed.

As I had come to this realization, Mary approached my position from behind and took her place beside me in the swing. She seemed to relish this moment as she was also warmed by the sunshine and cooled by such a gentle and refreshing breeze. I moved closer to her and gave her a small kiss on the temple.

"I wish that you didn't have to leave, Benjamin."

I smelled and replied, "I know, Mary. I have business to take care of before returning to New York." Mary had now hung her head. I gave her a compassionate look and added, "I would wish for you to visit me in New York. That or you could come with me. Leave Hillsborough behind and visit a whole new world."

Mary raised her head and gave me a longing look. I could tell that my words had moved her to consider the idea. Perhaps she had this longing to leave Hillsborough before I had arrived. I couldn't be sure now, but I did hope that she decided to travel with me. If not as a friend, but as a wife. Though I couldn't ask her to marry me in this moment. We sat there for a moment and reminisced about the night before. I could tell that Mary had enjoyed dinner together just as I had. I said, "The food was delicious, and I really enjoyed meeting your family."

Mary smiled and replied, "I enjoyed seeing you again and sharing dinner. I think that my family enjoyed having you for dinner. My uncle and aunt were nervous about meeting you, but they seem comfortable with you now."

I laughed and said, "I felt the same nervousness. I am relieved that they have accepted me as they have. I only regret that I didn't talk to your aunt as much as your uncle."

Mary nodded and replied, "That is all right. My aunt doesn't like to talk with anyone. She is very quiet. I know that she will warm up to you as she gets to know you. It took a long time for her to even talk to my father and mother when she married my uncle."

I found Mary's words interesting. "You mean that your aunt had not met your mother and father before marrying your uncle?"

Mary nodded and replied, "No one had met my aunt before she married my uncle. It was a very sudden wedding. My father had even mentioned this to my uncle when we arrived for the wedding. Of course, I don't remember this well as I was a very small child."

I was astonished at Mary's words. I then worked up my courage and asked, "Do you think that your family would have a negative reaction should you and I decide to marry and leave for New York?"

Mary blushed at hearing my words. "I am not sure. Is it that you have decided to ask for my hand in marriage?"

I was the one blushing now. "I have considered it. I will not lie. There is something about you, Mary, that I cannot ignore. I feel myself incapable of holding back from loving you. I have felt this since we first met. It is why I felt so horrible about accidentally kicking you."

Mary blushed again and added, "I felt the same. There was a

connection between us that was so strong. I have never felt it with anyone else."

As Mary and I had been completely engaged at this moment, her aunt had emerged from the home and stood watching as I hugged and kissed Mary. When I realized that she was there, I moved back to my side of the swinging bench. I acted as if nothing had happened. Her aunt simply stood there with a fond smile on her face as if remembering the love that she had experienced when she was our age. I smiled back and turned my attention back to the yard. In this moment, I could feel that my time to leave was quickly approaching. I was pained by the fact that this moment with Mary and her family would come to an end. I felt as if there had to be something that could do to stop the march of time. I looked at Mary and asked, "Would you like to walk with me?"

Mary looked into my eyes as if I had asked her to marry me. She seemed deeply touched that I would ask this. "You would wish to walk with me in the woods?"

I nodded and smiled. I could tell now that her heart was bursting with love for the idea. Before anything else could be said, I reached out my hand and grasped her hand. I stood and led her away from the porch. Mary then noticed that her aunt was standing in the doorway. "I will be back soon, Aunt Clara." Her aunt nodded and smiled fondly again. The only words that she offered were, "Be careful, Mary." I could feel the harmless suggestion of these words, and they were spoken.

Mary and I walked down to the next building and stopped to look around. Mary pointed into the distance toward what looked like a storage building. She said, "This is our spring house. If you look through the window, you will see all the delicious foods that we are preserving there." Mary then led me to the window of the spring house and led me in, looking through the window. I could see all the breads and cheeses were placed neatly on the shelves. There was quite a selection of different goods that were stored in the spring house. I did wonder why there was so much food here for such a small family.

"There seems to be a lot of food here for just your aunt and uncle."

Mary nodded and met my eyes. "The rest of the food is given out to the servants to eat on each day. This is the reserve of food for them all."

I seemed amazed at this idea. It was fascinating that the servants were provided for from this stock as well. Ben and Clara had really considered everything when building their lives up. Even thinking about the welfare of the servants. "Your aunt and uncle are very fair toward their servants."

Mary nodded and replied, "They are and I love it. People deserve to be treated with respect and compassion. I couldn't imagine wishing to be around my aunt and uncle if they were not the way they are now. They may be servants, but they are people too."

I nodded vigorously in acceptance of this idea. It was refreshing to know that Mary and my ideals matched up so perfectly in this way.

"Even when I am simply visiting my aunt and uncle, I am often sent home with more food than we can eat. My family believes in sharing our profits with everyone that has been good to us. We are all like a family."

I nodded once again. I could feel that my heart was truly connecting with Mary. I was truly feeling the words that she said in each moment, almost as if they carried their own energy and weight. I had never considered what a perfect meeting could be until now. I was connected with Mary in a way that I had never considered real.

Mary pulled lightly on my hand and led me off behind the house to the barn. We had to stroll through a small wooded area that protected the barn on one side. The sight was so beautiful that it seemed almost magical to walk here with Mary. I could not help but think that she too felt the same. We came to the front of the barn and stood in the doorway. Mary pointed to the upper loft and the corners of the barn. "We store our hay and some grains here for the market in Raleigh." Mary interested me in many ways. She spoke with such authority on each subject that we covered. She also seemed to connect with each topic. I could see the passion in her eyes for living things. It didn't matter to her. An animal was the same as a human, and a tree was just as significant. She was amazing. I had never thought about life being so sacred in any form to one person. I could see that she truly cared and loved on a much deeper level than anyone seemed capable. It was this fact that made me wonder whether such intense love was needed for me to be happy and complete.

Mary stood stark against the backdrop. She was beautiful in her flowing gown and elegant hairstyle. She was as of a goddess explaining her world to me. She was perfect in every way. I think that she could see this in my eyes as she blushed when she said, "I am often helping my family and the servants here to prepare for harvest and markets. If I am not gathering hay, then I am assisting in the fields. I also have been known to help birth animals when my uncle's hands are too large."

I smiled and simply said, "That is fascinating. I find it amazing that anyone has the ability to care for a farm. It is a lot of work, and hard work at that."

Mary blushed again and then once again took my hand. She led me further beyond the barn and into a wooded area. We ran hand in hand through the trees and out to an overlook. The area was beautiful. Below was a pond that seemed to glisten in the morning sun. The light illuminated the surface of the pond. It looked like a thousand fairies dancing in celebration of this day. I was glad to see that the world seemed so alive and carefree. Nothing of society mattered in this place. Mary and I were witnesses to the spectacular beauty of this place.

Mary and I had stopped at the edge of the overlook. She turned to me and said, "I am so glad that I met you, Benjamin. You are an amazing man, and I would be honored to be with you in New York. I feel that it might take some convincing for my family to accept, but they may be more willing given the dinner last night. I was happy that you bonded with them."

I smiled as Mary leaned in and gave me a passionate kiss. She was so bold in this moment that I couldn't begin to think about stopping her. Societal procedures didn't seem to exist here as Mary and I grew ever more passionate in this kiss. I could feel her heart bonding with mine. Could it be that I would make it possible for Mary to return to New York with me? I could want nothing more amazing than that in this very second. To share a life with Mary by my side would be a dream come true. She was a splendid woman and grabbed my attention every time with her physical, mental, and emotional beauty. She was a tree growing ever taller in my care of myself as I was the gardener that gave her life. I wished to bring her to her full potential and give her the life that she had dreamed. No matter what that life entailed. I only wished to support and help her in everything that she desired as I knew that I trusted her judgment fully.

As I finished this thought, Mary pulled back from me and said, "Please take me with you, Benjamin. I have often dreamed of a different life. Something beautiful and new. I want to find my home."

I nodded and replied, "I will do my best to make this possible, but we cannot simply throw customs out the window. How would your family respond?"

Mary looked at me longingly and responded, "I don't care what they want. This is my life, and I am choosing to be with you. I am choosing to leave everything behind in search of a new life with you."

I heard the intensity with which Mary spoke. She didn't seem to speak as a woman her age, but more like a woman that had lived life over and over again. It seemed as if her soul was speaking with the wisdom of many ages. That is if such a thing were real. I desired her now more than ever. She was the one that I desired, and I was sure of it now. Nothing would stop me with her blessing. We were bonded in perfection. Where she went, I would go as well.

"I will do whatever it takes for you to come with me. Though I want you to think about a way that we can do this without your family being left out. They are important to you. Maybe not now, but in the future, we will come to rely upon them." I had no idea how true these words rang. "I do not wish to upset you, but my friend Percy should be arriving to retrieve me soon. I don't wish to leave your side, Mary, but we will find a way to be together before I leave. I promise you this, my sweet love." I kissed Mary deeply and passionately as I placed my hands on the small of her back. When I pulled away, I could see that her face emanated a desire to share our passion for each other physically. I desired the same, but we would have to refrain.

As the passion of the moment reached its conclusion, Mary took my hand and walked with me back to the home. We rounded the corner of the porch to see Percy rolling toward the home. Time seemed to pass much more quickly here. It was the inevitability of my departure that hung over me. I was not in any way ready to return to the manor and face reality. I knew, however, that I would need to do so. Mary and I walked quickly back into the home just as Ben had returned from feeding the animals. Mary's aunt stood in the kitchen. I bowed to them and said, "I thank you both for inviting me into your beautiful home. I had too much fun last night."

Mary's aunt and uncle moved to where we stood as Mary's uncle replied, "The pleasure is all ours. Thank you so much for visiting us. Come back any time."

I nodded and thanked them again. Mary's aunt turned to grasp something from the table. "We would like you to take this with you, Benjamin." She turned back to me and handed me a basket of assorted foods. I could see that everything had been placed lovingly inside the basket and wrapped to keep it as fresh as possible.

I bowed again and said, "Thank you both so much. I hope to see you both again soon."

They nodded in acceptance of my words. I turned to Mary as she placed her arms around my neck and pulled me closer for a kiss. I couldn't stop her. She seemed to have an immense grasp of me. I kissed her passionately again as her aunt and uncle stood in awe of her boldness. I had expected them to say something about this event, but they simply stood silent and smiled. It was as if they were accepting our love without question. As our embrace ended, I could see that Mary's own parents did the same. Whatever had happened last night left a deeply positive impression on everyone. I was pleased to be accepted so readily. I turned in the moment and bowed my head to Mary's mother and father. I could see her father do the same as if to accept me. I then left the home to see Percy stopping the wagon in front of the porch. It was all that I could do to enter the wagon and leave Mary and her family behind. I was now leaving a sanctuary of peace and acceptance to once again be thrown into the chaos of my business in North Carolina.

Everything seemed to progress so quickly. In a flash, Percy had begun to drive the wagon out of the property and back onto the hardened road. There now was no mud to behold as the wagon creaked and bumped over the ruts in the road. I could feel that the wagon struggled at times to ride through such rough terrain.

"Good morning, Percy."

Percy reached out his hand and shook mine. "Good morning, Benjamin. I trust that your night has been joyous."

I nodded and replied, "It was and I have enjoyed myself. I have not forgotten about our issue with the manor, though."

Percy seemed to be reluctant to remember our issues himself. I turned and placed the basket of food into the back of the wagon. I did hope that the ruts in the road wouldn't compromise the basket and its contents.

"How was your night, Percy?"

Percy seemed to not hear my words as he stared into the distance ahead of the horses. "My night was eventful, to say the least. I was almost arrested by the sheriff, and I am sure that the minister will wish for me to not return to the church."

I was shocked at Percy's words. I could never have imagined that this was all so important to Percy. "What the hell happened?" I could not stop myself from asking this question so boldly.

Percy pulled the wagon over on a shaded area just off the main road. "I went to visit with the minister as we had discussed. He spoke with me without any pause. I showed him the journal, and he was quite disturbed by the words within. I could understand this. What I could not understand is why he accused me of lying and then ran out of the building screaming for the sheriff. Though I did grab a grouping of notes that he had produced for me before I told him whose journal it was. I am sure that the sheriff will not take kindly to my return to the town. That is why we will be traveling a different way to the manor."

I stared at Percy for a moment. I could not believe that this happened without his ability to represent himself. Though I, like Percy, didn't wish to tempt the sheriff into enacting the laws of the town. I didn't know much about this town and didn't wish to know if the town would burn someone for being a witch. I did doubt this, but I was not willing to stare into the face of death over it. Percy then turned the wagon to the left at the crossroads where we should have taken a right. We slowly rode past the side of the inn and out into the main street of the town. There weren't many other buildings to pass now. We had effectively ridden out of the town and out of the eyes of the law. I could see that the forest had now moved to surround us as we sneaked out of town. I looked behind me to check for any pursuers but found nothing. It seemed as if no one cared that we had avoided justice. That is if anyone knew. Without the evidence or in this case the journal, there was nothing to be arrested for besides the word of the minister. Last I understood, you couldn't be arrested for anything over hearsay.

Percy didn't seem to care about looking behind him. I could see that he was simply wishing to put the events of last night behind him. I understood this completely over the past several days. The only worry that I did have at this point was being trapped in the manor once again. I had felt the freedom of not having a demon living within your home, and I enjoyed it quite well. I didn't know what forces were at work within the manor, but I knew that this demon held dominion over everything on that property. I could imagine that Percy felt the same, though he didn't have to stay in the manor each night. The worst thing about staying in the town was that I felt that I couldn't bring myself to move into the inn. I felt that this would not be the proper thing to do. Perhaps it was that Percy had begun to infect my mind, but I couldn't bear to cleanse my aunt's memory. I couldn't bear to allow this thing to rule over her home and the lasting memory that it represented. I was not ready to admit defeat.

We continued to ride farther out of town and deeper into the forest. I felt surprised at the realization that the demon didn't follow me to Mary's uncle and aunt's home. I felt strange now that this thing had failed to terrify me as I slept. I felt as if I were no longer within the demon's gaze. This seemed to play over and over in my mind as I continued to feel what freedom was like. I couldn't seem to grasp the idea of not watching my back at every turn. I could now feel that Percy drove the horses harder through the forest. I wasn't sure why, but it seemed that he was running from something. I turned to look behind us and could see nothing. This gave me the most confused feeling. I began to look all around and could see nothing at all.

"Percy, is everything okay?"

Percy nodded and replied, "Everything is quite all right. I am simply rushing back to the manor. There is something that you must know about this demon. I am also worried that the sheriff might be lingering around my farmhouse and therefore the manor. Do me a favor, Benjamin?" I nodded and agreed. "Keep an eye open for the sheriff. I don't wish to be placed in jail anytime soon."

I nodded once again and immediately sprang to action. I looked all around the wagon as we moved ever deeper into the forest. Eventually, we rode around a right-hand turn and smoothly glided down a slight hill. The wagon seemed to be taking every maneuver that Percy performed. I had feared that the wheels of the wagon might give, but these fears seemed to be unfounded.

As we rounded another corner and straightened out again, I could tell that Percy began to push the horses harder. Now the horses moved at a full gallop, and I was not sure that the wagon could take a turn at this speed. Percy and I had scrunched down to fight against the wind that sought to dethrone us. The wagon bumped violently over the ruts in the road. I could feel the vibrations throughout the wagon. I felt that if we traveled any faster, I would be bounced from the seat. I reached down and held on to the seat tightly. Nothing seemed to be going as planned this morning. Though it was a positive indication that I had not seen the sheriff at all. That was not to say that he wouldn't be waiting for Percy at his farmhouse or nearby. It would make things so much worse to have Percy incarcerated. I continued to look about the woods while I desperately fought against the forces that sought to throw me from my seat.

Percy drove the wagon at full speed until we reached the drive to the home. I could tell that he was in a hurry not only because of the sheriff but also because of having my full attention now. Percy had now begun to slow up the horses as we weaved to the right and then the left. It seemed one fluid motion that had now brought us to approach the home. Percy once again slowed the horses and then pulled them to maneuver into a hard left. In what seemed like an instant he had brought the wagon parallel to the manor but had put the manor between his farmhouse and the wagon. Percy then leaped from the driver's position and dashed to unhitch the horses. I tried to follow suit but feared that I was much too slow. Percy now moved with the grace and speed of a madman. Nothing seemed to stop his movements. As Percy unhitched his horse and I my horse, he pointed to a side pasture and began to move his horse into the woods. I moved as quickly as I could and brought my horse into the pasture as he had. We then locked up the gate and dashed for the home. I wasn't sure why he would wish to move back to the inside of the manor when there was an even greater evil within. Surely Percy hadn't discovered a way to rid the home of this entity and free me from my torment. Though I followed Percy all the same.

We moved into the foyer as Percy slammed the front door behind us.

"Are you all right, Percy?" I asked.

He turned and began to catch his breath. He motioned for us to move into the kitchen, and I followed him. As we entered the empty room, I could tell that something had visited itself upon the bucket that had once held water. I moved to the far side of the kitchen and corrected the bucket's positioning. Percy continued to catch his breath and then sat down at the prep table.

"I am sorry, Benjamin. I wasn't sure that we were being followed. There is something important that you need to see."

I looked at Percy with alarm and said, "Hold that thought, Percy!"

With that sentence, I ran out of the back door and around to the wagon. I pulled the basket of food from the wagon and hastily returned. I placed the basket within the spring house just off the kitchen. I then moved back to where Percy had sat.

"All right, Percy. What was it that I needed to see?" I asked.

Percy removed a wad of papers from his deeper jacket pocket and placed them on the table. He seemed to be a man in a hurry still as he wasted no time in announcing what they contained. "These papers contain much information! Your aunt had been tracked by the minister for years. He had received word that Caroline was involved in dark practices. His notes are outlined as such:

> *March 14th*
>
> *I have approached the Tourney Manor to witness any unusual activity. I felt it better to approach the manor from the woods rather than the road to maintain my stealth. I pray that the good Lord is on my side. I had then come upon a very bright and flickering light as if a large candle were placed in the woods themselves. Upon further inspection, I am witnessing a bonfire with a large group of people. Too hard to tell how many. My heart skipped a beat as I have just seen a man have his throat cut like an animal. Two statues seem to be present to the right of the ceremony. Caroline and another strange woman seem to be inviting others to partake in a liquid. The man himself seems to be burning now in the bonfire. The others have begun chanting, "Burn! Burn! Burn!" I am trying to not be too loud. Just then I could hear a noise coming from behind me deep in the woods.*
>
> *I cannot make a note of the sounds as they are too distressing. I will return to the road soon.*

"The entry stops there, Benjamin," Percy said. "The next page is quite interesting as well. It outlines the minister's research into the cult. I cannot be sure from where this information comes, but it is alarming. The minister had outlined the cult as worshiping a major host of Satan. Though he didn't identify its name. The interesting thing is that the minister references a book that was used for darker rituals than could be performed alone. He also stated that the book had gone missing when Caroline began to fall ill. The last part of this page states,

Whomever shall bring forth this being,
Into themselves,
Shall know no rest in all sickness.
They shall be tested and shall reveal his name.
The host shall give way to the eternal reign of the dark king!

"The minister then writes that this is a reference to the Catholic clergy's belief in exorcism. He claims that his research shows that when the host of the demon dies while carrying the dark being, then the demon is free to pass into our world with the consuming of the host's soul. The last thing stated on this topic is that he tried to confirm this with his contact in the Catholic Church, but couldn't get a comment." Percy then gazed up at me, waiting for my reaction.

What could I say? This thing couldn't be destroyed. Surely it had taken the soul of my aunt and used it to bring itself into this world fully. Though I still didn't understand why it would only show itself from fear or the pitch of the night. I looked out the window as I thought. I couldn't begin to understand the implications that this document had over my situation. "Did the documents say anything else?"

Percy sat in silence for a moment and then replied, "I haven't been able to properly look over two pages of the papers. Give me a moment." Percy then fell into silence as he read. I couldn't tear myself away from the window. It was a horrid reality that I faced now. The possibility that this information could be correct chilled me to my bones. I also feared for the selling of the manor. If this beast began to terrorize the occupants, then I might have a liability to assist the new owners. This was something that I was in no way sure that I could accomplish.

Percy continued to sit in silence. I could tell that he was deep in study of the papers. Whatever they contained had to be something that the minister had discovered some way of stopping this nightmare. I turned from the window and faced Percy. "I think that this might work, Benjamin."

Percy stood from the table and walked over to me. He showed me the paper and said, "This is the last of the minister's notes on the demon. Unfortunately, the research has also confirmed that this demon has now moved beyond the scope of exorcism. The only thing that might work would be the removal of any item that the demon could hold important."

We both pondered these words for a moment. I then looked up and said, "What about the journal? There had to be some reason that the demon began opening and closing the door to the room down the hall."

Percy thought for a moment and agreed. I could see that something troubled Percy. "What is it, Percy?"

He responded with, "I left the journal with my family at my home."

My eyes widened and I thought for a moment. "I will walk to your home and retrieve the journal. Should the sheriff arrive, I will explain that I haven't seen you and I am retrieving my property from your care."

Percy nodded at this idea and added, "You're a genius, Benjamin! I couldn't have thought of a better plan myself."

I smiled and then sprang into action. "I'll return shortly. Where did you leave the journal?"

"I left it in the desk that is in my writing room," Percy answered.

I nodded and said, "I will retrieve it then. Is there anything else that I need to do while I am there?"

Percy shook his head and added, "Just grab the journal and come back here."

I nodded again and then pushed my way out the back door and began walking toward the road. It was not long before I reached the end of the drive and turned left to go out onto the road. I could see nothing to give me alarm or the idea that the sheriff had come to the area in search of Percy. Some part of me chuckled at the fact that the minister had been so upset over Percy's words. Though I did find it odd that the minister knew about Caroline's involvement in the occult but called for the sheriff at Percy's suggestion. I knew there had to be more than what Percy would be able to tell me. I wasn't sure what had really happened, but I didn't wish to be caught in the past. No. This was the time to focus on the present and deal with this demon. If indeed I was not able to sell the home, then I surely would not leave the home to this creature. I now sought to find a way to rid the property of the demon itself. Even if the house didn't stand anymore.

I moved swiftly down the road but maintained an eye over my surroundings. I didn't wish to seem suspicious, but I had to make sure that I wasn't surprised by anything. The journal had to be retrieved and burned. I would not allow this demon to be trapped within the home any longer. I was confused by how this demon had not been pulled to terrify Percy's family if it was really attached to the journal. Though I also questioned what would happen once the journal had been burned. Would that mean that this demon would be able to roam free? If so, what would that imply? The only way to be sure and answer these concerns would be to follow through with our assumptions. Even still, I hurried to the best of my ability to gather the journal from Percy's home. If indeed the demon had followed the journal, then Percy's family could be being terrorized as I walked.

It was not long before I reached the entranceway to Percy's home. I rushed up the walk and onto the porch. I could not hear or see anything strange to this point but still didn't wish to linger too long. I opened the front door and made my way cautiously into the home. I still couldn't hear or see anything odd. I also didn't find Percy's family within the home. I didn't waste any time locating his family. I simply moved down the hallway and into what looked like the writing room. I crossed the room with inhuman speed and began searching the desk for the journal. I had worried that Percy's wife would find me hunched over in the dimly lit room tearing open drawer after drawer. She would surely panic at this sight with the assumption that I was robbing their home. Though it would give me the opportunity to find out if his family had been visited by the sheriff. I still rushed to leave the home before anyone had seen me there. I opened the last drawer of the desk and found the journal intact. It had been placed among a grouping of other journals within the writing desk's main drawer.

I moved quickly to vacate the home while also covering my tracks and making sure that everything in the room seemed the same as before I had rummaged around in the desk. I knew that Percy would be pleased with my quick return. I left the writing room and moved to the front door. I peered out at first and could see no one outside. I also couldn't hear any sounds. This gave me cause to worry about Percy's family. I decided that it was my duty to make sure they were well, even if I didn't allow them to see me. I crept out the door and to the right. In seconds I was standing at the back corner of the home. I peered cautiously around the back of the home and could spy Percy's family working about the farm.

I was relieved to know that everyone seemed well. I rather swiftly moved to the front of the home and continued to travel back out onto the main road. I had determined that nothing could have happened at the home. I also considered that if there had been a visit by the sheriff, then he would have had the desire to stay and wait for Percy's return. I didn't see any strange wagon or anyone associating with Percy's family. I now had no wish to linger around the farmhouse in case anyone should arrive soon. I made it a point to move quickly back to the manor, checking for anyone approaching from behind as I went. There was no indication that anyone was roaming the roads either. No one could have driven a wagon through here recently without kicking up dust. I held out hopes that I would be able to return to the manor without delay. I continued to pay attention to the pasture to my right. I could see that the fence had been partially covered by vines that seemed to protect the wooden fence. I looked about the road and could see no one watching as I climbed over the fence and began walking toward the manor again.

I continued to check my surroundings and keep my ears poised for any new sounds. The closer I moved to the manor, the faster I began to walk. Eventually, I was flanked on my right by a row of trees that seemed to guide me into the drive of the home. I was relieved now that no one from the road would be able to see me moving back toward the home. Once I had climbed back over the fence and onto the drive, I dashed for the front of the home. In one graceful motion, I opened the door and moved into the foyer. I closed the door behind me and locked it firmly. I then moved as quickly as I could back into the kitchen.

Percy sat at the prep table and was once again looking over the pages that he had retrieved from the minister. I could see that Percy desired more answers in this situation. He held the same intrigue that drove me to search for answers as well. I moved over to the table and laid the journal in front of Percy. He immediately stopped his reading and looked up at me.

"I checked on your family and they are all well. I don't think that the sheriff has arrived to look for you," I said.

Percy seemed relieved at these words. "I thank you very much, Benjamin. My family doesn't deserve to be brought into this issue. I don't know how my children and my wife would accept such evil in our home as well. That is to say that I do not wish for you to have to deal with this at all, but you and I are much better equipped to handle such shocking actions." Percy took hold of the journal and stood from the table. He motioned for me to follow him down the hallway. We reached the end of the hall and stood in front of the rear door. "We will move out into the far pasture to burn the journal. You go first and keep an eye out. I will follow you," Percy stated.

"What is it that actually happened, Percy? Surely the sheriff wouldn't wish to find you over accusations leveled by the minister. I also find it odd that his papers have stated that he knew Caroline was involved in satanic rituals but wished to call the sheriff on you."

Percy stared at me for a moment and added, "We don't have time for that right now. Let's deal with the journal first."

I nodded and moved to open the back door. With a couple of looks around the back of the home, I knew that we were safe to move out into the yard. I motioned for Percy to follow and led him into the forest. It wasn't long before we had moved into a more secluded pasture that was being reclaimed by the forest. Percy produced a candle and some matches from his pocket and began to dig up the ground with a piece of metal. "Keep a watch for anyone that could be observing us," Percy commanded.

I nodded and immediately began looking around. As I did, I could hear Percy light the candle with a match. I turned my head back to Percy and witnessed him hold up the journal and begin to light it on fire.

It didn't take long for the journal to begin burning. Percy placed the journal back into the hole that he had dug out. The fire continued to consume the book, and in a moment the pages had been almost completely consumed by the fire. I could see a pleased look on Percy's face as he watched the journal transform into a charred black mass. The ashes began to blow away in the wind as the most foul smell engulfed Percy and me. We couldn't help but cover our noses as the human skin had been burned and singed by the flames. The smell was so distinct that I never wished to smell anything like it again. Once the flames had died, Percy recovered the journal and mixed the ashes around in the fresh dirt. I was relieved instantly at the sight of the journal being burned. I could feel a weight lifting from me. I also could tell that Percy could feel the same thing. We both began walking back to the manor.

8

RETURN TO DARKNESS

Percy and I didn't waste any time in returning to the manor. I could tell that Percy shared my relief after burning the journal. Even without evidence that the burning of the journal had changed anything, we both had high hopes that it had. I strolled through the back door to the home with Percy following shortly behind. We moved into the kitchen, and each began making something to eat. There was no assurance that anything had changed, and I worried that nothing really had. Though now it seemed that the air was lighter in the manor. I couldn't feel the presence that I had felt before. This had also been the case before, however. Only time would tell what would really happen after the sun faded behind the horizon.

This thought still left me with many questions. Why was it that a demon would wait until the sun was not present in the sky to truly display its power? I couldn't begin to understand the inner workings of the supernatural. I also did not wish to understand this darkness that we possibly still faced. Percy didn't seem to be following the same line of thought. I could tell that he seemed blindly relieved. We both stood for a few moments eating. The only sounds were those of our eating. I felt that neither of us wished to say anything for fear that it might spark an incident. We both simply stood in the kitchen eating.

The sun had now begun to hang lower in the sky. I could tell that the night was vastly approaching. I wasn't sure what Percy would do. I did hope, however, that he wouldn't abandon the manor without first assisting me in testing our theory about the journal. Though I simply had to trust that Percy would wish to test the hypothesis. I moved toward the door on the opposite side of the room. Percy seemed to pay me any attention. I slowly opened the door and peeked out. There was a small part of me that wished to see something peering back. Nothing was out of place. No demon, nor any signs that it had left the manor. I didn't wish to be paranoid in the moment, but I couldn't be sure. I just knew that part of me couldn't accept the journal as the answer to why the demon resided in the manor. Though I did wish to share Percy's optimism.

"Do you really think that I am accepting that the demon is gone? I am not blind, but I am hoping," Percy said. "We haven't been able to check whether this demon is gone." Percy's words gave me comfort. I could now be sure that he would stay at least for some time to see if this being had left the home. "I also will remind you that I cannot go home until much later. I want to make sure that the sheriff doesn't decide to pay me a late visit," Percy added.

I nodded in reply and suggested, "Let's move into the sitting room for a smoke then."

Percy smiled and led the way into the sitting room. We both took our seats with the window open behind us. The air still hung thick with humidity. We both produced our pipes and a bag of tobacco. It didn't seem to take long to spark the bowls and begin puffing. I did worry that Percy's family wouldn't understand why Percy had kept his distance, but that was not my concern. After all, it was Percy that would be expected to answer these questions. Though I did understand that Percy would return home but would be late.

Time was now progressing past noon. The day had progressed smoothly, and I could not help but feel that the power to stop this demon was on our side. Perhaps it was God not wishing to allow such a dark entity to gain domain over his creation. That or it was that we waited for something to change in vain. Each puff of my pipe brought more thoughts into my mind. I was considering the possibility that I would have to abandon the home and wait for someone willing to rid the home of this evil before I could sell. It would take more time, but I could at least place a representative to sell the manor. I had considered that the minister would wish to help, but that was now unclear.

"What was it that you had done when visiting the minister?" I asked.

Percy didn't respond immediately. He seemed to wait as if we would both forget about the reasons that the sheriff would wish to take Percy into custody. I waited patiently as Percy continued to smoke his pipe.

"I am not sure what came over me. The minister seemed willing to help, but he began resisting the idea that a demon could reside in the home. I raised my voice and scolded the minister but couldn't stop there. It was a combination of my yelling and slapping the minister for assuming that you and I were liars. I couldn't control my anger. I wasn't myself at all. I have never assaulted anyone over something so trivial," Percy said fervently.

I nodded and took a deep drag from my pipe. I could understand exactly what Percy meant. I had often felt as if I had begun to lose control over myself. Thankfully, this was not any time that I was away from the manor. I had considered, at this moment, that I wouldn't be able to stop myself around Mary or her family. I would have been embarrassed, to say the least. "That is quite all right, Percy. This demon has a way of getting the better of you. Though I doubt that anyone else would take this as an excuse," I said. My words of comfort didn't seem to help Percy. I could see that he was still worried that the sheriff would take him into custody and that he would have no reason to change the sheriff's mind. After all, it wasn't as if we could simply point to a demon as the cause for Percy's actions.

I felt that it was better to avoid this topic further. I didn't wish for Percy to stress himself further. The breeze continued to waft into the sitting room and provide a cooling effect to Percy and me. The home was quite comfortable now. I could feel myself falling into a comfortable state. My pipe was heated to the right temperature so that I didn't have to pull too hard to get a good puff. Percy and I sat in silence like this for some time until his words broke the silence.

"You know! I have never sat in this room before. I was always much too busy. I always saw visitors and Caroline utilizing this room from time to time, but not for too long. I always envied them," Percy stated.

I smiled and then replied, "Surely you didn't work all the time!"

Percy drooped his head and then sighed. "You know me, Benjamin! I cannot stop when there is work to do! Especially when your aunt was about. She was always giving us something to do. I can still hear her soft but forceful voice in the back of my mind. She was a fair taskmaster, but stern."

I smiled again at the thought of my aunt being such a woman. I never imagined that I would hear so much about her life until now. Though now I knew too much. Some things were left not being known. I knew that I could not simply dismiss all that had happened in the past several days, but it was Wednesday now and I could not help but feel that it would be a long time before I departed. If everything had gone according to plan, then I would be able to leave Hillsborough in peace. If not, then I would surely have to change my plans or figure out an alternative solution. Though it was the alternative solution that I feared most. It is in times like that that a man is truly reckless and spontaneous. I just didn't wish to do anything hastily.

I continued to sit in comfort. I could feel the chair in which I sat engulfing my body. I was happy to rest after a hard few days of constant motion. Percy and I sat in this room now worrying for nothing. The fact that I could perceive my freedom from this situation gave me an overconfident sense of peace. The thought then crossed my mind for Percy and me to prepare ourselves in the event that this being wasn't detached from our realm.

"Do you feel that we should investigate the manor again?"

Percy seemed lost in thought now but also made a humming noise to assure me that he had heard what I said. "I think that it would be the best course of action. Though we cannot investigate properly until late in the evening."

I agreed and we immediately began forming a plan. Whether it was paranoia or fear of being overheard, Percy briskly walked over to the sitting room door and shut it rather firmly. He then strolled toward me while puffing on his pipe. "I think we should explore the attic once more. Right now I doubt that we would get a reaction either way, but perhaps in a couple hours?" Percy produced his pocket watch and opened it. "It is half past two o'clock now. Would you agree on half past five?"

I nodded and replied, "That would be ideal. Though what will we do in the event that the creature attacks us again?"

Percy stood silent for a moment as he weighed his options. "I think that we should be cautious in either case, but running quickly would help," he replied.

I laughed for a moment and then asked, "Surely you jest?"

Percy seemed serious about this suggestion, which gave me reason to understand all the same that he had no idea how to rid the home of this being any more than I did. Though when I allowed myself to believe that he did, I had the utmost confidence. Now that confidence waned. I now faced the stark realization that Percy was just as in the dark as I was, perhaps more so. I agreed to Percy's suggestion in whole, and we both began looking out the window and planning our moves further. Percy suggested that we should start in the attic and move about the rest of the home if nothing could be sighted. I suggested that we should be cautious and look through the upper floors while maintaining a healthy view of the bedroom with the attic covering, then approaching the attic as the last resort. I didn't wish to go directly to its lair out of fear, but I knew that it was this fear that I would have to settle before the night was out. I felt ashamed of this fear. Never before had I been able to be shaken by anything or anyone in my life. Now I was being shaken by something that until recently didn't exist in my scope. This also caused problems with my beliefs. Now it was ever more apparent that the Bible didn't speak of demons as a simple tool to teach of the darker side of human nature.

Now it was all too real, and I didn't know how I could understand and quantify it. Perhaps being a skeptic was never my calling. Perhaps I had ignored another aspect to life that most didn't understand at all or even see. I had now become acutely aware that there were dark beings trying to gain control of the world and everything in it. I had now understood the calling that Jesus had placed on his disciples. I could now see the darkness that inhabited life in general and sought to corrupt even the most perfect. Yet to this question, how would a being such as God expect mortals to face such immense darkness without pause? Could it be true that even the smallest amount of faith could shield someone from the evil that lurked beyond this world? I didn't know the answer to this question, but now it was the only question that I had left to ask. All other queries seemed to have faded as if drowned out by this thought.

Percy puffed deeply on his pipe then said, "Have you heard any noises within the home prior to the demon showing itself?"

I thought for a moment and replied, "No. Though there will often be a feeling of dread that hung heavy over the whole home."

Percy seemed interested in my words. "So you mean to say that it is more of a feeling?"

I nodded and added, "Yes, but it is impossible to ignore. The feeling takes you over slowly. It is in no way subtle."

Percy seemed satisfied with this answer and turned back to the window.

"Why do you ask?" I said.

"I am just unclear on this manor. I worry that this being will hide in the home and not reveal itself until I have left."

I nodded and added, "I understand. I myself am worried that you will leave and the demon will attempt to settle a score with me. I cannot fathom what I would do in the event that I was left alone with this creature."

Percy made a face that shouted that he could understand this sentiment. Even Percy seemed to not know why I would continue to stay here. "I had checked with the inn in town, but they wanted forty-two dollars to stay in a room."

Percy looked at me with shock and replied, "That is a lot of money to stay at that inn. I would rather sleep in a barn. Though the innkeeper has claimed that he had renovated the rooms after my stay."

"When was it that you checked into the inn?"

Percy smiled and replied, "Before my wife and I had both moved here, I stayed at the inn until I could build my farmhouse. The room was despicable. I didn't understand how anyone would wish to stay in such a place for even two nights. I would rather build you a cabin on my property if I thought that I could complete it before your departure."

"What was so bad about the room, Percy?" I asked.

Percy took a drag from his pipe. "The bed is simply a frame with hay in it. The pillows are often infested with bugs, and the floors are just dirty. There is no furniture in that inn that is sturdy or reliable."

I winced at the thought of staying in the inn. Nothing could make me stay in such a place. A barn would be a much better place to stay and possibly more comfortable. I had now begun to understand that my situation was much more dire than I had once thought. I had nowhere else to go. I couldn't stay anywhere that would be more comfortable and out of the reach of this being. Though I still didn't even know if being in another place would help. I had never ventured to answer the question of what power this being truly held.

As soon as I thought about this, I had the most unsettling feeling. I didn't wish to know of any being that could get to me no matter where I resided. I also didn't wish for this thing to follow me back to New York. Though I did have to admit that it would make selling the manor that much easier. Percy and I continued to stand in silence as if watching the last drops of sanity vanish beyond the horizon. The sun wasn't too low in the sky, but I felt as if it wouldn't be long before the sun had fallen. I could also tell that Percy waited for the same to occur. We both hesitated to remain here after dark. Now it had become less interesting and more frightening. Nothing seemed to stop the anticipation of feeling such dread. Almost as if watching someone swing a stick toward your head. You anticipate the pain, which makes the feeling so much worse.

Percy and I continued to wait for five thirty. The time seemed to pass much more slowly the closer we came to our destined time. Eventually, Percy became too hasty and said, "I am tired of waiting. Let's go, Benjamin!"

I followed Percy out of the sitting room and back to the stairs. We both stood at the bottom of the stairs and looked at each other. The realization had set in that not only were we going to search the home for a demon, but we still had lit pipes. We each made haste to tamper our pipes and put them away. Percy and I seemed to be together in the thought that the demon might target the fire from the pipes to rid the home of our presence. I immediately moved to the stairs and began climbing up to the landing. I kept myself alert for any unusual noises. Though we both had confidence that our hypothesis was correct about the journal, we both didn't wish to be overconfident. After all, I was sure that fear and overconfidence were what this being had longed for since my arrival. Another victim to terrify and possibly control until their death. That is if the stories are true about demons only wishing to claim victims for Armageddon. This thought, however, made me more determined to examine everything around me. I was sure that I didn't wish to be caught off guard anymore.

As I reached the top of the stairs, I could feel a sense that I was being watched. The feeling had just started as I was about to step out onto the landing. At first, I was sure that it was Percy simply standing behind me, but it grew ever more present the farther that I went. I could now not distinguish from where this feeling emanated. I was sure that the demon was lurking about somewhere on the second floor. I moved away from the stairs and to the left. Upon peering down the hallway, I couldn't see anything that was out of place, but I did smell an overwhelming sulfur smell. It was as if the home was taken over by it. The smell grew and grew as I traveled down the hallway. Percy hadn't followed me down this hallway before but was now directly behind me. We moved as one person. When I entered a room, he entered the same room. I couldn't be sure, but I considered that Percy was feeling some sense of dread or being watched as I was feeling. I hoped that he now understood how it was to be in this home late in the day.

With Percy glued to me, I entered each room in this hallway and began moving back toward the right hallway. The sulfur smell that had once lingered in the home was gone. I thought this to be odd, but there was nothing odd otherwise. As Percy and I made the left turn to go down the next hallway, I could see that the sun was not falling behind the horizon. Time had seemed to blink by as it didn't take Percy and me long to search the other rooms. I tried to not turn my focus to the bedroom that was to my right. Everything in my mind screamed at me to not look. I could feel that this was the place where we would find the demon. I took the left turn cautiously and immediately went into the room at the end of the hallway. This was the room where Percy and the other servants had witnessed my aunt walking back and forth between the windows. The room was rather large and imposing but didn't seem to have anything in it. There was just some furniture that had been placed on the left side of the room and nothing else. No beds or any dressers. Not even a wardrobe or a closet. I found this to be rather odd.

"What was originally in this room, Percy?"

Percy didn't respond. I turned to see that Percy was gone. There was no sign of him in this giant room. I swiftly moved back to the doorway and looked back down the hall. I couldn't see Percy there either. I found it odd that he was right behind me the whole time but now had disappeared. I decided to check the other rooms in the hall. I left the room that I currently occupied and went into the first room on my right. This room was quite small but held a bed and an end table. It was reminiscent of the room that I had slept in at Mary's uncle's house. I also found it odd that it was a mirror image of that room. Perhaps it was a coincidence or it was intentional. Though without Percy, I would never know.

I immediately turned my attention back to searching the other rooms. I moved to the door of this tiny bedroom and heard a distinct yell.

"Benjamin! HELP!"

I ran out of the room and down the hall. I could hear that the yell had come from the bedroom containing the opening to the attic. I was sure that Percy had been taken by the demon. There was no doubt in my mind now. Percy was in mortal danger, and I had to rush to his side. I scrambled out of the bedroom and down the hall. I gave no concern now to my surroundings. Assisting Percy was all that was in my mind. I could consider nothing else. I didn't even waste my time or my energy by checking my surroundings for danger. The only thing to be sure of now was that I had to reach the bedroom. I moved to the doorway and turned into the room where the yell had originated. I could see Percy's head hanging out of the opening in the ceiling. He yelled again, "Benjamin! Help me!" I moved through the doorway and began climbing the ladder. I reached into the hole and grasped Percy's shirt. I was determined to not lose my friend. I pulled as hard as I could to try to recover Percy. It seemed, however, that the more that I pulled, the more that Percy slipped into the attic. He was now mostly into the hole and I was peering and reaching into the darkness of the attic. The sun had completely fallen, and I had not been able to obtain a candle for light. I feared that I would eventually be standing in darkness so thick that even I wouldn't be able to see. I pulled ever harder against whatever force was taking Percy into the attic. Nothing seemed to cause this being to relent. I now feared that Percy would be taken and I would be alone in the manor. I would be waiting for the demon to come for me next.

I stood in the middle of the ladder with my arms stretched out into the attic. It was all that I could do to not lose my footing and be jerked into the attic myself. The ladder was surprisingly stable at this moment and didn't seem to add to the problems at hand. I placed my feet into a bracing position on the side of the ladder and forced it against the wall of the closet. I then pushed with my feet as I pulled with all my might. Eventually, the creature released Percy from its grasp, and I felt myself crash to the floor with Percy landing on top of me. He rolled to his right and clambered to his feet. We both felt the impending doom of the demon approaching us from its lair. I now could understand this deep-seated fear that had consumed me once again. I was overcome with dread and a sense of giving in to my fears. Though this was not what I actually had done. I grabbed Percy by the sleeve of his jacket and jerked him out of the room and into the hallway. We both reached the stairs as we heard a noise to our left. I stopped just ahead of Percy to see the demon emerging from the doorway to the room. He held out his hand and began screaming in the most horrible sounds. Percy and I wasted no time in reaching the lower level. We both jumped over the railing to the stairs and fell down onto the floor of the foyer below. We had become more concerned with running from our doom than causing our doom. We also had no idea of the speed this creature held. Nor did we wish to find out.

I felt Percy grasp at the collar of my jacket and shirt simultaneously as he yanked me from the floor, and we both took an extreme pace back to the sitting room. I ran deep into the room and stood by the window as Percy slammed the door behind me and locked it. We stood now in silence as we heard the screams of the demon ring out throughout the home. The sound of this beast seemed to vibrate the very walls around us. It almost seemed as if the earth trembled at its roar.

This was enough to let Percy and me know that this demon was alive and well in this manor. I felt almost as if the being had gained in strength as opposed to waning. I had hoped that the journal would have the opposite effect, but perhaps the emotions contained within had now been released and the beast was free from all shackles. Perhaps Percy and I had given this creature freedom to rule within this world. Our fears had become real as we now had proof that the journal had no bearing over this being. Though I still found it odd that the room seemed to be protected by this demon or its lair. Could it be that the attic held something even more powerful that the demon longed to possess when it had freed itself of my aunt? Nothing could be investigated now, however. At least not until we could be sure that the creature had grown dormant again.

Percy and I now stood pacing about the room listening to these inhuman cries. I could tell that we both felt trapped with this burden now more than ever. I had been amazed also by the level of speed that Percy or I could possess when running from such a fright. We both had become the fastest men alive when facing hell itself. My only question in all this was how reaching this being was. The screeching from this demon was loud. How was it that no one else could hear such a yell and come to our aid? I then remembered that the only people close enough to aid us were Percy's family, and I didn't wish for them to come here and be involved with such a horrid thing.

"How long can this go on?" Percy asked. "We cannot deal with this forever!"

I nodded and didn't say anything. I couldn't find the words to say in such an event. Then just as the horrid voice had begun, it ended. No other sounds filled the home. No other noises could be heard for a moment. Then time stood still as Percy and I did as well. Silence had fallen save for the sound of the beast skulking back into the bedroom and then up into the attic. The only certainty now was that this nightmare had never left. Percy and I had never freed ourselves from anything. Now we could only stand in silence pondering where it all had gone wrong. Nothing could provide any answers now. I feared that all Percy and I could do was survive the night and then leave the manor by the morning. After all of this, though, I couldn't blame Percy for wishing to leave before sunrise. There was no telling if this was possible and whether the demon would allow us to gather Percy's horses without terrorizing us first. We could be sure of nothing now, and we could do nothing save for waiting.

The world itself seemed to fall silent as if I had become deaf. I wasn't sure how long this peace would last with the demon in the home. I sat down in the chair closest to the window as Percy continued to pace about the room. "There has to be some way to rid this house of this evil!" Percy seemed as if he were focused too much on killing the demon. I had to admit, though, that I was guilty of being just as stubborn.

Fear didn't seem to matter now. There was only the urge to eliminate what plagued our lives. Only during times of relaxation did I stop to think about the insanity of everything that had happened. I had never truly considered how normal a demonic presence in the manor had become. All the same, I couldn't allow this thing to take the last of my life from me. I had to resist its presence as much as possible.

"Perhaps if I were to talk to the minister and allow him to visit the manor to perform an exorcism," Percy said excitedly.

I shook my head vigorously in response. "Nothing can change what has happened. The demon pushed you into the actions that you took for a reason. Perhaps the minister was the only one who could have stopped this being. Thus the demon pushed you into attacking him so that he would turn his back on us," I said.

Percy stood with an inquisitive look upon his face. I could tell that he was now considering my words to be truth. "If this is true, Benjamin. Then how can this being know everything that we were attempting? That is only the power of God himself to know all."

Percy had a point. This was a most unusual quandary. I was sure that something had to explain this knowledge of the future. "All I am saying is that this demon has us right where it wants us. It has cut us off from anyone that could aid us. This helplessness that we feel is feeding this thing. He is growing stronger from our fears and doubts. This is the battle plan of a cunning foe indeed," I said.

Percy stared at me in amazement at this thought.

"If this demon was summoned when I was a younger person during a visit by my mother, then it has had a long time to plan all of this. No one could have known about its plan either because no one knew it was here until my aunt's life began to fade."

Percy nodded. "Are you sure that you don't know more about this than you are telling me, Benjamin?" Percy asked.

I looked at Percy with a worried look as I said, "I am not sure where these thoughts are coming from, but I am just formulating all of this now."

Percy still stood in amazement at my words. My thoughts seemed to have a clarity to them that I had never felt before. It was as if I was no longer reacting to my doubts and fears but was acting upon all thought and emotion that I felt toward defeating this being. As if overcoming this foe aligned myself in such a way to hear all thoughts and knowledge that was contained around us all. As if the universe was speaking to me through my thoughts. I could not be sure of this, but I knew it to be true since my thoughts weren't my own. Though I now felt as if I had been backed into a corner with no choice. Though I would rather not lash out at this being.

"Didn't you say that the minister has connections to the Catholic Church?" I asked.

Percy nodded and replied, "Yes. His notes had stated this."

I continued, "Then I should pay this minister a visit and hope that I am not overcome with the same urge to trap myself with anger. If he has connections with the Catholic faith, then he may know of tools that can be used in this case to drive the demon out."

Percy stood once again in amazement at my words. Though now his expression leaned more toward annoyance.

I didn't know much of what I had spoken other than it made sense. I had always known about the Catholic Church. I also knew that they had talked about utilizing tools to defeat the devil and his minions. Perhaps these were tangible tools that can be used to overcome the demon. It was an idea that seemed to be a stretch, but I was inclined to trust them as I knew they weren't my own. I could tell that these thoughts felt no fear or worry. They were concise and motivated. To what end was unclear, but I still felt better when they were formed within my psyche. I could see that Percy seemed to have a paranoia about my words now. I could tell that he was troubled by my sudden understanding of this situation.

"Why is it that we have been running from this beast the whole time, but now you suddenly have an understanding about what should happen next?"

I shrugged my shoulders and replied, "Everything has a reason to exist. Perhaps the reason that this demon has infested this home is so that you and I could bond over trying to defeat it. Perhaps we are supposed to learn such things. I do not know why, but I know that the minister seems to be a key in all of this. Logically, the demon doesn't want to be defeated. So it would do all that it could to make sure that you weren't successful in talking to the minister and gaining his help. Perhaps it knows that his contacts in the Catholic Church would be its demise."

Percy nodded as he couldn't refute this thought process. Though these thoughts were now mine, I could still tell that the overall idea was not. This gave me pause in all that I would say around people. After all, I didn't want anyone to be suspicious of me and feel that the demon had infected my mind as well as the home. It wasn't my intent to distance myself from others but to find the answers in this moment about saving this home and myself from this being of evil. Now the only thing that I had to be aware of was my feelings toward harming the minister or myself. I didn't wish to have a repeat of Percy's visit.

I understood now why it all happened that way. This being was truly conniving, and I didn't wish to be a pawn in its game. I was now committed to ridding the world of this being and freeing myself and Percy from this possible torment. No one deserved to be used for such nefarious things. I just had to find out the ending of this story. I could not live with the idea that someone else would be tormented by this creature. That another family possibly with children would have their innocence robbed from them. I could not live with that factor. No matter how long it took now, I would stop this being and take its control away from it. Percy and I had begun to form a plan now. Though our plan didn't include what to do on this night. I had hoped, however, that this demon would be finished with us until the next day.

The silence was eventually broken. I could hear creaking coming from the floor above us. Percy and I eventually stopped in our tracks. We now sat not even puffing on our pipes. We were frozen, just waiting for the next set of sounds. Percy looked at me as if to say, "Did you hear that?" Though nothing came out of his mouth.

We waited as the sounds continued. The boards above us continued with their creaking as if someone were sneaking across them. No other sounds were heard. Even the noises and sounds of life from outside the window could not be heard. Percy and I still stood frozen as we heard the sounds of the creaking floor moving toward the door of our room. Whatever was making these noises had now left the room above us. I waved for Percy to follow as I led him out into the hallway. We could hear the sounds now moving down the hallway and toward the stairs. Percy and I now stood in the middle of the hallway, waiting. I could feel myself longing to return to the sitting room. Now, however, we were completely frozen.

The sounds continued as the being crept down the hallway further and reached the landing. There was a distinct sound of someone stopping on the landing of the stairs and waiting, almost as if they were waiting for us to move out into the foyer to meet them. Percy and I wouldn't dream of moving from our position. I waited ahead of Percy, who still clung to the doorway to the sitting room. I knew that if I moved farther down the hallway, then I would do it alone. I struggled to fight against the curiosity to walk down the hallway and look up the stairs. The sounds that we had heard were not like that of the demon. This was different. It sounded as if someone who was older was moving slowly down the hallway but with sure footing.

Percy and I waited as long as we could before I began to walk forward down the hallway. I was most interested in knowing who this entity was as I could not feel any sense of dread. I simply felt interested in what was happening. Percy pulled at the back of my jacket. I could hear him begging me not to go. The whispers of his voice didn't feel strong enough to stop my advance toward the foyer.

I continued to move down the hallway in a slow and methodical motion. I hoped that my slow walk and silent footsteps would cause this entity to not realize that I was now approaching the foyer. Percy still stood in the doorway of the sitting room, and I could see now that he was reaching out, waving his hand for me to return to the sitting room. I could see this because I was now approaching the bottom step of the stairs and had begun turning to look up the stairs. As I peeked around the banister, I could see now that there was a woman in a gown standing on the top landing. She was simply looking forward and didn't seem to react to my presence. I considered the possibility that she was not aware that I was present because of my creeping down the hallway. I couldn't be sure of anything at this moment. I now motioned for Percy to follow the hallway to my position. Percy stood in the doorway still and didn't seem to trust my beckoning. I could tell that Percy was completely frozen in fear still. He had even stopped motioning for me to return to the sitting room.

Suddenly I could feel something telling me to look toward the top landing of the stairs. I could not explain why until I looked up. The woman in the gown was now peering down at me. She still didn't move at all but was just standing there looking at me. I felt the feeling of being isolated. I couldn't stop the feeling that Percy had abandoned me. It was almost as if I was completely alone in the home. I focused through these emotions and could see that the woman's face was covered with a thin veil.

There was a darkness that hung around her face and concealed her features. I could also see that her gown now flowed down onto the landing and seemed to cover all of her. Even her feet were covered by this gown though her toes seemed to stick out from under the bottom of the gown. Her toes were white and pale, so pale in fact that her skin seemed to hold a green hew. It was as if she were covered in some sort of sickness that had infected her skin. She didn't seem to be of an imposing stature or to be a large woman in any way. She instead seemed to be a smaller and more frail woman. She held a shape that didn't seem curvy or fat. I found it odd that she was even alive at all. She was stood at a hunch that seemed as if her spine were bent at a wrong angle. I could see that she seemed to be older but younger at the same time. I found it all very odd, and it almost made me feel as if I couldn't trust my own sight.

Before I could witness anything more, the woman lifted a bony and dead-looking finger to her mouth. She seemed to be telling me to be quiet, but it was all in the most odd way. She then moved her finger out to a point. She was now stood, pointing just behind me. I could now hear her, "She's behind you!"

She didn't seem to say this with any volume to her voice. It was like a whisper that filled the whole home. Yet it seemed effective enough to cause me to be struck with a deep-seated fear. I felt completely uncomfortable. My mind seemed so unsettled by the woman's words that I felt as if I were in complete danger. I feared to look behind me, but I had to be sure that nothing was waiting to kill me. I stood motionless, save for my head turning toward my right. I looked as far to the right as I could and could see something standing behind me. It was a brooding mass that seemed poised to grab me and wisp me away.

I dared not show any fear, but that had now become almost completely impossible. I had no idea what was happening or how to stop this. I turned to my right to get a better look at this thing and could feel my mind screaming for me to run. I also wasn't sure how Percy hadn't begun to yell for me to look behind me. I slowly continued turning until this thing was in my full view. It was the hag from the other night that had been floating toward the door. She was now standing in front of me with a half-decayed face. I couldn't recognize her in any way, nor did I wish to do so.

Though now it was all that I could do to look at her horrid features. She was smiling at me with the most jagged and broken teeth that I had ever seen. I could see that her tongue was rotten and swollen and black. Nothing could have prepared my mind for such a sight. I feared everything had come to an end, but I couldn't do anything about it. She had me where she wanted me, and nothing could stop that now. My only hope was that Percy would get me out of the situation or at least assist me in driving this thing away. I had no idea what to do as she began lifting her arm toward my face. She seemed to have a look of arousal in this moment. I felt that she had desired me as if we were on our wedding night and she was the only one to satisfy me.

I could now feel a bony and cold finger brush against my face. Her smell was horrendous now. She smelled rotten and dead, decaying where she stood and desiring for me to do the same. She gently brushed my cheek as I stood in fear. I had thought that I would meet a swift end at her hands, but now it seemed that I was to suffer at her hand. She ran her tongue out of her mouth and licked what was left of her rotten smile.

"Do not fear me, Benjamin! I am here to take you home! Don't you recognize your dear mother?" Her words rang inside my head like a bell had been rung. I wasn't sure what to do, save reaching deep into my pocket and producing a match that I had all hopes would light on the first try. I had no other options now. Percy had obviously fallen into his own fear, and I couldn't scream or do anything to stop this. I simply had to drive this thing away before it made its plans fully known to me. I was to strike the match and light her wispy, matted hair on fire. I was to bring down the flame of purification upon this creature and drive it out of my sight once and for all.

I slowly pressed the match against the toughest portion of my coat and dragged the match top outward. To my amazement, the match lit in a grand fashion. No words could find me as I held the match up and heard the terrible shrieks of this woman being lit ablaze. Instantly the smell of burning death filled my nose. It was all that I could do to not vomit from this stench. Her screams echoed throughout the home as she burned away into the form of smoke. She was now nothing more than ash and blackness. The ash seemed to be her flesh and the blackness - her soul. Both vanished before my very eyes as I still looked on in amazement.

If this thing had been my mother, then she didn't act as such. A mother didn't seem to lust after their children in such a way. Perhaps if she was my mother, then she was twisted and evil like this demon that infested the home. Either way, she was gone now, and I felt somewhat at ease. With the match still lit, I turned to the other woman and hoped that I would be able to burn her as well. This was not the case, however, as she rushed from the top of the stairs in an ear-piercing scream and pushed me through the front door. I was amazed that the door simply opened and then began to close behind me.

My mind struggled to keep up with all that was happening. I couldn't believe that I was once again being thrown from the home and out into the drive. I could tell that I had reached some height as I was now parallel to the top of the front door before I came crashing down to the gravel drive below. I could now feel each stone punching into my flesh through my clothing. They each felt like tiny daggers trying to cut their way through my flesh. I slid across the gravel and now lay in the patch of grass in the center of the entrance to the manor. I rolled onto my stomach and quickly gained my footing again. My only thoughts were now of Percy and the danger that he was in. Though I couldn't hear any of his screams. It was as if the world had fallen silent. If Percy had become trapped in the manor, then he was surely hiding quietly in the sitting room. Though my mind could only imagine the worst things.

The pain of my fall seemed to be all that I could feel as well. I wasn't sure why the world seemed dark and hazy now. It was as if a fog had rolled in over the manor grounds and I was exposed to this. The manor had also become dark. Not even the dim light that had shone from the sitting room could be seen. I was sure that this was due to Percy being tormented by this being or worse. At this thought, I sprang into action. I moved back to the front door and beat upon the wood. I yelled out loudly so as to gain Percy's attention. There was still no sound, and the door wouldn't open. I ran frantically to the left side of the manor and began trying to open the window to the kitchen. I could see a bright light shining from inside the sitting room, but it was different. There didn't seem to be a flicker of the flame of the candle. It was as if the light was constant and didn't have a flame to it. I was confused at this discovery and now wished to run to the other side of the home.

I turned to my left and continued around to the back porch. The back door didn't seem to budge either. I felt completely alone and cut off from my only friend in this place. I willed to not allow these thoughts to affect me. I simply continued on the other side of the home and peered through the sitting room window. I could see that Percy and I were still there. I was struck by this immediately and completely confused. It was as if I had been dreaming the whole time about the events of earlier.

Could I have died and this was God showing me something that I had done wrong in my life? I could see that Percy stood from the chair and was moving to the window now. I wondered if he could even detect my presence in the window. I worried that he would not, but I still could do nothing. I was beyond any rationality now. I was stuck in a place that I had never been and worried that this was some-place closer to the demon, closer to being grasped by this demon and dragged into the gaping maw of darkness that followed. I tried to think rationally about it all, but nothing seemed to help.

Percy approached the window but didn't seem to react to me. His face did react to the me that was in the room. I was reliving the events just prior to going toward the stairs. I was sure that I was in this place to learn something about what had happened. I could now under-stand why the doors wouldn't open. I simply didn't belong in this memory. I didn't belong in the realm either but felt that there was no way out. I was only left to watch as the events of this night played out before me. This could only mean that I was, in fact, dead. My heart wept at this realization, but I didn't wish to lose my hold over my own sanity. If I was dead, then I had been lied to my whole life. I was supposed to ascend into the heavens and be with the rest of my family.

I could feel the worry taking over my mind that I was tainted by this demon and not able to join anyone in heaven, that I had been separated by this evil from resting for all eternity. Though, if this was true, then why should I feel anything? Why would I not feel despair on a deeper level? Why was I not being cast into a lake of fire for all eternity? These questions didn't seem to have an answer. I willed myself to return to the scene as if watching a play unfold from the stage itself. I forced my eyes to watch the events unfold. I did so until I could see that Percy was standing in the doorway to the sitting room, yelling for my return. I found it odd that he was yelling for me to return. I heard this as a whisper that was slowly being drowned. I realized then that I had been bewitched. This demon or other beings had placed a form of control over my mind.

All other sounds had been drowned out. I moved quickly to the foyer windows and could see myself facing this woman that I had burned. I recognized that I had to find out what had happened to Percy in the now. I moved back to the window of the sitting room. I could hear Percy yelling for my return, but he was now standing in the hallway outside the sitting room. He motioned more prevalently for my return. I then could see that he moved farther down the hall-way, and I could no longer hear or see Percy. He seemed to have moved out of range for me to detect him in any way.

I moved back to the foyer window and once again peered into the window. I could see that Percy had now moved to the door and was trying to open it. The woman that stood at the top of the stairs now descended to Percy's location. She held out her hand as if calling Percy to assist her. I now knew that this woman was Caroline. She was the woman possessed by the demon, and it showed. She was frail and weak. Her life had been drained away. I could tell that a darkness hung over her now.

I found it odd that I could see a sight beyond normal sight. I could see the corruption in her soul. She had once been my aunt but had now been taken as a servant of this demon. I feared that my mother had shared the same fate. If the being that I burned was, in fact, my mother. I could see Percy struggling to open the door. I was shocked by this. I had felt this many times, but it was much more different when I am watching someone else being affected by the same thing. I could also feel the fear in the room as Percy tried with all that he had to open the door. I continued to watch this woman float across the floor toward Percy. She now seemed to be consumed with hatred. I could hear her say, "Percyyyy...I am coming to take you to your home!"

I yelled out, "Percy! Run!" The woman immediately stopped and looked at me. I could see her intense gaze peering at me with all hatred in her. She then turned and started to float toward the window. I could also see that Percy was confused by this and immediately ran back down the hallway and into the sitting room. I immediately rushed back to the sitting room window and yelled for Percy. I beat on the window, but this seemed to be counterproductive. I could see that Percy had heard me beating on the window and fled into the kitchen. I was also in grave danger as I looked to my left to see my aunt floating toward me. Her voice had changed to be grating and high-pitched. "You cannot escape your fate, Benjamin! Your mother and I will not allow you to leave!" With these words, she began coming toward me faster. I ran as fast as I could toward the back of the home now. I couldn't allow myself to be taken any further into this darkness. I continued around to the kitchen side of the home. I decided to not stop so as to not allow this ghost to grasp me.

I moved to the window of the kitchen and yelled again for Percy, but he didn't seem to react. I once again beat on the window to get his attention, but he simply backed away from the window and ran again. I watched him move out of the kitchen and toward the back door. I ran to the back door but couldn't see anything through it. I tried again to get into the home through the back door but couldn't. The door didn't even budge. Just then I remembered the bedroom with the window. I then realized that my aunt was still out here somewhere. I turned to see her float down from the upper floor and hover in front of me. I couldn't see any way to move past her as she blocked the opening. To my right was where the home jutted out with a storage shed. I turned to my left and dashed around the house. I could hear her screech as she floated swiftly over the ground toward me. She moved just as swiftly as I did, but seemed to not tire.

I rounded the front of the home and continued running ever faster. I rounded the far front corner of the home. I could now see a light on in the bedroom. Percy was surely hiding there. I looked to my left and could see that my aunt was quickly catching up to me. I dashed down the side of the building, yelling for Percy once more. I reached the window, feeling the pressure from Caroline bearing down upon me. Without regard for any safety, I punched through the window and once again began yelling for Percy. He stood from the bed and looked through the window with alarm.

"Percy! Help me out of here!" I yelled louder and louder. Caroline had begun to close in on my position and reach out to grasp me. I could feel now that Percy had grabbed my hand and arm and began pulling me. I slowly rose from the ground and began to go through the opening. "Keep pulling! I am almost out!" It didn't take long now for me to reenter the real world through the window.

I fell out onto the ground in front of Percy. "Thank you," I said exhaustedly. I wasn't sure that my aunt was not following me still. I looked up at the window and could see that there was no damage. My mind began to calm as I realized that everything that I had witnessed within this other realm didn't affect this realm. Though I was still unclear how these entities were able to enter the home randomly and move throughout the building. Could it be that the windows were a passage of some kind between these two worlds? I didn't wish to think about anything at this moment. I simply stood and brushed myself off. Percy seemed to look me over so as to see if I was all right.

"What happened to you, Benjamin?"

I looked into Percy's eyes and said, "I am not sure. I went into a realm where everything relayed before my eyes. I was knocking on some of the windows to try and contact you, but you ran."

Percy looked away and replied, "I am sorry about that, Benjamin. I thought that they were all trying to terrify me. I was scared for my life. I didn't realize that you might have needed my help."

I reassured Percy that everything was okay. I couldn't have been sure what had happened but felt that nothing could be known about it. This demon seemed to control anything and everything that it could in order to trap its victims. I felt terrible about my aunt, but she was now under the control of a demon that twisted her soul for its own use. I felt that this was all far too insidious to remain. I looked toward Percy and said, "You have to leave. I understand that I cannot stay anywhere else, but you must go. These beings are heightened by you being here. I am not sure how I know this, but it is imperative that you leave for your home now."

Percy nodded in acknowledgment. I could tell that his leaving me in the home disturbed him deeply. I could tell that he had planned on staying in the home with me till the sun rose. Though I wasn't sure where he would sleep either, especially not with the demon inhabiting the upper level. Percy began walking toward the back door. I followed and assisted Percy with the horses. With both of us working together, it didn't take long to hitch the horses back to the wagon. Percy took his place on the seat of the wagon and began to turn the wagon around. He stopped midstride of the horses and said, "Be ready for me to retrieve you at dawn. I am worried about leaving you, but if I must, then I will return as quickly as I can in the morning."

I nodded quietly and waved Percy on. He turned the wagon the rest of the way and began driving toward the road. I could feel that it was time to enter the home and rest. I swiftly walked into the home and kept my eyes focused on the door to my bedroom. I also could tell that the home was dark, save for the only light being in this bedroom. When Percy had fled into this room, he had grabbed the candle and moved it into the bedroom. I was glad for this as I could see very well in this room. I hoped that Percy would have a safe journey home and that he wouldn't be tormented further tonight.

I lay down on the bed and began trying to rest my mind. I hoped that the night wouldn't become any worse. I closed my eyes and began to feel myself drift toward sleep. I had hoped that I could rest until morning, but I was sure that this would be much harder now. As I grew closer to rest, I could hear a shuffling sound. There was also some murmuring. The sound moved from the upper floor and down the stairs. I waited as I could hear it move to just outside my door.

The murmuring seemed to become louder but was still indistinct. I feared that it all had started again. I braced myself for anything that could happen next. The murmuring grew louder, and I could hear that it was my mother's voice. The louder the sound became, the more distinct the words. I still couldn't tell, however, what was being said. My mother's voice seemed to be traveling to my ear from a great distance. She seemed to be speaking from within a void of some kind. The voice echoed and reverberated about the room. The voice became so loud that my ears began to burn and hurt. I pulled the sheets over my head and tried to protect my ears. I could not, however, as the burning sensation continued. Her voice then instantly stopped. Silence fell over the room. Instantly I heard the door being hit really hard just once and at the same time heard, "You've killed me, Benjamin! You've killed me!" I was horrified at this sound but didn't wish to move or provoke this any further. I simply closed my eyes and prayed that it was all over.

9

RELAXATION

The morning sun rose slowly over the horizon. I found myself sitting on the porch smoking this early in the morning. I had awoken just before the sun arose. I waited for Percy to arrive as the day broke. I could feel such peace once again. I had hoped that I would be able to sleep well last night, but that didn't seem to be the case. Though I was glad that the spirits and demon didn't bother me any further. The true relief, however, would come when Percy arrived. I could hear the world springing to life around me as all the animals began making their usual morning noises. I could tell that the day seemed to be bright and peaceful. I hoped that this fact would assist me today when talking with the minister. I couldn't afford to allow this demon to interfere.

I did find it odd that the demon had not been involved in the events of last night. Perhaps it was only able to allow the spirits to torment me rather than being involved in the work itself. I could not understand why I was not taken further into the darkness by this being or why it hadn't made an appearance. Perhaps my hypothesis was correct and it fed solely on fear. This would mean that the time that I spent away from the manor had weakened the demon, ultimately forcing it to hide away and send its servants after me to horrify Percy and me. Though I felt relief that the demon had not made an appearance. After all, I could have died in the darkened realm forever. I was sure that this would cause my soul to be trapped into serving this demon forever. I could not prove any of this, but then again, who could?

I could see now that Percy rode slowly along the road toward the porch of the manor. I could tell that he didn't sleep well last night, if at all. I could understand given this being his first night within the manor. Though I am sure that Percy wouldn't have faced this torment. I was sure that he would have left the manor completely. I was sure that Percy wasn't a coward, but he also had somewhere else to sleep at night. I could not see a man staying in this situation unless he really had no choice. Though I knew that a woman wouldn't tolerate any of it. Percy rode ever closer to the drive of the home and began to prepare for the turn. The wagon went to the left and then turned into a hard right. The horses didn't seem to struggle at all when making this turn and seemed to move in one fluid motion. The wagon now moved swiftly up to the porch.

I didn't waste any time or words to climb onto the wagon. Percy immediately snapped the reins and began to drive the wagon away from the home. We made a smooth left turn out onto the road again as I looked back toward the manor. I could now see that the silhouette of my aunt stood in the window as if pleading with me to not leave. I ignored these pleas and looked forward again. Percy pushed the wagon faster and faster as we neared his home. I could tell that we would not be stopping for breakfast this morning. I was agreeable to this as I had made a sandwich from the food that was in the spring house, but worried that I was now out of food.

Percy drove around the corner in the road and out toward town. We rushed through the forest as we went, and I could tell that I was getting used to the layout of the town. Everything seemed to take half as long to reach now. Though I wasn't sure what Percy would be aiming to do once in town as I was sure that the sheriff would still be looking for him.

"The plan for the day is that I will turn myself into the sheriff. He will most likely give me a stern talking to and let me go. I will do all of this while you talk to the minister. If I am not outside in the wagon when you are done, then please head directly to the sheriff's office. It is down the street and to the right at the end of town. Do you understand?" Percy said with conviction. I nodded but didn't speak.

"I hope that the minister will be able to help us further. Please refrain from talking about me and my actions. I think that he will be able to help you if he doesn't suspect that you are affiliated with me. I also hope that he will want to wait to cleanse the home after you are already there," Percy said adamantly.

I nodded once again and replied, "Is everything all right, Percy?"

Percy didn't seem to pay my words any attention as he pushed the horses harder to reach town. I was not sure what had happened through the course of the night and this morning, but I couldn't worry about that now. I had a clear job to accomplish. I didn't wish that Percy waste his time with the sheriff for nothing.

The wagon rode over the rough road swiftly but was not the most comfortable ride that I had taken in a wagon. We bounced all over the seat and even had to brace ourselves. I worried that Percy had been at odds with his wife this morning as he seemed on edge. I could not intrude in his personal life, but I did worry that he was making hasty decisions. I longed to warn him, but I ultimately could not. I just had to trust Percy's judgment. Though I wasn't sure that his judgment was sound. I simply rode along quietly as Percy slowed the horses and began to make a right turn. We did so with a little sliding to the left as we rounded the first building and moved out onto Main Street. Percy didn't waste any time in pulling over to the left just beyond the carriage house. He moved the wagon parallel to the church and stopped the wagon.

I leapt from my seat and said, "Thank you, Percy. I hope that the sheriff will not give you too much trouble this morning."

Percy nodded and replied, "Thank you, Benjamin. I hope that you will be able to gain assistance from the minister with this issue."

I nodded as well and walked around the corner of the church and into the main hall. I couldn't see the minister anywhere. I wasn't sure why he wouldn't be here practicing his sermons but decided that I would look around. I moved over to the right and began looking into the room behind the podium. I could smell that someone had recently extinguished a candle in this room, but it was now dark. I turned around and continued to look. I moved back to the front of the church and then climbed up to the choir loft. I was amazed that the church was so well built and so elaborate. I could easily see where all the money of the town was used. Though I did think that this town was not capable of supporting any population. I was now found to be wrong.

I moved into the room at the top of the church and looked around. I could see that there was a door open in the far portion of this dimly lit room. I yelled out, "Hello?"

The person in the room seemed to rummage around for a moment and then poked his head out.

"Yes? Can I help you?" the man said.

I paused for a moment and replied, "Are you the minister of the town, sir?"

The man nodded and moved further out of the door.

"I was asked to speak with you about a matter in my home," I said.

The minister looked back into this room swiftly and replied, "I am sorry, but I was trying to grab something from our storage room."

I nodded and added, "That is quite all right. I shall wait for you down in the main hall." With those words I turned and left the room as I could hear the minister rummage through the storage room. I walked back down the stairs and took a seat in the main hall. I had hoped that the minister would be quick about his mission to gather something from the storage room. This proved to not be the case. I feared that Percy would be waiting for a long time outside the church for me. Though that was if he wasn't held up in the sheriff's office. I could feel time passing slowly as I pulled my pocket watch from my pocket and checked the time. I was sure that I had been waiting for almost thirty minutes now. Though the passage of time was much slower than I liked to believe. I could only hope that the minister would appear soon so that I might beseech him for assistance with the manor. Though I was not sure that he would accept, and I was also unsure as to what I would do if he was not willing to assist me.

I was, however, sure that I could make an impressive enough case for him to get involved. I was worried, as well, that he would catch on to me being involved with Percy and would deny assistance to me based on this fact.

I had not waited much longer when I could hear that the minister had now began moving out of the choir room and toward the stairs of the loft. He descended the stairs swiftly and moved toward me. "I am very sorry about taking so long, sir. How may I help you?" the minister said.

I could see that he held a stack of paper in his right hand and a journal in his left. I stood from where I was seated and bowed my head slightly. "My name is Benjamin Price. I would like to—"

The minister interrupted me, "If you're here about the Tourney Manor, then I can help you. If, however, you are here to speak with me about Mr. Merivel's actions, then I will not be helping you."

I gave the minister a most troubled and puzzled look. "I am not here for anything other than the manor itself, sir. I have nothing to do with any issues that you have with Percy," I said emphatically. "I have been having issues with the manor. I am here to proclaim that I have had experiences within that home that I need your assistance to deal with. I am not saying that the home is haunted, but I have witnessed several spirits within, as well as a dark being that I believe could be a demon."

With these words, the minister gave me a shocked look. I was sure that he didn't know what to think of the words that I had to say, but I would wait patiently for his response. "A demon you say? Surely you're mistaken."

I shook my head and replied, "I know that it is hard to believe, but I have seen a dark entity within the home. I have seen it move things without touching them and have even been moved by the demon itself. I do not wish to make this matter public and simply wish for your help in removing this thing from the manor. I intend to sell the manor to someone that can care for the home."

The minister seemed deeply troubled by my words, and I could see that he believed me. Though I was never sure that he fully heard and understood what I had meant.

I waited for a moment as the minister considered his next words. He didn't speak, however; he simply motioned for me to follow him. We both moved into the back room as he shut the door and lit the candle on his desk. I couldn't understand what was happening fully until I could see that the minister was placing the journal and the paper into his desk. He pulled out another journal and laid it out on his desk. He opened the journal to the middle and then read for a moment. I waited patiently.

"Mr. Price, I have a lot happening today. Could I come by tomorrow and assist you with the manor?" I nodded as the minister continued, "What is it that you would like for me to do to help you?"

I thought about how to reply to the minister. "I wondered if you could provide a means to remove this demon from my home."

The minister gave me a most skeptical look. "I will say that I have known people in the Catholic faith that have performed such cere-monies, but I do not necessarily believe that your home could be infested with a demon. I am not sure that I would be the one to assist in this matter. Though, I do not know anyone in the area that could help you. The notes before me are a collection of documents that a friend of mine in the Catholic Church mailed to me. I have studied them, but I doubt that I can do anything in reality to help you."

I looked down toward the floor of the study and replied, "I under-stand that this is something that is unconventional, but I would like for you to at least take a look. I am out of options, and I have been tormented every night since I have been staying in the manor."

The minister thought for a moment and said, "I will arrive tomorrow around ten in the morning. Please be ready to receive me."

I nodded again and replied, "Thank you, sir. I will see you tomorrow at ten o'clock. Thank you for your help." With those words I bowed my head slightly again and walked out of the room. I had hoped that Percy had enough time to talk to the sheriff and return to the church.

I walked through the main hall and toward the front door to the church. As I opened the door, I had the thought that Percy wouldn't be there, but he was waiting on the wagon. I hurried out of the church and down the small wooden steps. Nothing could have gone smoother about this morning. I walked around the back of the wagon and took my place on the passenger side of the wagon.

"How was the sheriff?" I asked.

Percy smiled and replied, "The sheriff is fine. He simply asked me why I had struck the minister, and I told him about the altercation. He didn't seem too worried about it. He was waiting for me to come to his office and explain what had happened."

I smiled at the news that Percy shared. "And you were worried about nothing then!" I said.

Percy nodded and chuckled. Percy snapped the reins of the horses, and we began rolling forward.

"The minister has agreed to come by the manor tomorrow morning around ten o'clock. He was hesitant like you had told me, but he agreed."

Percy seemed happy with this news. "So we have a real chance to drive this demon out, but what happened last night?"

I looked away from Percy as we rode farther down the main street of the town. "Last night was different. I have never experienced anything like that. The two spirits that tormented us were my mother and aunt. Though I set my mother on fire."

Percy looked at me in shock. "How are you sure that those things were ever alive?" Percy asked.

"I was hearing what they were saying. It was loud and very intrusive to my hearing. You didn't hear anything?"

Percy shook his head. "No. I didn't hear anything," Percy replied.

I thought for a moment. I found it all interesting that I was the only one to hear the voices being spoken by the spirits. Could it be that they had only appeared because of me? Perhaps they sought to lure me into giving myself up to this demon.

Percy drove the horses farther now and out of town. We followed the same path that we had before toward the manor. I continued to ponder what all this had meant. I was unsure of anything at this point but knew that I was away from the manor now. Percy didn't seem too concerned with anything now. Where he had once seemed on edge, he was now comfortable. Perhaps there was no rift between himself and his family. I could only guess that everything in that portion of his life was good. It might have been that the meeting with the sheriff was all that troubled Percy. Though I still didn't wish to ask as I felt that it wasn't any of my business. I simply would ride along patiently and await Percy's words about today's events.

Of course, I hadn't stopped to consider that Percy might return me to the manor, but I felt that this wouldn't be the case. After all, Percy had seemed to shudder at the thought of staying in the manor for any length of time earlier. He seemed to be wary of the manor as was I. Percy seemed to slack up on the reins more now and didn't have the look of bloodlust in his eyes. I could tell that the situation with the sheriff had troubled him deeply. I didn't know the sheriff nor had I ever met the man, but perhaps Percy and he were friends. In a town this size, I would be amazed if Percy didn't know everyone here.

The road now seemed to smooth out as we proceeded down the small hill and out of the woods. I could see the drive to the manor directly in front of us now as we banked a right turn slowly and continued to move on. "We will go to my farmhouse this morning and relax. If you wouldn't mind, I could use some help around the farm today."

I nodded and smiled as I felt the relief of not having to face the manor yet again. I felt that it was enough to stay in the manor overnight, but not all the time. Percy pulled on the reins of the horses and gently guided them to the left. The sun was now higher in the sky as we drove up to the front of the farmhouse and stopped in front of the porch. Percy's children greeted us as they played on the porch. Percy looked at them with a smile and said, "Are you allowing Mother and the servants to work this morning?" Both of them stopped what they were doing immediately and nodded in acknowledgment. "Good for the both of you. You may both go play in the back field now, but don't get into any mischief." Percy was stern as he said these words. Both children nodded and replied, "Yes, Father!" then ran off toward the field. They both seemed rather well-behaved. I could see that Percy had raised both of them in manners. He seemed a proper man with a stern disposition toward manners.

Percy looked at me and said, "I am sorry for their rudeness, but they are eager to run out into the fields and play."

I smiled and replied, "That is quite all right. They are just children after all."

Percy seemed to agree and added, "Could you help me with the horses again?"

I nodded as Percy snapped the reins yet again and drove the wagon in front of the wagon shed. I could tell now that I was beginning to become accustomed to rural life as it didn't take any time to unhitch the horses and guide them into the grazing field. We closed up the pen and walked back to the wagon. It didn't take much for us to muscle the wagon back into the shed. The wheels seemed to settle into the ground in the shed, and we closed up the building.

Percy and I made our way into the home and toward the far end. Percy turned to his right, and we entered the sitting room of the farmhouse. The room itself wasn't much, but the vines of the ivy outside had a calming effect on the room. They also provided shade and cool air. I felt as if I were sitting near a cold waterfall on a hot day. Percy didn't waste any time in producing his pipe as did I. We both smoked in silence until he said, "I am sorry about leaving you there last night. Your words were true, but I couldn't sleep much as I feared that those things would take you again. No man should die like that."

I nodded and took a drag from the pipe. "That is all right, Percy. I was fine, and neither the spirits nor the demon bothered me at all after you left. They tried but I was exhausted and fell into sleep. I will say, however, that it was the best sleep that I have had in the manor."

Percy seemed surprised at my words. "You mean that you haven't slept well since you arrived?"

I shook my head and added, "I did at Mary's house, but that would be all."

Percy shook his head and said, "I am sorry, Benjamin. I had high hopes that you would be able to have a good experience in our town. I understand now why you have been so eager to return to New York City. A man should be comfortable in his home and not have to worry about being dragged to hell every night."

I wasn't bothered by this fact without being in the moment. I simply had the need for rest without being tormented every night. Percy and I puffed on our pipes for a moment. "When did you wish to work around the farm?" I asked.

Percy replied, "The time is not now. We will begin shortly. I have to work with you on feeding the animals today. I had fed some of them this morning and cleaned out some of their pens, but I couldn't get everything done before I had left."

I sat for a moment and puffed on my pipe as Percy seemed to be deep in thought.

I couldn't begin to understand the level of fatigue that Percy had since he didn't sleep well last night and had to be up early this morning. I had, after all, slept quite well. Even with the possible torment from these beings, I still seemed to rest deeply. I would attribute this fact to lost sleep over several days. I had slept well before last night, but it would still take time to recover from such events. I could be sure, however, that Percy was alarmed after seeing the events of last night. He seemed to be especially shaken by my vanishing from this world and being stuck within another realm. I must admit that I too was shaken by this and didn't wish to be trapped in another world again. The effects were not simply losing sleep. I also had pain in my muscles all over my body. I was sore beyond belief after being cast out of the door of the manor twice and falling down the stairs. I could fight through the pain, but it, mixed with the fatigue, had made me less capable of movement. Whatever assistance I could provide this morning to Percy would be minimal.

I waited and smoked now. Percy didn't seem in too much of a hurry to finish feeding the animals. I suspected that he too was sore. I was not able to see anything happen to him, but there was time for me to run around the home trying to move back into this world. I did hope that he too was not assaulted by these spirits. Though I did doubt that he was completely exempt. Percy continued to smoke and think.

"How was it that you were able to gain freedom from our world last night?"

I looked at Percy. "I am not sure. I was pushed from the home and out the front door. The next thing I knew, I was on the gravel outside and had to get back to my feet. When I stood up, the world had changed. Everything seemed to have a darkened haze hanging over it. I couldn't see very well either. I don't know where this realm was or how it was that I had arrived there, but I knew that I was not in our world anymore."

Percy seemed to be hanging on my every word. "How did it feel when you were there?"

I considered the question that Percy asked and replied, "I felt cold. Like there was no source of warmth. The air was no longer thick with humidity, but was light and wafted about. Everything seemed unnatural in some way or another. Even the home was dark save for the lights in the areas that we inhabited within the home. Even the outside of the home was cold and damp."

Percy seemed alarmed. "I am glad that you survived, but it seemed impossible. Once second I could see that you had been thrown out the door, and the next I was pulling you into the room from the window. I feared that I wouldn't live through anything. That I would never escape the home into my normal life again. Though I am curious, what was that screeching that I could hear when you broke through the window?"

Without missing a moment, I replied, "That was Caroline. Her soul was troubled and twisted. I think that she had been taken by this demon without being able to rest. She made horrible grunts and screams. That is what you heard when you pulled me through the window."

Percy now seemed more troubled than interested. "I am sorry,

Benjamin. I should have stopped you, but I didn't know what to do. I was frozen in fear. I felt like a child that couldn't control themselves in order to assist in any way."

I looked down for a moment and then smiled at Percy. "It is all right, Percy. I assure you. I was able to free myself with your help. It doesn't matter what you had done or hadn't done, but what you were able to do when I really needed you to pull me from the other world."

Percy seemed relieved once more. "I understand, Benjamin. I will try to be there going forward. Though I am sure that I do not wish to stay within the manor again."

I laughed at Percy's words and replied, "I know. I am not willing to do it either, but I don't have a choice at this point. Though I think that I could talk to Mary's family and try to stay with them, but I am not willing to ask at this point." I could see that Percy understood my point of view.

"I will never understand how you can stay in such a situation, but at least you can bar the doors at night and sleep without worrying that these things can get to you."

I nodded emphatically. "That is the best thing to remember. Up to now, I have not had any one of these beings try to get into my bedroom without using the door. I am glad this is so since I would really like to keep being able to sleep at least a small amount."

Percy continued puffing on his pipe until he said, "I think it is time that we feed the animals. They are not restricted to the food that I provide, but I would still like to get that done before any more time passes."

I nodded and we both stood from our seats.

I turned toward the door and could see the whole of the room in a better way. I could see that the whole room was a bit shabby. The furniture seemed dated but still comfortable. The flooring in the room matched the rest of the home as it was all a lighter color of wood. It was well taken care of and seemed to have a sheen across the top of the wood. The walls were also similar to the rest of the home as they were made of boards that had been painted white. The paint had seemed to run slightly but still looked uniform and nice. The room held bookshelves on each side of the room with books filling every inch. I was interested in why Percy would have so many books, but I understood that he was a highly educated man. I could tell now that he valued knowledge. I did find it interesting as well that the windows at the far top portion of the room seemed to be of a custom design. They were longer than they were taller and seemed to swing open into the room. I was amazed that the room was so comfortable to be so simple. I had always seen sitting rooms that were grander and that held a fireplace within one wall. I had never felt so cozy in a sitting room before, however.

The one other thing that really caught my eye was the vines that partially covered the window at the far end of the room. I felt invited to sit in the room and take time to relax while reading a book or studying something new. I could tell that Percy had planned to spend a lot of time in this room.

I followed Percy out to the back porch and stopped. He stood on the edge of the porch and began telling me about his property.

"To our right is our main growing fields. The crops that I grow here are from seeds that your aunt donated to me. We are helping to provide food to others throughout the town and to Raleigh and other larger towns in this area. My wife and the other servants mainly work in these fields. Though now they are resting. This hot sun doesn't help in harvesting these crops. I have worked with my wife in the fields and am not too keen on it some days, but it must be done. I am more focused on the barns and pastures." Percy pointed across the yard to the barns and part of the pastures behind.

"I work on maintaining the fences and feeding the animals. It occupies a lot of time, but not as much as growing the crops. I am mainly an animal petter." Percy chuckled at these words. "The woods that surround the property remain a place where I always have to look for my animals. I expanded my pastures into the wooded areas so that the animals can rest in the shade. I did all this last summer, and I have now had two cases of the animals breaking out of the pastures and trying to run into the forest. They don't seem to like it here, but with all that I know now, I wonder if this demon is assaulting their minds as well."

Percy seemed to be sorrowful at this thought. I could tell that he cared deeply for the animals on his farm. Not to say that he didn't care as much for the people that worked to harvest his crops. Percy continued to explain the history of his farm, and I could tell that he was very proud to work on a farm. He seemed a shrewd business owner in respect to selling his crops and making sure that he could pay and feed his workers. He even began to describe how he hired workers and why he kept a smaller group of servants on the farm. Though I was sure that he didn't need a large force of workers on this farm anyway. Not that the farm was not of an impressive size, but was not complex. Everything seemed much better laid out than Mary's uncle's farm. Though Percy had not branched out into producing wine or other such goods on the farm. I could appreciate the simplicity with which the farm was constructed and laid out.

Percy and I now moved away from the porch and out onto the property. I followed Percy out to the barn and began lifting buckets of feed and carrying them along with Percy. He stopped and turned to me. "Could you take that feed and spread it out in the chicken pens?" I nodded and waited as Percy explained to me how to feed the chickens. I was pleased that I would have the opportunity to learn about a different way of life. It was one thing to question what it would be like to own a farm and another to work on a farm. Percy then turned and walked farther out toward the pastures. I moved over to the chicken pens just behind the barn and began to spread the feed out over the pen. I was worried that the chickens wouldn't trust me enough to emerge from their coops and eat. I threw a good helping of feed in the first pen and waited. It wasn't long before the rooster and a couple of hens strutted out of the coop and began walking around to collect food. Not long after this, the rest of the chickens and their chicks emerged from the coop and began feasting upon the seeds.

I moved on to the next pen now that I was satisfied with the chickens trusting me enough to eat in front of me. I found it fascinating how chickens and other small birds ate. They seemed so entertaining when they did eat. I felt like a new mother after moving about the pens and feeding the chickens. Each little chick followed its mother about the pen and chirped loudly as if thanking me for the food they now could eat. I was happy beyond belief that I was able to assist Percy and his animals on the farm. I moved farther beyond the pens and began looking for Percy. I could see that he had now moved far out into the pastures and was feeding his horses. He threw buckets of apples and carrots out into the fields and even spread some hay about near that. Percy seemed intent on making sure that these animals were comfortable. Since the day was so hot, I watched him move about the pens and check for clean and cool water. Percy didn't seem to have access to water, but I was sure that he had a creek or well that he could pull water from for his animals.

Soon, I moved out to where Percy worked and assisted him in checking to make sure water had been supplied to his animals. I then returned to Percy and awaited the next set of instructions. "We have all the animals fed, and I can now not worry about the animals. Would you be willing to help me pull fresh hay down from the loft for the horses?"

I nodded without delay and followed Percy back to the barn. I could see that the old hay had been moved out of the barn and partially taken out to the crops. "You use the hay for the crops?"

Percy nodded and said, "Yes. We pack it around the plants and allow it to rot away. It keeps the plants cool and carries dung for the plants to have more nutrients and be fertilized. Your aunt showed me that trick. You get better and much richer plants."

I was interested in these words. I was sure that nothing would work quite as easily as this for plants to be fed and have a cooling effect on such hot days. After all, each plant continuously set in the sun without relenting. I thought it was nice that Percy and his family considered everything with caring for the animals as well as the plants. Percy had now moved into the barn and began climbing up into the loft. The ladder that he used had been built onto the side of the barn and allowed him to move out onto a ledge before he reached the hay. I could tell that he had been able to have a lot of hay here as the whole loft was full. Percy moved out onto the ledge and began using his pitchfork to move the bales of hay out of the loft and allow them to drop down onto the ground.

Percy had called my attention to a pitchfork that leaned against the wall of the barn. I was instructed to use this pitchfork to sift the hay and break the bales into groupings of hay to spread about the barn. I was curious as to why Percy would feed his animals this much, but couldn't take the time to ask him just at this moment. I spread the hay about the barn and made sure that each bale that I broke apart was able to cover the stables completely. The barn was huge, so I was not able to reach the farthest stables easily. Eventually, however, Percy and I had covered the whole barn.

Percy climbed down from the loft and was now standing on the ground level again.

"Why is it that you spread the hay even in the summer?" I inquired.

Percy smiled and said, "The animals sleep outside in the summer mostly, but we give them a chance to move into the barn before the nighttime and rest on the soft hay. They use the bathroom on the hay, and it helps to fertilize the fields. That is why our pastures are positioned around the barn. This makes it much easier to move the animals about the farm.

"Of course, the pigs and chickens will stay where they are, but the cows and horses are brought in for a bit. Most would think that this is a lot of work, but it doesn't happen every night. The hay takes some time to rot into the ground around the roots of the crops. Instead, the hay can dry out after being spread around the barn like this. Once we do need the animals to lay in here for a bit, then it has usually been several days to a week."

I understood now how this was such an intelligent plan. I was happy that I could learn this and understand more about how to farm. I was enthralled by the level of care that had been put into taking care of these animals. I knew that Percy was serious about his farm and seemed to learn a lot from my aunt about farming. I was sure that it was still hard work, but the benefits of being able to eat food at any moment that it was needed were amazing. The people that I had most surrounded myself with were all enthralled with purchasing any food that was needed to eat and live. Imagine the ability to be able to grow your own food without going to a market and purchasing it. I found this to be quite advantageous.

As I assisted Percy around the farm, I could not help but think of Mary. I immediately thought about what she would say about all the happenings that had gone on. I also felt as if I could better understand now what she had been called to do around the farm that her family owned. I knew that this was the work that she was accustomed to and had lived with for her whole life. I wondered if Mary would really wish to leave this life for something that was much less physical work and much more relaxation. I wondered if she would be able to adjust to such a life. I also wondered if she was thinking of me also. If she wanted to see me again after my visit. To tell the truth, I thought about Mary often but most of the time had to push it from my mind. I feared that these spirits would know who she was to me and would haunt her as well. I could not allow that to happen. I didn't wish to bring her into all this or to cause her to be tormented as well. Mary was pure and sweet. She was innocent and kind in so many ways. I could not live with the knowledge that she was being haunted as well. I also worried about what her family might do should everything begin after I left their home. I didn't wish for them to think that I had done anything to cause an infestation of negativity within their home.

Percy and I moved back into his home and sat at the dining table. Percy seemed to be waiting for lunch as it was now just past noon. "I thank you for your help this morning. Most of the time I have all this work done before the sun even rises. Even if the animals are still sleeping. The farm is not immense as you have seen, but there is still a lot of work to be done. I also move out into the fields and assist with spreading any hay or pulling out the weeds from the fields."

I nodded and replied, "You're welcome, Percy. I have enjoyed helping you on the farm. I have often wished to see what it is like working on a farm such as this."

Percy smiled and asked, "What did you think?"

I smiled back at Percy and replied, "I liked it. Though I am not used to working on a farm. I am sure that I would be able to do it after a period of time. The barn was a lot of work, but nothing that is out of my grasp."

Percy chuckled now and said, "There is much more to do, but it is better than being within the manor with the demon and his ghost friends."

I smiled and chuckled as well. "I would be willing to work more with you if you need."

Percy shook his head and said, "We have nothing more to do today. My wife and the servants are coming back from the fields now and beginning to move toward resting. We try to get everything done before the heat of the day sets in. I know that it would be easier to work at night, but we are not able to see. Also, the ground needs time to recover from our working with it each day."

Percy seemed sincere with his words. I knew now that Percy was attached to this farm and the way of life associated with it.

As we talked at the dinner table, we heard the servants and the rest of Percy's family come into the home. I wondered what more would be done for the day. Chloe entered the room where we sat and said, "Hello, dear! Would you and Benjamin care to move into the sitting room or out onto the porch? I will prepare some lunch for all of us."

We both agreed, and Percy told her that we would be out on the back porch. Percy and I moved outside to the back porch and sat down as the servants moved off in different directions.

"Where are they all going?" I asked.

Percy looked out across the property and replied, "The servants have different homesteads out at the edge of the farm. Beyond the pastures, they live at the edge of the forest around the farm. I helped many of them erect their homes when we all had time. Most of the homes have their own little garden plots that they work in, and we all help each other. This evening I will probably go out to see the servants and make sure that everything is well. Most of them live near to each other, but some live away from the farm and back toward the manor. Before you ask, I have asked them if they have had any strange activity around their homes, and they have not. I haven't been able to talk to any of my servants who have had issues with anything odd. I was sure that the servants that resided toward the manor would have something, but I was wrong."

I nodded in acknowledgment. "I find it refreshing that everyone works together in Hillsborough. I have always imagined more labor that is not so honest."

Percy chuckled and said, "Most that visit the area have the idea that we all own slaves and don't work on our own to maintain our farms."

I understood now about the misconceptions of the South. Nothing could have prepared me to think that rural farms could be so quaint. I had feared that I would have to bear witness to such events as slaves being punished or even running off. Though I would not tolerate that on any property that I would own, how would I stop someone from doing such things on their property? Still, I was glad that I didn't have to bear witness to such things. Though I still had to bear witness to a monster stalking the manor in which I stayed.

Percy and I sat for a moment and smoked our pipes. The sun was not very high in the sky and gave off a heat that was too much for any person to work in. I could not imagine working on a farm at this level of heat and humidity. Percy smoked for a moment as he drew in a deep breath and said, "I would like to let you know that Chloe and I are wanting you to stay the night with us. We have made a spare room available. It isn't much, but we feel that we cannot allow you to stay within that manor anymore. Think on it if you'd like, but please let me know."

I didn't react immediately to what Percy had said. I didn't wish to stay with them, but I really considered the option because of the fact that I was tired of being tormented within the manor. "What room have you made available?"

Percy smiled and replied, "The writing room. I have moved the desk around this morning and made space enough for you to sleep upon the floor. I am sorry that I don't have a bed dedicated to you, but we don't have as much space as the manor."

I nodded at Percy and continued to consider the option. I didn't wish to sleep on the floor, but I felt that it would still be better than the torment that I surely faced within the manor. Though the thought of bringing all these negative beings into Percy's home didn't help my decision either. I couldn't allow anyone else to be dragged into all this. I wouldn't allow it. Percy and I continued to smoke our pipes until the bowls had burned to ash. I turned my pipe over and popped the back of the bowl. The ash dumped out onto the ground in a pile with some ash wafting away in the wind.

I couldn't understand how that Percy and his wife had considered assisting me. Surely Percy hadn't mentioned anything that he had witnessed within the manor to his wife and family. I could not see how Chloe would take such news that these things existed. Though I didn't know Chloe in the least. Perhaps she had taken such a notion and continued on with her life without any pause. I doubted this as she would now be living beside a demon-infested home. I didn't imagine that anyone would wish that upon their lives. Instead, I chose to believe that Percy had not mentioned anything to Chloe and had just convinced her in another way. Percy and I didn't sit for too much longer before Chloe emerged from the home and invited us to eat lunch. We stood from our seats on the porch and immediately moved back into the house.

The table was being set for lunch as Percy and I approached the table. Today it seemed that there would be a serving of vegetable soup and bread. Chloe had set out butter for the bread, and there was a large pitcher of water on the table. Percy and I took our seats in the middle of the table as everyone else was already in their seats. The family said grace and we all began to eat. The soup was delicious and had so many flavors of the vegetables in it that I found it hard to just taste one specific thing. The bread was also delicious. I especially enjoyed the homemade butter that had been churned. I had never tasted butter like this in my life and couldn't understand how it was so much more delicious than any that I had tasted before. I wasn't sure if Chloe had put something in the butter or if it naturally had such a fine flavor.

The lunch was simple but filling. The flavors were sumptuous, even by the standards that I was used to in New York. I wondered if Chloe had ever studied to be a chef at one point or had worked for anyone as a cook before. "The lunch was delicious, Chloe. Have you ever been a professional cook?"

Chloe chuckled and replied, "No, sir. I just learned from my mother and grandmother."

I smiled at Chloe and said, "Then you learned from the best!"

She laughed now and began carrying the plates back into the kitchen. I was happy that I was able to share this meal with Percy and his family. Nothing could have been better in this moment.

This was the feeling of family that I had always longed to experience. Even when I was younger, my mother and father seemed to be estranged from each other at times. I always believed that it was due to the fact that my father traveled for the military and was always being assigned to new duties. Mother and I never knew how long he would be gone or if he would be called to fight away somewhere else. Luckily, he had not been sent on a long engagement, but there were times that I knew he would have important work to do elsewhere. I was never bothered by this idea as he would often bring home exemplary pay for the family. Mother never had to work at all and would always have plenty of money to deal with anything that arose around the house. Even our trips to North Carolina were paid for with ease. Though we never lived like we were wealthy.

Mother always returned from North Carolina on the times that I didn't go with more money as well. No doubt I now know the reasons why. Perhaps financial gain was a part of worshiping this demon. I was always blessed to have anything that I wished for as a child, but never knew what I would want. I was dressed in suits from a young age and allowed to go to school at an earlier age than most. My family was always simple in our style of life and never wished for anything more. We even lived in a simple home but with plenty of room.

Though I never knew anyone to visit our home. I always imagined that this was in case my father ever had his superiors visit from the fort. I always worried that nothing would come home from him other than a letter, but those were thoughts that I tried to not entertain. That is until it happened. I lost my father at the age of eight. There was an accident at the cannonry, and he was killed in a blast of gunpowder. I had never known such sadness until my mother was visited by others of the fort and given a letter of his last wishes. She cried for weeks alone in her room. That was when I was sent away for school.

I had always imagined that she didn't want me to see her in that state. Though I never really knew as she rarely visited me. The boarding school also rarely closed for me to return home, and when it did, no one would be there to pick me up and take me to see my mother. I had often wondered if Mother was away in North Carolina at that point. I always thought that she would return one day and inform me that I had to leave the school because of our financial ruin. This never happened, of course, and I was never asked anything about financial issues. I assumed in my later years that my mother had simply forgotten me and I was to move on to something else in my life.

Later on, I was introduced to more suffering as my mother would also pass when I was at the age of seventeen. By this point, I was already in New York City and was being apprenticed at the bank. I never had the time or the finances to visit our home and see my mother laid to rest. Though at that point, I never wished to see her again. I was used to being alone in the world and having no one to call for me or to visit. I slowly became used to not seeing my mother so when she passed on, I felt nothing different than usual. Most would say that this is a sad way to live, but it was all that I had ever known. I never imagined that I would grow to be a man modeled after my own father, but I had. I was resilient in every way and pushed myself harder and harder to overcome anything that I faced. I had even forsaken my responsibility to myself to be with anyone else in favor of my studies and advancing my career. That was a fact about myself that I had hoped to change now that I had met Mary.

Percy and I moved back out to the back porch and talked for a while. I continued to ask him about life on a farm until he finally asked, "Are you thinking of owning a farm at some point in your life?"

I smiled and continued to smoke as I said, "No. At least not now. I have often thought about living on a farm, but I don't think that I could at this stage in my life. Perhaps someday though."

Percy chuckled and replied, "That is the exact way that I used to think. Then I began working for Ms. Caroline, and my ideas about living on a farm changed. Then again, Caroline helped me with that decision as she often showed me the 'proper' way to farm." I chuckled with Percy, and we both moved on from that subject.

Time passed and we moved to the topic of family, and Percy asked, "Have you thought more about having a family someday?"

I nodded and said, "To tell you the truth, I have often thought about marrying Mary before my departure, but I am not sure that I should."

Percy looked at me with surprise and responded, "Why not? You're interested, and it doesn't matter what's right, just that you both want to be together."

I nodded and thought for a moment. Percy was right. I had waited so long to meet a woman that I had found intriguing enough to marry. She occupied my mind at times now, and I worried that I was becoming obsessed. The only thing that I could do would be to be with her as I had dreamed. Many things had now become clear.

Percy and I continued to talk about many different things until I asked, "Do you know if there is such a place to buy a ring around here?"

Percy shook his head and replied, "That is not something that we do here. Many people are too poor to afford such things. The only place that I would know that would have jewelers would be in Raleigh. That is a journey I am sure that you wouldn't wish to make again unless you needed to do so."

I thought for a moment then asked, "So what is the custom for this area if I wanted to be married to someone?"

Percy smiled and then replied, "The best thing to do would be to talk to Mary. You both would need to decide. I would say that if she is the right woman for you, then you would need to understand what she wishes and see how that matches to your own desires."

I nodded in acknowledgment and continued to smoke. I was not sure when I would be able to talk to Mary, but I did plan for it to be tomorrow afternoon. I wished to settle the matters with the minister before doing anything else.

The day slowly drifted into the late evening, and I implored Percy that I would need to gather my things from the manor. I also wished to bathe as it had been a couple of days. I feared that I could no longer cover my odor now. Percy was sure that we could gather some of my things from the manor before the night had fallen, but we would have to be swift. I could have gone alone, but I felt that this would not be the best course of action as I didn't wish to be stuck in another realm again.

Percy and I departed his home for the manor as we walked along the road. Thankfully, the manor was close enough to be able to walk to the property without much effort. The walk was interesting as Percy shared ideas with me about starting a farm. He also shared knowledge about caring for the land and animals that any farm would need to operate. I was amazed at his level of mastery over farming. Though I also knew that he was telling me all this because his nerves had worn thin as we approached the manor. We did reach the manor with little effort, and I left Percy to stand in the foyer as I grabbed my clothes bag. I also managed to grab my book so that I would be able to read tonight before bed. I emerged from the back room in time to see that Percy had remained right beside the front door. He was poised to leave the manor at a moment's notice. I had wondered what would have happened if the spirits or even this demon had returned for me. Would Percy have simply fled the house and left me to my own devices, or would he have stayed and assisted me in leaving the manor as well?

It didn't take long for Percy and me to return to the farmhouse once again. The walk back had been uneventful, and I could tell that I would be at peace from this menace tonight. With the last light of the day, Percy and I moved out into the woods to the usual bathing pool.

"During the summer, we bathe in this pool cause of the cool water. In the winter we bathe in the water from the well that is heated and poured into a bucket. It doesn't take long to relax in the dead of winter with a hot bath, but I prefer this pool to anything."

I was amazed at this style of bathing but was happy that I had a pure source of water to bathe within. Percy bid me a good bath and left for the servants' homes to check on them again. I could tell that this was his usual night as he seemed to move in the direction of the farthest homes to work his way back. He had given me instruction to meet him back at the barn once I had finished bathing. I quickly moved down into the water without clothing and began splashing around. I could feel the water cool upon my skin.

I worried that there would be some sort of creature hiding within the pool, but Percy assured me that there were none and even plunged a stick deep within the pool and moved it about. The stick was not harmed, and no animals had come out of the water in a rage. I was not used to bathing in such conditions and had no idea what I must do. I splashed about in the water for a bit and dove below the surface. I was still vigilant, however, because of my worry that the spirits would find me here. I didn't wish to drown as I knew that this was a horrible way to go. I wished for my death to be a noble death. To die defending someone I cared about or to die while helping someone across a street, but never in a dramatic way such as drowning. I also didn't know to what need that these things would go in order to kill me.

I moved about the pool of water once more then walked up the bank and began dressing myself. Percy had built a seat beside the pool so as to allow me to dangle my feet into the water and clean them from the mud of the bank. I slipped my socks on and then my shoes and was finally ready. I felt different now. Not really clean, but not as dirty as I was. I welcomed this feeling as I felt naturally clean. Like my ancestors would have done before me. I truly felt connected to this way of life but wasn't sure what level of dedication I could give to this life.

I slipped back out of the woods and began walking back to the barn. I could see that Percy was moving toward the last of the servants' homes ahead of me. I thought of calling out but felt that it was better to leave Percy to his normal rounds. I couldn't begin to become involved in Percy's life further as I didn't want to give the impression that I would be staying. I didn't take long to move to the edge of the barn and lean against the wall until I could see Percy walking in my direction. I called out, "How are the servants this evening?"

Percy continued to walk until he was closer and replied, "They are all well. I had the fortune of being able to see everyone tonight. How was your bath in the woods?"

I smiled and chuckled then replied, "Good, sir! It was well."

Percy laughed as he moved to the barn beside me. He didn't say anything at first and then produced his pipe from his pocket as he said, "Do you ever think that we smoke too much?"

I laughed and replied, "Perhaps. Why?"

Without missing a beat, Percy replied, "My wife had told one of the servants that she worried that I was too addicted to smoking my pipe. She had seen an increase in this habit since you'd arrived!"

We both laughed and stood smoking as the sun dipped behind the trees. I looked at Percy and asked, "Why are we at the barn so late?"

He didn't respond immediately and just watched the sunset. I gathered from his demeanor that we would be doing something important tonight, but what exactly was a mystery.

"We are going to walk the fences tonight. I would like to check on the animals in their pens to make sure they are resting well."

I nodded and said, "How will we see?"

Percy looked at me as if my head had fallen off and said, "With a lantern of course!"

I laughed and felt relief that I wouldn't have to carry a torch through the night air and around trees. I knew that this would be a bad idea in the heat of the summer. The farm wouldn't fare from a fire that filled the woods surrounding the home.

Percy turned toward the barn and reached inside the doorway. He pulled out a lantern and immediately lit it from a match in his pocket. The lantern shone brightly into the night as we began to make our rounds. I was happy that I would be able to experience yet another factor of living on a farm. We moved out toward the pasture and then followed the fencing around to the far side. Percy and I continued to inspect the fence. Each side was nothing more than wood that had been stacked together with a huge spike driven into each joint. I was amazed that Percy had built such a thing to protect his animals from wandering off. I also dreaded the sight of the manor sitting alone in the night.

The fence here was solid but was the closest one to the manor that I could get on Percy's property. I couldn't help but peek at the manor from where we stood as if expecting to see something. Nothing seemed out of place, so we continued on. Just as we had turned and walked toward the other side of the fencing, we could hear something in the woods behind us. Percy turned and held out the lantern for a better view. I looked toward the manor again and now could see that all the candles in the home were lit. This couldn't be. The candles on the upper floor had never been lit. Only the bottom floor candles were used ever, and I feared that something might be happening. Before I could make my way to the manor, however, Percy grabbed the collar of my jacket and pulled me backward. "Not tonight, Benjamin. They are toying with us."

I replied, "But, but..." Percy didn't seem to care. He simply held me there then turned and began dragging me away. "What about my belongings? What if the manor burns down with all of my belongings?"

Percy turned and looked me in the eye. "I wouldn't be happier, and we would outfit you with some clothes." His face revealed how serious he was about this statement as I looked at him. Eventually I stood upright and began walking with him away from the home. We could hear a howl coming from the woods now. Percy opened his jacket and pulled out a very capable revolver. He turned and swiftly pulled the trigger to scare anything that would be hiding in the woods. Smoke billowed out all around the woods, and I waited and listened for anything that could be moving away from our position. Nothing. Percy wiped the barrel of his gun on his vest and placed it back into its holster under his jacket. I felt as if I had watched a villain from the Western frontier claim the life of a man. The action was cold and swift. I could tell that Percy had become accustomed to defending his farm from any threat. After a moment or two, we moved back toward the barn.

We checked the rest of the pasture fences on our way back to the barn and made sure that everything was all right. Nothing seemed out of place now, and I felt at ease to relax for the night. I could tell that Percy also shared this sentiment as he continued on with his normal pleasant attitude. I was amused by the thought that the demon could have been startled by the gunshot and stopped what it was attempting to do immediately. This was something that Percy also found humorous as we moved back to the farmhouse and then inside. Percy latched the door into a locked position and invited me back to the dining room.

"In an area this rural, why do you lock your doors?"

Percy took a moment and then replied, "In any normal time I wouldn't. But I am now trying to protect us all from this demon. I fear that it might stalk my farm at night and cause harm to me or my family as we rest."

I was taken aback by Percy's statement. Could it be that he was really this alarmed? I thought nothing more about Percy locking the doors and moved off into the dining room with him. We sat in the dim light of the candles and talked for a moment. We talked about many different subjects and even our pasts. Percy didn't seem to wish to tell of his own background, but he eventually did.

"My family and I are not from here, as I told you. We moved from northern Virginia. I married my wife two months before we moved to Hillsborough. My brother had died just after we were married, and we lost our real-estate ventures. I used to be quite wealthy, but the area wasn't able to sustain its growth. We were forced to sell the properties that we held and either move into another profession or leave town. I was always interested in farming and was contacted by a friend here in town to move here and live a quieter life. So I packed up my wife and I and we moved here.

"Not long after settling here, Chloe became pregnant and we built this farmhouse. It took some time, but I felt that I had to do it. Caroline was nice enough to give me the land for the house, and I worked with her until I paid it off. I then purchased the other portions of land for my farm as she got older. I never wanted the farm to grow much bigger than this, so I am happy with how it all turned out. Chloe was skeptical of moving here, but like me, she had known Sheriff Duns for a long time and trusted his judgment. My mother and father died from consumption and left us the homes and land that we used to begin our business, but we lost it all."

I could see now that Percy regretted his past, and this is why he was so unwilling to share it. I asked more questions about his past, but he wouldn't budge with any more information.

Eventually, Percy stood from the table and bid me good night as he moved down the hallway and into his bedroom. I followed his lead and moved into the writing room after blowing out all the candles except one. I now saw what Percy had been talking about. A makeshift bed lay on the floor of the room, and all the furniture had been shifted to give me just enough room to sleep comfortably. I moved farther into the room and then turned and latched the door to lock it. I also wouldn't take any chances with this demon or spirits that seemed to follow me. I simply knew that I would have to take these precautions while remaining within the town. I did hope that upon leaving, I would be able to rest without closing and locking a door.

I moved back toward the bed on the floor and began dressing down to sleep. I stretched my clothes out across the furniture that had been moved so that I would have a place to sleep. I then lay down on the bed and slipped underneath the thin sheet that would cover me throughout the night. I was now comfortable and ready to rest.

Once again I found myself looking forward to the next day to relieve me of the burden of a haunted manor. I read for a moment as I put everything out of my mind and then slipped down into the bed. I puffed once to blow out the candle and settled into the bed for the night. I had left the windows open in this room so as to feel a nice breeze but feared that this might not be a good idea. Eventually, however, I didn't care at all.

10

THE MINISTER

I awoke the next morning feeling rested. I knew that I had dreamed of something, but I couldn't remember. I assumed that it wasn't important, so I continued to put on my clothes again in preparation for my day. I also packed my bags to leave for the manor house this morning to await the minister's visit. I knew that I would likely request for Percy to allow me to go back to the manor on foot. That way he wouldn't have to risk being seen by the minister or causing the minister to not help me. I checked my pocket watch and saw that it was only 7:00 a.m. I had plenty of time to get started this morning. I gathered my things expertly and moved out into the dining room. I shared a pleasant breakfast with Percy and his family and then helped to straighten the room that I had slept in. We shifted the tables and chairs back into their positions and then moved out onto the front porch. I was ready to face the day with the hopes that this demon wouldn't be able to survive the minister's visit. I was also hopeful that I would have enough time to visit with Mary and see about her decisions toward marriage.

I talked to Percy for a few moments before I told him about my plans to walk back to the manor alone. Percy seemed worried about this, but when I explained that the minister would be at the manor around ten o'clock, Percy was agreeable. Neither of us wished for him to see the minister again so soon in case the minister still had an issue with Percy. I then stood from my place on the porch and resumed moving back toward the manor. I moved with a swiftness that I didn't think I possessed. I refused to enter the home alone but realized now that it was only nine o'clock. I was sure that I would reach the manor in the next twenty minutes or less.

I felt a tug at my heart when I realized this. I couldn't bring myself to even thought of entering the home by myself. I didn't wish to be tormented further. I also didn't wish to work myself up so that I would interrupt anything that the minister would be able to do to help me with the manor. That would have been catastrophic since the minister seemed very busy. I hurried down the road and toward the manor. I hoped that the minister would arrive early and I would be able to meet him outside the home. Though I was sure that this wouldn't be the case.

It wasn't long before I came to the porch on the front of the home. I quickly moved inside to set my bags in the bedroom before the minister arrived. I didn't give any spirits or demons a chance as I moved too quickly for me to even notice a sound at all. I made sure that I also kept my focus on the space in front of me. I moved into the bedroom and placed my bags in the far end of the room. I was sure that I didn't have much time, but I felt nervous about stopping what I was doing and wasting any time in this manor. I didn't even give myself time to make sure that I placed the bags upright. I placed the bags and moved back out of the manor. I took my place on the front porch and began to relax. Though this relaxation involved keeping my senses alert for any odd sounds in or outside the manor. I produced my watch from my pocket and checked the time. It was now half past nine, and I was sure that the minister would arrive in the next twenty minutes.

The sun was now moving farther into the sky, and the day was heating up. Unfortunately, it seemed that the humidity was thicker today than it had been since I arrived. The only thing that I could hope for now would be a storm to wash out all the humidity. I was amazed, however, that this morning seemed to have much more heat than earlier in the week. I sat quietly just taking the whole world in and could see that the forests were already alive. I could see that squirrels ran about as deer seemed to play farther in the distance. The birds were chirping, and the whole morning seemed to be bright and lively. I had been ready to see a relaxing morning that was also inviting around the manor. Though I did fear that this wouldn't be long-lasting as it felt impossible that such evil would rest for long. I also worried that the minister's presence would stir up the home and cause much unrest. I also thought about Mary and what she would be doing on a hot morning like today. I could feel that she was also wondering the same. For a moment I thought that it might be her that would pay me a visit this fine morning, but those hopes were unfounded.

I watched both directions of the road and searched along the road in front of the manor to see if there were any signs that the minister would be along soon. I knew that I seemed desperate to any that would see my actions, but I could not worry about that now. I was deeply concerned that the home would continue to be riddled with such a deep level of evil and that I would find myself with a property that couldn't be maintained, a beautiful home just rotting away in this remote sector of the world. I didn't wish to have this thought as I would like for such a good property and amazing home to go to someone that would utilize it or be able to start a farm that they had dreamed about. I looked in front of me for the minister to arrive, then to my left. I could see now that there was a small cart moving toward the manor with some hay in the back of it. There was only a single horse, and I could see two men on the cart. One drove the cart, and the other sat on the very back of the cart as of a child but was protecting the hay from falling out of the cart.

The road seemed to present a problem for the small cart as it bumped wildly over the ruts in the road. Even though the road had been flattened considerably since I arrived, it still held its share of bumps and ruts. The horse that pulled the cart seemed to not mind the road at all but did seem to struggle slightly against the drag of the cart as it moved over the road. I could see that both men not only held on to something in their hands but also held the cart to try to not fall off at a moment's notice. I found this to be slightly humorous but didn't wish to laugh in case the minister had conscripted a small cart to carry him out to the manor. I could see now that the man driving the cart was not the minister, but the man in the back didn't turn to face forward at all. He also seemed to be dressed rather plainly with a farmer's hat on his head. Though this was not to say that the hat was odd, but I would have expected the minister to work in the same dress that he did when he gave his sermons. I waited patiently to see what this cart would hold as it passed.

The odd thing that I hadn't counted on was that the cart slowed in front of the manor and came to a stop in front but was still out on the road. The man on the back of the cart stepped down onto the road. I could feel the man's trepidation as he began walking up the drive. I didn't get up to greet him at first, but eventually, I did wave.

"Hello, sir!" I yelled out to the man. I could see that he was waving but couldn't see who he was from this distance. It wasn't long, however, before he approached the porch.

"Good morning, Mr. Price. I hope that you haven't been waiting too long for my arrival."

I shook my head as I stood from the rocking chair. "I have only been out here for maybe forty minutes. It is good to see you this morning. I am well, and you?"

The minister approached and shook my hand. "I am well. I do hope that you will be able to explain all that is happening within the manor."

I nodded and said, "I can. I have experienced a lot of troubling things within the manor."

The minister looked up at me and gave me a very different reaction to what he did yesterday. "I am not surprised. Your aunt was a very generous woman, but as my papers that I am sure that Mr. Merivel shared with you stated, Caroline was a treacherous woman in the end. I could not have expected under any circumstances that she would be the one to worship the devil."

I nodded and added, "I could agree to that, sir."

The minister looked me in the eye and said, "You can call me Minister Bryant."

I nodded and then replied to him in this way. "I thank you for coming out on such a short notice to see the manor. I am working to try to sell the home, but I haven't wished to move forward on that point since I have had this haunting." I continued to tell the minister about all the events in the home. I gave him a detailed account of everything as we both sat on the porch. After I had shared these details with him, I said, "I am sorry, sir. Would you like some water?"

The minister smiled and said, "I sure would. Thank you, sir."

I nodded and then led him into the manor. I didn't wait for the minister to enter the home but left the door ajar. I moved swiftly in the kitchen and retrieved the bucket. I moved out into the hallway and said, "I will have to pull the water from the well. Please make yourself as comfortable as you can!" I then moved outside and began pulling water from the well. I wasn't sure that I should have left the minister alone in the manor, but I felt that I would only be gone a short time. I did, however, keep an ear out for any sounds that might come from the home. I also moved as quickly as I could muster. My fear was not that the minister would be prey to this demon, but that he wouldn't wish to be within the home without support. Though he didn't seem to need it when I addressed him before I grabbed the water from the well.

I moved just as quickly back into the manor now and placed the bucket on the preparation table. It didn't take me a long time to fill two cups with water and move out of the kitchen and back into the foyer. I handed the minister his water and took a sip of mine as well. The minister turned to me and said, "I would like for you to accompany me throughout the home and show me where all these events have occurred. I also would like you to tell me about how you felt when everything started each time that the ghosts or the demon appeared. I can then understand what areas I need to target."

I nodded and said, "Follow me this way then."

We didn't waste any time getting started. I moved throughout the whole home and pointed out all the areas where Percy and I had experienced the evil in the home. The last room that I took the minister into was the bedroom that now sat empty with the hatch to the attic. He immediately paused at the door and looked toward the hatch. I could tell that he didn't wish to go any farther, but he did with prayer. He had now begun to pray as if chanting for protection from God. I couldn't be sure that he would be attacked, but I felt that I should be cautious in this room as well. I didn't wish to provoke anything that might harm the minister.

Minister Bryant moved to the hatch and began to pull out the ladder and place it underneath the hole to the attic. He continued to pray as he progressed toward crawling into the attic. I stood in amazement as he slowly worked toward the attic. He now had moved up the ladder and stood on it with his head poking through into the attic. He signaled with his hand for me to grab a candle. I moved faster than I thought that any human could and grabbed a candle and brought it back to the minister. I also provided him with a match, which I could hear him use to light the candle.

Once the light began to glow out of the hold that the minister had moved halfway into, the minister climbed completely into the attic. I reached up and handed him the Bible that he had left on the ladder. I then moved into the attic myself. I stood mainly in the dark and kept my eyes open and shifting around the room so that I wouldn't be surprised by anything. Minister Bryant moved deeper into the attic and continued to pray. I could see that there was no darkness here. I found this to be an encouraging sign. What I didn't find encouraging was the fact that I felt as if I were being watched from all directions. I wasn't sure if this was my feelings or a true feeling from the demon. The minister didn't seem to notice this at all. At least if he did, then he didn't give into it.

I stood there in the partial darkness in a sheepish manner. I was still focused on making sure that I wasn't ambushed from any direction. I was so engrossed in this effort that it took longer than normal for me notice that the minister was motioning for me to follow him. I moved swiftly across the attic and to the minister's side. He handed me the Bible that was opened to a passage. I held on to it and continued to stand in silence. The minister's prayer had now moved into a song, it seemed. I wasn't sure what he was saying right off as I was still cautious toward my surroundings. The fact remained that I was not ready to focus into what was happening. I instead was focused on the surroundings.

The minister continued to walk about the attic for a moment and then motioned for me to move down the ladder and back into the bedroom. The feeling of being watched had now subsided. I found this to be a good sign indeed. I took my time now moving back out of the attic and into the rest of the home. I now held the ladder in one hand and the Bible that was still open to the passage that it was before. The minister slowly descended to the floor below him. I hoped with everything within me that he would be all right and that this demon wouldn't show itself or attack the minister. I knew that he probably wouldn't run from this thing, but I did wish for him to be able to complete his walk through the home. I handed the Bible back to the minister and backed out of the room. I kept my eyes on the hole that led to the attic until the minister and I left the room.

The minister and I now moved away from the bedroom and down the stairs to the foyer again. I could feel that the air had changed, and I was happy that I felt free from this burden. Whatever the minister had said during his prayer felt as if it had worked even if it was for just now. Once the minister and I had reached the floor at the base of the stairs, we talked for a moment.

"How do you feel that everything proceeded, Minister Bryant?"

He thought for a moment and said, "I am not sure. I felt something in the attic, but nowhere else. I now don't feel anything, but I don't live within the home. How do you feel about everything?"

I smiled and replied, "I think that the air feels much lighter than it felt when I first arrived. I will be honest. I thought that you would be attacked immediately when you entered the attic. Percy and I never entered the attic without being attacked immediately."

The minister didn't seem to say much now. He simply told me that I should begin to feel relief from all this evil that had been contained within the home but that I should still be careful. He also told me that he would stay for a moment to make sure that there were no occurrences after his walk through the home. "I am sure that something else will happen, Mr. Price."

I stopped the minister and said, "Please call me Benjamin."

He smiled and continued, "With something like a demon, I have studied that it can take several days to deal with a being that strong. If anything else happens, please don't hesitate to inform me at the church. I will make myself available immediately if I am there."

I nodded and said, "Let's move into the sitting room then. Anything that will happen within the home can be heard or felt from that room."

The minister nodded, and I began leading him into the sitting room.

We arrived at the sitting room door, and I motioned for Minister Bryant to sit within. I then moved back into the kitchen to fill our glasses with water. I still kept my ears open for anything that might be going on within the home. I also kept a keen awareness over my feelings so that I would be able to tell the minister if anything was about to happen within the home. I once again moved at an increased pace back into the sitting room. The minister stood by the window and took in the morning air. I walked in and set his cup on the end table beside his chair.

"I want to thank you so much for coming by this morning. I am grateful that you were able to assist me. How is it that you knew what to do?"

The minister didn't turn to acknowledge my presence but said, "I have been many things in my life. When I realized that I wanted to be in the church, I moved toward the Catholic faith. I felt the most drawn to their way of worship and their beliefs. I had been raised differently though. I also grew up in town 'ere. I always wanted to travel to the north and become a part of that lifestyle. I always entertained myself with stories of the big cities that you all have there. God saw to it that I would find my place within the church, just not the one that I thought I wanted. I did, however, see much in my time.

"The good Lord led me to different areas to learn all that I could. I met several Catholic priests and bishops as well as members of other faiths as well. I found that I never really connected with their beliefs as much as I had thought that I would. So...I stayed 'ere. I did keep a lot of friends that did introduce me to many new things.

"Now I'm too old to travel outside this town, so I correspond with my contacts through the post. That is how I knew all about this cult in our town. It took time, but I was sent several books from a bishop in Massachusetts. He told me in the letter to be cautious and to check into these cults and gather evidence for the sheriff."

I found his words extremely compelling. "Why is it that you didn't notify the sheriff then?" I asked.

He continued to stand in the window and said, "I did. The sheriff at the time wouldn't do anything about it. He said that he would check into it, but I knew he never did. Once I realized that they'd gotten to him, I just kept watchin' 'em from the woods. I hoped that one day I'd be able to expose 'em to the town, but by that time, your aunt had grown ill and stopped her practice.

"I found it odd that she didn't seem to remember anything about the cult in her later years and deemed that the consumption had taken 'er mind. I never could find out who'd taken over the cult, but it all seemed to stop after she died. No one was practicin', and no one cared that they ever did. So I kept quiet on the whole matter."

I was struck with the sound of conviction in his voice. Here was a man who had seen everything firsthand and had somehow never been caught for spying on anyone, a man that stood in the way of evil but could do nothing in the end. I didn't know the previous sheriff, but I hoped that the current sheriff wasn't the same.

I moved my chair to face the minister now. I sat in the chair and waited for the minister to focus in on our conversation again. "I am sorry that no one believed you then. I just hope that that cult is gone for good now and you can clean up the manor and be done with such things."

The minister turned and said, "Thank you, Benjamin. I hope so as well. The Lord doesn't have a place in this world for such people, and good people like us are left out in the cold waiting for our world to return to normal."

I felt as if these words could apply to any age. Though I hoped that it didn't to the future of America. The minister now moved to his chair and sat facing me in the sitting room. I could see that he regretted not doing more for the town, but why worry now? The minister was a much older man anyway. His life should not be filled with such regrets, but instead the triumphs of his life. I wondered if this was why he dressed so simply and didn't seem to draw attention to himself.

"Do not worry, Minister Bryant. I am sure that the people of this town will be saved and be able to live happy and fruitful lives. The work that you have done in this town has surely been good, right?" I asked.

The minister didn't seem to respond to or even hear my words. He simply sat in thought and stared at the chair that I sat in.

"I am sure that I have had many accomplishments in this town, Benjamin. But people are often hard to change. I know everyone 'ere. I know 'em all. They're good people, but I worry that this cult has moved throughout the town and are working to take down the church. I will say though, Benjamin. My life has been good. God has truly blessed me, and I know that I can die in peace. This town will be fine without me, but I hope fervently that the next minister won't 'ave to deal with anythin' like that." With that statement the minister simply sat quietly.

We both now waited for any signs that the blessing of the house had failed. Though I could see that we both hoped that it hadn't. The minister and I didn't have any other deep conversations, and I could see now that he was deeply troubled by his past. I felt sorrow for the elderly man. He seemed stout and of good faith but very tired and weary from a long and healthy life. My only regret was not being able to hear of his younger days as I was sure that he was old enough to remember the wars that had come before or what life was like long ago. I so craved the opportunity to learn such things that only museums sought to capture. It was all such different knowledge when relayed by someone that was there.

The minister visited with me until it was a quarter past one o'clock. He stood from his chair after checking his watch and said, "Thank you for your hospitality, Benjamin. It isn't often that I meet a young man with a hunger for life. Just make sure that that hunger is for wholesomeness and nothin' else."

I stood from my chair and thanked the minister for coming to visit. We moved back into the foyer, and the minister prayed with me. I felt strength in this moment that I wasn't alone against this being, that I had another point of reference on this haunting and how to proceed. I then showed the minister out the door as his friend with the cart waited outside the door.

"Benjamin. Please let me know if you have any more trouble. I'll be happy to assist you."

I nodded and thanked the minister again. He had been a great help. I watched as the driver of the cart snapped the reins and began rolling away with the minister riding on the back of the cart. They took an abrupt left turn out into the road and then moved off into the distance. I knew now that I didn't have to worry about the manor or its contents.

The minister's prayer had obviously worked, and I was now free to move on with my life. I now wouldn't have to concern myself with fear or trying to keep my mind on track when being assaulted by the devil. I did, however, wish to talk with Mary before the day was out. I wasn't sure that Percy could take me to her aunt and uncle's house, but I wanted to try. Without even taking into account that the front door wasn't locked, I strolled off to Percy's home.

The day was beautiful, and much of the heat of the day had subsided. I could feel the gnats flying about and attempting to latch on to my ear, but I was happy nonetheless. It seemed that nothing could bother me now. I felt that my best chance of having enough courage to talk to Mary would be after striking a final blow against this demon and his host. I also felt sure that Mary would understand why I hadn't visited her in a bit of time. Sometimes I did worry that she would be upset that I hadn't been able to visit, but I knew that this wouldn't be the case. Mary would be happy to see me as I was excited to see her. She was the one that I was falling for deeply, but was also the one woman that I knew would understand what I was dealing with in the manor. Her family, however, didn't need to know anything about what was happening. The last thing that I needed was their family spreading any of this around the town.

This would not only shock the whole town but also make the minister look as if he hadn't done anything about this at all. I didn't wish to mar his reputation. I knew that this would cause the trust that we had built to falter. I also knew that I would no longer be able to gain help from the minister in this regard should the demon return. That is if it had ever left. The most apparent thing to me now, however, was that I could no longer fight the urge to see Mary's beautiful face and to feel her warmth. I had never known any love at all especially one as strong as this. I wasn't sure if I was ready for the level of commitment that I now faced, but I was willing to find out.

I had now arrived just in front of Percy's farmhouse. I moved down the drive to see that Percy was not outside. I thought this was odd as I knew that he had told me to find him there should the minister leave. I ignored this and moved farther into the home. I called out to Percy, "Hello? Percy!" Nothing. I then moved out onto the back porch and called out again. "Hello? Percy?"

I paused for a moment here before I could hear, "Yes! I am in the far pasture!"

I smiled at Percy's words and immediately began to move out to the far pasture. I knew now that Percy was checking the fences in the pasture and possibly visiting with his servants. I moved closer to the pasture and still couldn't see him. I looked about for a moment and then heard, "Benjamin! Over here!" I looked around but couldn't see Percy anywhere. I could hear rustling in the leaves slightly. I turned and looked in the direction of that sound before the thought dawned on me. *Where is his family and why had they not answered my yells?* This gave me pause. I felt odd about this now. I wasn't sure what was happening, but I felt that I should freeze in my tracks. I felt as if something was wrong but wasn't sure why that was happening.

I waited for a moment as I could hear more rustling from the woods. Everything in me called to me to run as quickly as I could. I still didn't move. I wasn't sure that anything was going on, but I was sure that I would find out soon as I could now see that the limbs to the trees in the distance was now moving back and forth. I was now frozen in place. My legs wouldn't work even if I could will myself to run. I was sure that I would not like anything that would come out of the trees and approach me. I felt that the best course of action would be to attempt to move myself backward slowly so as to not startle anything that might emerge from the forest. I still couldn't feel my legs enough to move. I even tried to throw myself backward in order to get away from the forest. This still didn't work at all. I simply watched and waited as the rustling of the leaves and the shifting of the branches of the trees grow more vigorous.

When the trees finally broke open, my heart sank. I could hear nothing. No breathing or any indication that this was Percy. I waited until I could get a better look at what was approaching. Eventually, Percy emerged from the forest and I could let out a sigh of relief and resume breathing. My heart returned to normal, and I felt that the world caught up again. Percy moved out of the forest and up to me to shake my hand and said, "Are you all right, Benjamin?"

I nodded and shook his hand, "I am sorry, Percy. I just thought that after everything that the minister had done that the demon had moved out here to torment me."

Percy chuckled and replied, "I am sorry, sir. I didn't mean to scare you."

I laughed in relief and caught my breath. I stood for a moment and then said, "I came here to let you know that the minister had left. I also wanted to ask for a favor."

Percy smiled and said, "What is it that you need?"

I wasted no time in asking, "Would you be willing to take me over to Mary's uncle's farm this evening?"

Percy stood back for a moment and smiled. "Oh, I see! Yes, I can!

For who am I to stand in the way of love?" Percy laughed for a moment and then stopped when he realized that I was not laughing in any way. Percy placed his hand on my shoulder as he and I moved back toward the home. "I am sorry, Benjamin. I couldn't resist."

I chuckled for a moment and then continued on. As we moved toward Percy's home, I noticed that Percy was dressed more as a farmer now. He had a lighter-colored pant and a white shirt with the sleeves rolled up. He had a brown vest over his shirt that had some grass and dirt on it and held onto his pocket watch. Then there was his hat. He wore a straw hat with a wide brim that protected him from the sun. I didn't find that this was odd, but it was different as I had only seen Percy with a suit on in his normal days. Now I could see him more as a farmer than a businessman. He also seemed more relaxed.

Percy and I moved back to the wagon barn and began gathering the horses from the corral and preparing them to be hitched to the wagon. I felt that it was my focus on what I needed to say to Mary that caused this process to progress so much faster. Percy and I then pulled at the horses' reins and led them to the wagon. Without much effort, Percy and I hitched the horses to the wagon and took our positions on the seat. With one snap of the reins we were moving down the drive and out onto the road. The wagon bumped along the road for a moment until the surface of the road had smoothed out. Percy drove the wagon into a hard-left turn and then gently worked the wagon back straight in the road so as to miss all the deeper ruts. This maneuver gave me the sense that we were moving much faster than I was sure we were moving. Percy then slowed the horses to a steady trot as we moved through the forest and out toward the main road that ran through the town.

The wind that blew across my face was a welcomed feeling to offset the heat of the day. The forest didn't seem to mind that the world had heated up so much. The sun bathed the forest and road in a pale green light. The verdant look of the dirt now seemed to make the forest look like it held a deep green stained glass. I was amazed at the aura that was now all around the wagon. I had imagined that the rural areas of North Carolina would be beautiful, but I hadn't imagined that it would be this beautiful.

The light that shone through the trees seemed to dance along with the wagon. I could tell that Percy felt the same as I frequently could see him looking out into the forest from the corner of my eyes. This was a day that I would imagine when I would think of being free from this entity. Though it remained to be seen if I was truly free from the hauntings in the manor. I did hold the hope, however, that I was truly free and able to enjoy the rest of my visit to Hillsborough. My time in this simple town was growing short now, and I feared that I wouldn't be able to relax as I had hoped before I arrived to the town.

Percy drove the horses onward toward the left fork in the road. He gently guided the wagon around the corner and onto the Main Street of the town. It was now that I could see that the whole town was out walking around. People were greeting each other in the streets and walking back and forth from building to building. I couldn't have anticipated such a sight. It was now Wednesday of the last week of my visit, and I felt as if the day were more of a Saturday. I looked toward Percy and said, "Why are there so many people in town now?"

Percy waved to some of the people that he knew and greeted others with a hearty hello. "Today is a beautiful day. People are building supplies and visiting the town. Most farmers and people that live on the edge of town wait for clear sunny days to buy supplies as not everyone has a covered cart or wagon. They are all buying things like sugar and coffee to take home for the rest of the month. Some will even come into town today to buy vegetables as not everyone in the town is a farmer."

Percy's words gave me a sense of intrigue. Often people assumed that everyone would be a farmer here, but could it be that some were able to survive here as we did in New York City? This gave me reason to feel closer to this town. My own biases had changed in this town now, and I was more understanding of how people lived in a wide range of lifestyles here on the fringe of the civilized world. At least it seemed this way to me. Percy guided the cart to begin a right turn as we began to drive out of the town. Even on the edge of town, people were moving about the street carrying various goods in different packages. Some were carrying sacks, and others were carrying boxes of different sizes.

I often imagined these to be presents of shoes or tools that another would need in their everyday life. I also imagined that this was Christmastime in the summer of North Carolina and everyone rushed to buy gifts or the parts to build a gift. One gentleman was even carrying wood across a porch of the supply store and placing them onto the back of his cart. I found a kinship now in the life that people lived here in rural America, that some would have the ability to live as in a city and others made their own way and lived from the land itself. This was the meaning of existence in my mind. Too often had I longed to start a farm where I lived in the city but could not as it was much too developed and urban.

Some did ride horses into the city and hitch them at the town hall, and some would even ride utility carts through the streets to building and work sites. I now felt a sense of love for this town and reasoned that I should visit this place again. If not for Mary's sake and that of her family, then for my own and the knowledge of living in rural Hillsborough for a time.

Percy now steered the horses to the far right of the road and followed the curve out of town. We straightened out on the connecting road to Mary's family farm. Excitement jumped in my chest now as I could feel her nearing to me. I worried now that I wouldn't be able to say what needed to be said. I feared that I wouldn't work up the courage to move forward with Mary and my life together and be so bold so as to suggest marriage. Life was now setting in, and my future with the woman that I felt so close to was hanging in the balance. It felt sublime in its simplicity yet complex in my head. What would I be if I were to have wasted Percy's time in coming to her uncle's farm and not being able to utter the words? Though I still didn't wish to face the thought of her rejection.

Eventually I was staring fate in the eyes as Percy guided the wagon onto the property and circled around to the farmhouse. It was now that I would have to be a man in every way and speak to the woman that I desired above anyone else. Today I would set aside self-ishness for the love of another.

Percy and I stepped down from the seat and moved toward the farmhouse. I assisted Percy in unhitching the horses once again and tying them to the hitch post outside the farmhouse. The wagon now set with the wheels chocked in silence awaiting our return. I moved to the front door and knocked lightly as I moved into the home. One of the servants met me at the door and said, "Good evening, sir. Are you here to see Ben?"

I shook my head and politely replied, "I am here to speak with Mary if that is possible."

The lady servant nodded and asked that I follow her. She led me out the back door of the home and motioned toward Mary resting under the tree of the backyard. I paused for a moment at the sight of her beauty. I was frozen where I stood without any ability to move toward this woman. Mary was sitting in a simple dress with a small bonnet upon her head. She seemed to be writing in a journal of some sort, but it was hard to tell at this distance. I took in a deep breath and willed myself to stroll casually to her side.

The lady servants yelled out, "Mary! You have a visitor!"

With these words the anxiety welled up inside me. I was struck with stupidity at knowing that I would soon speak with Mary about a future together. Mary stood from the seat under the tree as I approached and smiled widely. I couldn't help but kiss her on her cheek as I moved under the tree and invite her to sit down again.

"Good evening, Mary."

She smiled again and closed her journal. "Good morning, Benjamin. How are you this evening?"

I paused for a moment and then replied, "I am well, and you?"

She replied, "I am well also. Why have you come to visit me?"

It was then that I took her hand in mine and said, "I am sorry that I haven't visited in several days. I have had a lot of business to attend to for the manor. I have been thinking about you every moment, and I was worried that I had waited too long to visit. I wanted to ask you how you felt about our marriage before I left for New York and taking you with me. Would that be acceptable to you?"

Mary giggled at my choice of words and nervous tone. "What do you mean acceptable? Of course, Benjamin! I would love to be your wife!"

I paused at the sound of her words. I had really said everything right off. I had asked her to marry me, and I didn't even know what I would give her for a ring. "I don't have a ring right now. I could buy you one in New—"

Mary interrupted, "I couldn't care about a ring. I know that you and I are meant to be. Just live in this happiness with me, my love. If you want to buy a ring for me or not, I don't care about that." She smiled in a deeply loving way and put her arms around me. Without worrying about anything or even what anyone would say, she kissed me passionately on the lips.

This moment couldn't have been any better. The whole world could have erupted into flames and I wouldn't care in the slightest. Mary was to be my wife, and I didn't wish to leave her in this moment. I didn't even pay any attention to anyone around or what had happened to Percy. I didn't even feel bad for that admission to myself. I simply hugged Mary and kissed her again and again. Finally, after all the time that I had spent worrying about meeting with her, I was at a happy resolution.

Mary and I were so enthralled in the moment that I didn't even notice Mary's uncle and father approaching us. Mary's father called, putting, "Who is it that is making advances toward my daughter!" He said this with a gruff and deep voice.

I froze instantly and let go of Mary. Without a pause, she moved to her father and gave him a hug. "Benjamin has asked for my hand in marriage, Father!" she said excitedly.

Mary's father looked at me with an approving demeanor. Though I wasn't ready to say that I had his approval until he said it out loud. I simply stood there watching the scene as Mary's father embraced her and gave her a kiss on the top of her head. I could tell that he was accepting of his daughter's decisions. I felt good about this but still reserved. Ben moved away from Mary and her father and came over to me with his hand out. I could see that everyone had been working in the fields today as they were all dressed simply. Though Uncle Ben seemed to be more a settler than a farmer as he was dressed like a Quaker. This amused me in every way. Though I wouldn't say this to Ben in this moment as I didn't wish to cause any issues just after asking for Mary's hand in marriage.

Ben shook my hand vigorously and said, "Welcome to the family, Benjamin! I knew that this would happen after the other night. Mary seemed to be so sad when you left, and I realized the looks that you both gave each other that night was similar to the looks that I have Mary's aunt."

Mary and her father now moved to where Ben and I stood. Mary's father moved closer and stretched out his open hand. I shook his hand as he said, "Welcome to the family, Benjamin! I had worried that Mary would marry into another farming family and live in the rural world for too long. I am glad to see that she will be able to see more of the world with you than staying here."

I smiled and nodded and added, "Thank you, sir!"

Mary's father held up his other hand as we shook hands and said, "Please call me Martin."

I nodded in acknowledgment and then smiled. "Thank you both for welcoming me to the family."

Ben hugged his niece and congratulated her. Martin looked back to Mary and said, "It is too late in the day to celebrate, but we will throw a party tomorrow. I trust that you will both be married on Friday?"

Mary nodded and I smiled as I knew that this would all be perfect for my schedule.

The rest of the family began moving into the backyard, wondering what was going on. Martin yelled out, "Mary and Benjamin are to be married on Friday!"

The rest of the family now ran toward the home and joined us in the backyard. Mary and I were greeted with happy smiles and embraces. Mary's mother approached me and said, "You had better take care of my daughter, sir!" She then smiled as I did and hugged me. I was welcomed to the family in a very loving and happy manner. I could only imagine that my asking Mary to marry me would turn out this way. I thought that there would have been someone within the family that would object to our marriage, especially with Mary being so young.

Though I wasn't sure that the people of this area would follow the social norms. I was surprised by the fact that everyone seemed to accept me without any trepidation. I was pleased by this, however, and didn't wish for anything to happen now that would harm this bond that was being formed.

I looked around and could see that Percy was now standing on the back porch with some of the servants. I could see that he too had been touched by this moment as he was smiling and clapping. I was elated by my success and felt that nothing could change this moment. After a few moments Ben moved into the house and appeared carrying two bottles of wine and began opening them and pouring them into glasses that had been set out onto the outside table. We all took a glass and began celebrating. Everyone talked and partook of the wine. Even Percy seemed to join in on the celebration.

Eventually we all had had enough wine to empty both bottles before Martin announced, "I would like to invite you all to the wedding on Friday here in the backyard! We will have a celebration that we cannot have tonight and celebrate the marriage of these two lovers!"

I was amazed at how smooth this was all moving. I was glad now that I had allowed myself to speak out and tell Mary how I felt. I was now destined to share my life with the beautiful woman that I loved. Once we had all talked for a moment and Mary and I had received our congratulations, I bid Mary a good night and returned to the wagon in front of the farmhouse. I could see now that Percy had hitched the horses himself and prepared the wagon to return to the manor. I would not be able to rest in comfort with anticipation for the coming joy and celebration. I was ready to face the next few days and hoped that I would be able to visit with the sheriff and allow him to know that I wished to sell the manor.

Everything was coming together now as Percy and I returned to the road and began rolling toward the manor. I would now have the ability to be at peace in my mind with settling my affairs in the town and return to New York without worry. I just hoped that Mary would also be able to rest easy tonight in anticipation for a celebration of our love.

Percy continued to drive until we reached the manor and left me at the beginning of the drive. I could now feel that there was a peace that hung over the property. The night had done little to cast a spooky appearance over the land and the manor itself. I was ready now to head into the manor and sleep well on this calm and beautiful manor. I also would be able to consider on this night how I would be able to ask anyone for money in return for the deed. Though I would have to make it a priority to gather the deed from the sheriff after showing my aunt's will to him. Tomorrow I would gather this deed and then announce my official selling of the property to the sheriff and the whole town.

I now strolled inside and prepared myself to sleep. I gathered all my thoughts so as to make sure that I wasn't focusing on this demon anymore. I didn't wish to call this being back into the home through my fear and longing for it. I also didn't wish to spook myself before bed. Nothing would allow me to sleep with the memories of such terror within the manor if I was not mindful of my thoughts. I shut the door to the bedroom and locked it just in case I was wrong about the demon being gone. I then hunkered down in my bed and pulled my covering around my body. The thin sheet seemed to follow my form completely. I felt as if I were wrapping my body for a final rest within the ground. I could only hope that I would be able to sleep like the dead.

I also wished that I would be able to have fond dreams of beautiful things. Perhaps I would now be able to dream of Mary and our life together. I would be able to see the amazing life that I had so imagined for myself and the wife that I would have with whom to share my life. In either case, I was ready for the deepest and most restful sleep that I could obtain in this small bed. I reached over to the table beside the bed and blew out the candle. I now lay in complete darkness. I was ready to test my theories about this demon departing the home for whatever world from which it had emerged.

The darkness was thick within the home, and I could be sure that I would not be able to see anything that could approach me. I waited in silence for any noises that would confirm or deny my theory that this demon had been removed from the home. I continued to wait as I could only hear the sounds of the typical creatures of the night outside. I was not able to feel or hear anything strange within the home. The sense of dread that I had associated with these beings was now present. I also couldn't hear any footsteps or creaking of flooring.

Some part of me longed to be at peace now and simply fall into sleep. The other portion of me wished to hear anything that I could know that this demon had returned. I didn't wish to be tormented, but I found it all hard to believe that this being could be gone. I eventually came to the conclusion that I was accustomed to the demon, to the torment that had been visited upon Percy and me. This made me feel that I was alone in the home for good. Nothing would be there to intrigue my mind. No issue to solve and no puzzle to solve. I was now able to be at peace, and I refused to realize it. After all, I was used to solving the problems of others. Eventually, however, I stopped my mind from these thoughts and closed my eyes. I could now feel the world bleeding away from me as I drifted into a deep sleep.

11

FIGHTING EVIL

The sun shone through the window into the bedroom. I could see that there were intricate shadows that were being cast on the walls from the sun shining through the bushes outside. I was awoken suddenly and without warning. I found it odd that I had awoken to the sun being so high in the sky. I felt rested and relaxed in every way and felt that my dream had come true. I was relaxed in this manor as I had never been before. I lay there for a moment and awaited any signs that there were others in the manor. Eventually I remembered that I was alone within the manor. I had had a dream of being with Mary and her family sharing the celebration of Mary and my life beginning together. I could smell the fragrance that suggested the world was waking from its nightly slumber. The smell was light and wafting in the gentle breeze of flowers. I thought that perhaps Percy's family had awoken late as well. I immediately thought of sharing a warm breakfast with Percy and his family. I also thought of Mary as I had done through the night and could not help but miss her.

After a moment of imagining, I climbed out of the bed and sat on the edge, rubbing my face and eyes. I did not want to stay awake and felt the allure of falling back to sleep in this bed. I knew, however, that this would be impossible as this was an important day. Today Percy and I would travel into town and collect the deed and make it known that I wished to sell the manor.

I stood from the bed and put my suit on my body. The fit was a little odd as it had been in my luggage for longer than any other suit. I decided that I needed to wash my clothing today as well to prepare for my return to New York. I knew that I would be able to wash my clothing in the manor as the thought that I had defeated this evil being. I tried to push the thought from my mind so as to not feel so much excitement. After all, I didn't wish to be disappointed should the latter be proven. I didn't wish to have a false sense that I had defeated this demon once and for all.

I walked out of the room and into the kitchen. I then filled my cup with water and drank deeply from it. My fear that I had awoken too late to enjoy breakfast was now present in my mind. I moved into the spring house and checked the food within the basket. I could see now that there was nothing left save for crumbs. I removed the basket from the spring house and placed it out onto the preparation table in the kitchen. I was satisfied now that I would need to travel to Percy's home and see if I was welcomed for breakfast. I finished off the rest of the water and moved quickly out the front door of the manor. I then followed the drive out to the road and swiftly began walking toward Percy's home. Just then I looked up and could see Percy walking toward me.

"Percy! Good morning!" I called out. Percy raised his head and waved. I jogged over to him, "Why are you walking toward the manor this morning?"

Percy stopped in front of me and said, "I was coming to invite you to breakfast. Chloe and Catherine are preparing breakfast this morning."

I nodded and thanked Percy. I then began walking with Percy back toward his home. I felt that I should ask Percy at this time for his help with going into town. "I wanted to ask you, this morning, if you would like to go into town for me to see the sheriff. I need to collect the deed to the manor and impress upon the sheriff that I wished to sell the manor."

Percy walked with me and seemed relieved. "I will assist you, sir. Though I wanted to ask you how your night went."

I nodded and said, "Everything is perfect within the manor. I think that the minister was able to clear the demon from the home."

Percy was relieved even more now. We briskly walked back to the farmhouse and into the dining room. I sat at the end of the table and could clearly see into the kitchen of the home. I watched both Chloe and Catherine work in the kitchen with grace. I enjoyed watching the arts that were incorporated into cooking. I loved the movement of the hands and the way that Chloe was articulating the knife in her hand. She was using it to cut through the chicken that would be for breakfast this morning. I felt intrigued by the way that these women worked in a uniform fashion to finish breakfast and also begin working on lunch.

I watched Catherine finish stirring what I now knew was gravy on the fire. She then removed the cooking pot and moved into the far side of the kitchen. She poured the gravy into a giant bowl and then placed the pot back onto its rack and pulled it out from the fire. I watched as Catherine brought the gravy bowl into the dining room and placed it on the table as she took her seat at the table. The bacon and sausage were still sizzling as Chloe placed them on the table. I was starving and ready to fill my stomach with a wholesome breakfast. I put a slice of bread and two pieces of bacon and sausage just on top of that. I would have asked if eggs had been prepared, but I didn't wish to be difficult. I covered this all in a small amount of gravy and began to eat. I cut the corner of the bread off along with a piece of bacon and sausage. The bacon was crunchy and the sausage was juicy and fell apart in my mouth. I loved the taste of pork for breakfast, and that had not changed throughout my life. It seemed that the opposite was true. The more that I aged, the more that I seemed to enjoy pork even more. The gravy was smooth and delicious and was the perfect garnish upon my makeshift sandwich. The bread was moist and had a very earthy flavor in contrast with the meats.

Eventually Chloe returned with a plate of fruit. I imagined that the sweetness of the fruit would go well with my coffee that I was enjoying with my meal. The fruit was sweet and juicy and also complimented the other items well. I could not have imagined a better breakfast for a day like today. I would have everything I needed in order to be properly prepared to face the day. After some time, Chloe sat at the table to eat as well. I looked to Chloe and asked, "Excuse me, Chloe, but would you all have a wash bucket that I can use for my clothes today?"

Chloe looked up from the table and replied, "I can take care of your clothing today as long as you can bring them by."

I could not help but feel ashamed that Percy's wife would be washing my clothes. To have someone else to clean my dirty clothes seemed odd to me. I also had not had a week that I didn't wash my clothes often so as to be clean and pressed for work every day. Although this was easier when you live in a large city. I continued to eat breakfast with Percy and his family.

After breakfast I moved down the road with Percy to grab my bag that held my dirty clothes. I hoped that Chloe would be swift with cleaning my clothes as I did still wish to visit Mary and her family tonight in a clean suit. It didn't take long for Percy and me to grab the bag and move back to Percy's home. I walked through the doorway and was immediately greeted by Chloe. She beckoned for me to follow her down the hallway and out the back door. I followed her around the home to a small platform that held a bucket and a scrubbing rack. There was also a clothing line here to hang clothes on. Chloe took my bag from me and began putting a substance in the bucket of water. I watched as she removed my clothing and lay the suits on the platform. With a uniform movement, Chloe washed and scrubbed my clothing one piece at a time. I was interested to see that Chloe was using a wooden bucket that was quite large. I had never seen a bucket that was this big for washing clothes. She sat on a chair and bent over slightly so as to reach deep into the bucket and drench the clothing. She then scrubbed the clothes, one article at a time, over the scrubbing rack that was beside the bucket. Water flooded down to the platform and out into the yard. Chloe worked with a vigor that I had never seen before. I felt truly sorry for the labor that Chloe had to endure to clean my clothing. I had never seen anyone that had washed my clothes when I would drop off my dirty laundry at a cleaner. This really put the labor of everyday life into perspective for me now.

Eventually I interrupted Chloe's work and asked, "Is there anything that I can assist you with now?"

Chloe looked up at me with a smile and said, "No, Benjamin. I have everything from here. Though you could hang the clothes that I have finished on the line there." She pointed to a line that was ran across two trees. The line was positioned to be just away from the forest. I quickly moved back and forth placing the washed clothing on the line to dry. Before I walked away from Chloe working, I said, "Thank you for washing my clothes, Chloe. I truly appreciate the help." Chloe smiled and nodded as I walked away.

I moved back toward the back porch now as I thought about how spoiled the city had made me. I enjoyed the wild of the rural areas. It seemed surreal to see life in such a remote location. I listened to the birds sing and watch the animals running around in the trees. The breeze was a little cold, but somewhat comfortable. I sat down on the porch. I sat there for a moment as I felt the cool breeze. The chill in the wind tickled my face as it went by. I was happy to sit in the morning light and watch the day. I didn't know how long that I would have to wait for my clothing to dry, but I did hope that I would at least have one suit to wear that was clean. I thought about borrowing a suit from Percy, but I decided that this was not so serious as that. The only other idea was to wear a damp suit, but I did not wish to wear wet clothing for any period of time.

I sat there continuing to think about my day and the clothing that I wished to wear to visit Mary again tonight. As I thought, the curiosity of where Percy had gone sat heavy on my mind. I suddenly realized that I had not seen Percy in some time. Not since I had left the home to follow Chloe to the washing area. I found it strange that Percy was not hanging around the farmhouse after breakfast. I felt that I owed a debt to Percy and his family for being so gracious. I did hope that I would be able to send some money to Percy and his family to cover any costs that they might have incurred.

Of course no amount of money could cover the level of devotion that Percy had to me and the situation that I found myself in. Percy had never been asked to become involved in anything, but he did it anyway. I was amazed as I sat there and thought about how quick that Percy had been willing to jump into the fray and assist me with a demon. There was no expression of words that could describe the level of appreciation that I felt toward Percy. I continued to sit on the porch for a moment as I waited for Percy or his wife to appear. I was sure that Percy had begun working around the barn for the day. I decided that I would walk out to the barn to check on him.

My thoughts then turned to the manor. I found it nice that I had been able to stay in the manor alone without worrying about my safety. I didn't wish for my stay there to turn into anything like it had before. I only wished to rest now and get the enjoyment of the trip that I had taken to relax and sell this home. Though I could not deny that the demon had made things interesting. I didn't expect to learn this much about another world that most definitely did exist and haunted our world.

I no longer thought about demons and spirits as a lesson. I now know that I had faced the evil that most would not believe exists. The manor truly was such a beautiful home, but with its own issues. That was only compounded by something that could not be seen or felt until it was too late. Then the terror set in and it was too much for any normal person to wish to deal with. I could no longer dismiss anything with scientific explanations without considering the supernatural first. Sometimes I could feel myself considering the possibility that these terrible beings could follow me to my apartment in New York.

This seemed to be a leap as nothing had given me the idea that the demon would be able to leave the property. Then again, I was still not sure that it was even defeated. I just hoped with everything in me that it was defeated. I didn't wish to attempt to sell the home and destroy my good name by selling a haunted home to the unwitting purchaser.

My thoughts continued to move toward the desire that Percy would still wish to buy the manor. I would even wish to make the manor more affordable for his family to afford without having to break themselves financially.

I continued on to the barn and could not see Percy anywhere. This confused me as I desired to speak to Percy about the remainder of the day. I rounded the corner of the barn to begin moving toward the far pasture in the hopes that I would find Percy out in the pasture. As I did, I could see Percy in the far distance talking to a servant. I felt that something dire had happened, but I began to approach the area anyway. The day was warm but held a strong breeze. I no longer felt the deep level of humidity that hung over the area. I felt the relief that I knew that everyone else could on this day. I hoped that the day would continue this way and this would govern the days to come for the rest of the week. I approached Percy directly as I could see that the servant had moved away and toward their home on the edge of the property.

Percy turned to me and said, "Hello, Benjamin. Is something wrong?"

I shook my head with a confused look upon my face. Percy put his arm around my shoulders and pulled me closer to the pasture. "I am sorry to alarm you, but my servant named Jessica stated that she heard weird noises outside her home last night. I fear that a predator has been stalking the woods recently. That or there is a sign that this demon has returned. Please act as if I haven't told you this."

I nodded as Percy turned and said goodbye to his servants. We briskly walked back to the barn. Percy entered the doorway of the barn and moved off to the left. I followed his lead until he stopped in front of me. "I don't wish to alarm my family nor the other servants with this information. She said that she could hear a growling outside that was very gruff. I asked her if she could see anything out in the forest and she said no. She did say that it shook her door back and forth for a moment then seemed to walk away from her house slowly."

I rubbed my chin with my hand. "Where does this servant reside?"

Percy looked around him and replied, "She lives just away from the manor."

My eyes widened, and I feared that I was no longer able to say that the home had been cleared of this evil.

"She didn't seem to say that she felt the sense of dread that we have both felt, but she did say that the creature seemed odd as she couldn't hear four feet but two," Percy said.

"Do you think that it could have been another creature?"

Percy paused for a moment and thought. "A bear maybe, but I doubt that as we don't get any bears in this area."

I nodded.

"If anything, she seemed to say that it may be a mountain cat. Though I am not sure cause we would have all heard a scream that loud."

I paused and replied, "How does a mountain lion sound when it screams?"

Percy swiftly replied in an animated manner, "A mountain cat sounds like a woman screaming. It is a horrible, ear-piercing sound. Everyone around the area would have been able to hear it. I also would like to mention that there is another servant that lives a little farther away from this woman. I asked her if she had heard anything last night just before Jessica approached me and she said no."

This all seemed just a little odd. I was struck by the level of detail and care that Percy had put into this investigation. I could see that he too seemed to lean toward the idea that this demon had returned. This was the last thing that I had imagined that I would hear from Percy in this moment. I was struck dumb by the thought that this demon had returned to the area. Though I was still questioning why this being would wish to haunt another property. Perhaps it was simply to terrify someone else into giving it the power that it craved. I would have imagined that this being would have appeared to me in the night. At the very least, it would have been able to affect my dreams more and more as I slept. Though I wasn't sure that this would have solved anything for this demon.

My mind raced with these thoughts until Percy brought this all to the worst level. "Could it be, Benjamin, that the minister simply pushed this demon out of the manor and made it free to terrify anyone that it wishes?"

I instantly felt a deep pang of fear. This would be the worst case indeed. I responded, "I am not sure, but we should be cautious here, Percy."

Percy nodded. I looked about as I could hear voices approaching the barn. Percy seemed to notice and did the same. It was the sound of Percy's wife and son. They were steadily moving toward the barn. Percy held his finger up to his mouth, and we both began walking out of the barn and back toward the farmhouse.

Percy's wife and son ambushed Percy and me as we emerged from the barn. "Percy! Your son has to talk with you!" I could see Percy roll his eyes as he felt that his son had been in trouble with his wife. Chloe then turned to me and said, "Your clothing is drying well, Benjamin. I will have them all to you by the end of the day."

I smiled and thanked Chloe once again for her help. She then turned toward the farmhouse and walked inside. I was not sure why the servants as well as Chloe weren't moving out toward the fields in order to work. Though I decided that there might have not been any work for them to do. I turned to see that Percy and his son had moved to the back porch and were talking rather quietly. I feared that the boy would have to be punished in front of my very eyes. I didn't wish to witness such an awkward event. Eventually, however, Percy stood from over the boy and motioned for him to return to his play. He then walked from the porch over to me.

"My son has confirmed my worst fears." With these words, my heart sank. "Something was lurking around his room last night. He said that he could hear scratching on the outside of the house in his and his sister's room. Come with me and let's see if there are any signs as to what this is."

I nodded and immediately followed Percy. We walked around the corner of the home and over to where the window to his son's room was located. We looked at the wall below this window and could see what his son was talking about. There were deep gashes in the wall. The gashes were long and seemed to be made my slender claws being scraped slowly over the wood timbers.

Percy turned to me and said, "Are you seeing this?"

I nodded without reply. I was amazed at this sight. Nothing could have prepared me for this image. I would now have to worry that this being had returned or, worse, that it had been freed to terrorize the town. I couldn't even imagine the level of terror that such a being would sew over this land. People would be massing to hunt this thing, only to realize that they couldn't kill it. The even worse idea would be if the remainder of the cult that summoned it would be in the area. They would be able to gain control of this thing and use it to their advantage. This would be an absolute nightmare descending upon this town. Though it didn't matter now. If this was to happen, then I would make sure that I would stop this thing.

Percy rubbed his hands across the scratches. He shook his head for a moment and then said, "Do you know what this looks like?"

I shook my head and waited for his response. "These look like nothing that I have seen. Anything on a big cat or bear would be much thicker and deeper. There would be much more wood removed from the timbers. This is something different. This looks like something more like a smaller animal but with long claws."

Percy seemed genuinely concerned now. I could see his face covered in worry as he and I feared the worst. My mind instantly sank into the darkness of the whole town being haunted by this demon. I couldn't even imagine the fear that Percy felt as this thing had seemed to move deep into his property. I too was alarmed by this prospect as I was not sure that this thing would wish to reveal itself to Percy or me anymore since we had caused this beast to lose its home. I knew now that Percy and I had to truly be careful of our next moves.

Percy stood from examining the wall and turned toward me. "We have to keep this quiet for now. I will consider ways to explain the scratches in case anyone notices them. In the meantime, we must go about our day in a normal fashion. Did you have anything that you needed to do today, Benjamin?"

I nodded and replied, "I do. I must go to the sheriff's office this morning to recover the deed as well as announce to him that I am looking for a buyer for the manor. I fear that I have little time left to be able to sell the home."

Percy looked around and said, "I understand. Let's get out of here before anything else happens. If you don't mind, I would like to talk to you about what we should do next."

I nodded, and Percy and I moved to the wagon shed. We hurried to hitch the horses to the wagon and move toward town. Percy launched himself onto the seat of the wagon as soon as we had hitched the horses. He snapped the reins as I grabbed onto the wagon and began to lift myself up and into the seat. I could excuse his hurry but still felt odd that we were abandoning his farmhouse and the families contained within. I did understand that this demon wouldn't affect these people again until the night had set in, but I worried that I would be spending the night with Mary's family as Percy would wish to return tonight. I was sure that we were worrying about nothing, but the fear of this demon returning overrode my desire to be rational.

Percy snapped the reins again and pulled the wagon to the right as we rounded the first curve and began moving toward the town. Percy didn't seem to wish to talk in this moment but instead concentrated on the road. We broke into a full stride as the road straightened and began guiding us through the forest. Percy seemed to not adhere to safe conditions when operating the wagon this morning, and I feared that we might roll the wagon over. I looked at Percy and said, "I also wished to know if you would be willing to take me to Mary's uncle's house this evening so that I may see Mary."

Percy nodded but didn't utter a word. He drove the wagon like that of a man consumed with madness. I thought for a moment that Percy wouldn't be willing to meet with his friend the sheriff or accompany me to the minister's office in the church. Though I hadn't presented that idea to Percy. I wasn't sure what the minister would do in this case but was sure that he should know in case anyone else was being affected. My only thoughts now turned to the safety of the town and those that resided within it. Surely, we were making a larger issue out of this situation than needed, but I couldn't be sure of anything now.

Suddenly my thoughts turned to Mary and my betrothal. She would, no doubt, wish to spend our wedding night together in the manor. I feared what might come about in that situation. Nothing could be more alarming than dragging my wife into a meeting with the devil. I had to protect her and her innocence at all costs. I knew that Mary was a tough and gracious woman, but this was too much for Percy and me to bear.

How would a decent woman of the town be able to cope with an evil so dark that it blackens her soul? I could imagine now saying no to her when she proposed that we spend the night in the Tourney Manor. She would be devastated, and the option to not trust our marriage would be firmly revealed to her. I knew that she would understand if I explained it to her, but I knew that I shouldn't lay this at her feet. After all, what would I say? *"Welcome to my haunted manor, my dear! Don't allow the things of the night to carry you away!"* She would be horrified at those words. I felt a responsibility toward this situation and all who would be affected by it. I believed in my mind that, in this case, I was now responsible for this whole town.

I did hope that a visit to the minister would be able to shed more light on why this being would be able to move about the town. That, or show that this was not how any of this could function. I did hope that this demon would not be able to torment the whole town. Perhaps the minister would say that this demon would still be bound to the manor and offer another solution. I could only think about everything in this capacity. Nothing in my mind would allow me to be negative on the day before my wedding. Percy pulled the wagon gently to the right but also allowed the wagon to drift onto the far side of the road. The wagon straightened and began roaming toward the sheriff's office. We pulled up outside as Percy tied the horses to their post to drink. I could feel the wood creaking under my feet as I moved across the boards of the walkway outside the sheriff's door. Percy stood outside and kept an eye on his horses as I entered the building. The sheriff was a pleasant man as he stood from his desk and said, "Welcome! Come in! How can I help you today?"

I smiled and reached out my hand to shake the sheriff's. "I am well this morning, sir! I would like to pick up a deed that has been left in your care."

The sheriff motioned for me to take a seat in front of his desk. He then moved behind his desk and took a seat in his chair. The sheriff then began rifling through his desk drawers until he pulled the deed out of his desk. "I am sorry for your loss, Mr. Price. I have been waiting for you to come by so that I could meet the nephew of Ms. Caroline. Her will entrusted that I care for the document, but I wasn't sure that you'd come by."

I smiled at the sheriff's thick Southern drawl. "I am sorry that it took me so long to come by your office, sir. I have been trying to get the manor in order to sell."

The sheriff looked at me with surprise. "Sell?" he asked.

I nodded and replied, "Yes, sir. I am wanting to sell the manor to a good family within the town that might really need a farm to work."

The sheriff seemed disappointed as he looked down toward his desk. "I am sorry, Mr. Price, but I had hoped that you'd be able to take over the manor and operate a farm yourself."

I laughed at this idea and replied, "No, sir. I am a banker in New York City. I have a lot of work to do when I return. I don't have the means to operate nor the time for a farm. I hate to disappoint you, but I think that another family would love the home and be able to grow crops on the property."

The sheriff forced a smile on his face and then leaned back in his chair. "Mr. Price. Do you know why our town is so small?"

I shook my head silently.

"Because no one wants to settle here. We are on the edge of wilderness here, and we don't have a lot of the luxuries that other towns possess. I hate to say it, but we need people moving here to maintain the town. There aren't any families that would be willing to buy the manor."

I smiled with an absurd look on my face. "Why would there not be anyone in town that would need this manor?"

The sheriff leaned over the desk and began playing with a pencil. "I am not one to share other people's business, but there aren't any families wealthy enough to own the manor. People in this town don't live by money alone. We all help each other, and folks are doing without. Sometimes the town has to provide food to one another because a farm dries up."

I looked around the room for a moment and then said, "What families have seen their farms 'dry up'?"

The sheriff smiled and chuckled. "They have become workers on someone else's farm. Many here desire to be a worker and not a farmer. Times are hard in this town, and I am left to deal with it all. The mayor is more concerned with appeasing politicians in Raleigh and bringing in outside wealth. Things are turning around, but the only hopes that we all have are those pertaining to the Starnes family and their winery."

I nodded and added, "I have met the Starnes family. They are pleasant people. Do you think that they would be willing to purchase the manor from me and start another farm there?"

The sheriff raised his eyebrows as if he were intrigued. "I am not sure. I do know that you are marrying into Ben's brother's family. Why don't you ask them?" I thought for a moment as the sheriff said, "What? You thought that everyone in such a small town wouldn't hear about a wedding on Friday? We know each other personally."

I continued to sit silently then said, "I am sorry, sir. I hadn't meant to insult your intelligence, but I will ask the Starnes family about the manor."

The sheriff leaned back in his chair and nodded, "I hope that they will buy it. I don't know of anyone else in this town that would be able to buy a property as pricey as the Tourney Manor."

I smiled in frustration and said, "Thank you for your time, sir. Have a good day, and I will inform you of any sale that takes place."

The sheriff nodded and I stood from my chair. I then walked quickly to the door and stepped out into the sunlight.

Percy was standing beside the door and followed me from the side of the door as he said, "How did it go?"

I didn't even turn around when I replied, "It went well. He thinks that I won't be able to sell the manor and was expecting me to stay and farm the land. I cannot do that in any way."

Percy caught up to me and said, "I know that the sheriff is gruff at times, but he means well. I think that he is simply worried that everyone will slowly abandon the town and that the mayor won't do anything about it. He has been trying to get the mayor to advertise the town to his friends in Raleigh and promote people to move."

I turned and looked Percy in the eye. "I am aware of this, but I am not able to live on the hopes and dreams of a town. I have a life in New York that I must return to shortly. I don't have time to deal with politics that block me from selling the property."

Percy stopped in his tracks and seemed taken aback. "I am sorry, Benjamin. I didn't mean to support the sheriff's fervor. I understand your situation, but I agree that there isn't anyone wealthy enough to buy the manor."

I turned back around and said aloud, "Then I will have to give it to someone!" I then walked across the street and down to the church. I could see that the minister was sitting on the stairs that led into the church. I approached him and took a seat to his right. "Good morning, Mr. Price!"

I smiled and replied, "Good morning, Minister Bryant. I have come to ask some questions."

The minister immediately placed his journal on the steps beside him and gave me his full attention.

"I am sorry to inform you that I have heard of some strange occurrences going on with Mr. Merivel's farm. I fear that this demon has been moved out of the manor and now is free to terrorize the whole town." I stated.

The minister chuckled and said, "I am not sure that it works like this. A demon latches on to a person or a place and tries to hold that person or place in its power. If a demon loses its power over that person or place, then it will move on to somewhere else. Most believe that it will return to hell. It doesn't simply move into another property like a vagabond.

"If the demon is truly haunting the farm of Mr. Merivel, then it hasn't truly been removed from the manor. It is probably attempting to terrorize the others in the area to regain its hold over the land. I would say that this will be outside my help. I would recommend that you allow me to call for a priest to come here and check out the manor for himself."

I lowered my head. "I am sorry, Minister Bryant, but I do not have that much time. I am expected to leave on Saturday morning for Raleigh."

The minister didn't seem happy at my words. "I am sorry, Benjamin. There is nothin' more that I can do. Please consider my words and let me know if you would like for me to contact a priest. I wish that I could help, but I am clearly out of my area of knowledge."

I nodded and said, "Thank you for all of your help, sir. I will let you know if there is any further help that I will need." I nodded to the minister and stood from the steps.

The minister stood and shook my hand. "It was an honor to meet you, Benjamin. I hope that God watches over your return to New York. I will be presiding over your wedding tomorrow, so I will see you then."

I smiled and thanked the minister again. As I moved back toward where Percy was sitting on the wagon, I couldn't help but feel that I was now out of my league. I had no other ideas in my mind as to how I would defeat this creature. I was sure that it would finally win out and I would have to sell the manor from New York City. This would be no small task, and there would be a lot of waiting. I also was not sure how I would be able to transfer a large sum of money through the post. This would be difficult, to say the least, and I would likely have to insure the package. I was willing to do this, but I didn't wish to if I didn't need to insure it. My mind was racing with thoughts that I wasn't sure that I trusted. Though I wasn't sure what choice I really had in this situation.

I now approached the wagon and took my place on the seat. Percy turned to me and asked, "What did the minister say?"

I sat in silence for a moment and replied, "The minister said that he would need to call a priest. I tried to find out why, and he simply said that one of his friends would know more than he would about such things. I think that this is our only option. Though I wouldn't be here when they arrived.

Percy turned his head forward and snapped the reins. "This is most disappointing." I tended to agree with Percy on this point.

I was not sure what I would do from this point, but I reasoned that Percy should be the one to help me decide since he had been dragged into this now. I would not like to have any other person oversee that this task was completed. Percy was the only one that I knew would have an interest in hiding this from the town and still being able to cleanse the home. Though if a priest did arrive in the town, then it would surely stir up conversation over what was happening in the town. Especially if the sheriff had anything to do with it. I was sure that the whole town didn't need to know my private affairs either.

Percy continued on with driving the wagon toward the farm-house. I was sure that he would wish to have a smoke after all this bad news. The wagon rounded the curve and back toward the forest. The building that we usually passed when we entered the town was now behind us on our left. The forest began to slowly approach us now. I was satisfied that Percy wasn't pushing the wagon to move faster and faster as he'd done this morning. I was thankful that I didn't have to hold on to the wagon tightly for fear of falling out into the road.

Percy and I continued to ride along the road at this pace for some time. Percy pulled into his drive to the house and then returned the wagon to the porch. "I will be inside shortly, Benjamin. We can get underway to Mary's family farm soon."

I nodded to Percy as I stepped down off the wagon. Percy pulled the wagon forward and had begun the process of unhitching the horses. I moved into the house and could see that everyone was performing chores. The children were dusting the home and straightening the table. I thought that this was odd for the children to clean as I had been used to children not knowing how to clean. I could see the level of discipline that had been instilled in these children from a young age. They both stopped what they were doing and turned to me. Neither of them said anything at first and just looked at me as if I had come to take them away. I could tell that they cowered a little.

"Is everything all right, children?"

They both nodded as they stood silent. Then Catherine worked up her nerve, "We hope that you take that monster with you when you leave, sir."

I gave them a puzzled look. "What monster are you mentioning?"

They looked at each other. Then the boy piped up, "The monster that visited last night. I don't want to see that again."

These words made my heart tear. I now had confirmation that this thing was affecting these children in the worst way. I had not wished for any of this to happen, and now my deepest fears were coming true. I approached both of them and kneeled down. "Nothing will happen to you both. This monster cannot get you as long as you stay inside. I am trying to search for a way to make this monster leave you both alone."

The children seemed relieved by these words but were still terrified. I could hear Percy enter the house behind me. "What is happening in here?"

I stood and turned to Percy. I motioned for him and me to talk in the kitchen. We both walked into the kitchen and kept an eye on his children. "I am not sure what will happen, Percy. Your children are terrified of this demon. I just don't know of anything else that can be done to make this thing go away." Percy hung his head, and I could tell that he was thinking the same thing.

Percy and I continued to talk in the kitchen about resolutions to this issue. We could see that the children had returned to their cleaning. They didn't seem bothered by anything at this point, so Percy and I slipped out to the back porch. We both sat and smoked while talking about every plan that we could devise. The only issue that continued to make each plan ineffectual was that we didn't know what state the demon was in currently. Meaning that if this demon had been removed from the home and now terrorized the town freely, then we would not have a chance to fight it off until the night came. I warned Percy that the minister had said that this demon would not be able to exist in this manner, but we both felt that we should explore all possibilities. We also had begun to think of ways that we could deal with this demon from within the manor. Every possible solution seemed less of a solution and more of a compound of the issue.

A few minutes passed, and I looked at Percy, "Do you have a Bible?" He nodded as he stared at me blankly. "Then we will use that tomorrow before my wedding to clear the home. Surely with reading and prayer, we can drive this being out of the manor and it will no longer afflict anyone."

Percy seemed reluctant to agree to this idea, but he had little choice as nothing else seemed to be an efficient plan. We both nodded and agreed on this final course of action. Perhaps it would be better to clear the home ourselves than to wait for a priest to come from the north and take his time to clear the home. This was the least that we could do, and it didn't seem too complicated. Surely the minister didn't possess some power that we could not possess. Still, we both felt trepidation toward the idea of tussling with that foul being once more.

Eventually, our planning turned to events of the day again. We both debated the current state of the South and still could find time to puff away on our pipes. This day held so much wonder and happiness still. Lunch would not be served on this day as we had all eaten such a large breakfast, but I was sure that Percy would be able to have a delicious dinner with his family. Though I still was not sure what plans Percy would have for me. I did hope that I would be able to return to the manor tonight.

The thought hung heavy in my mind that I could attract the demon to myself to prevent the children in Percy's home from being targeted by this entity. I was not sure that I would be able to help in this way, but I had to try something. I felt that it was more likely that Percy would leave me with Mary and her family while he dealt with the manor. I hoped that this would not be the case as I was not sure that the demon would not seek to trap Percy within its world.

Though I knew that there would be nothing that I could say that would change Percy's mind from this course of action. I just had to hope that Percy would not do something so foolish. I had never known Percy to be a rash man, but when one's children are involved, then people have a tendency to do rash things. I would not allow this thought to fill my mind, however. I didn't wish for Percy to put himself in harm's way just for my account. I had to deal with this issue, and I trusted that Percy would know that he could not act without someone to assist him.

We both sat in silence for a moment until Chloe approached from the right side of the porch. She moved to where Percy was seated and kissed him passionately. "I have done all of the chores for now, my love. The children are still working in the house, and I have finished with Benjamin's clothes. I am going to plant some flowers with the servants."

Percy nodded and thanked his wife with another kiss. I also thanked her but without a kiss. She then turned and moved out toward the barn. I could tell that Percy didn't wish to lie to his wife or family, but he was worried for them. The look that he gave his wife as she left for the barn was one of regret. Somehow I felt that he regretted getting himself into this situation.

After some time of smoking on the porch and allow Percy to be in his own mind for a moment, I said, "I am sorry that you are involved in this, Percy. It was never my intention to bring you or your family into all of this. Please do not do anything without me. I fear that you might become trapped within the world that I had the other night. Can you promise that we will work diligently on this matter without being separated?"

Percy nodded and the replied, "Then I think that we should stay here and work on the manor rather than you going to visit with Mary."

Percy wouldn't even look me in the eye as he said that. He just sat forward in his chair and cradled his pipe in his hands. He was not going to allow anything to harm his family in all this situation. I could see that he had a face that was prepared for war. I knew that if I didn't agree to stay here and assist him, he was going to do something rash in this moment. His words had cut me deeply as I wished to see my future wife tonight, but I knew that this was just as important if not more so. After all, I had been the cause of all this. It was my family that allowed this evil into this world, and I felt that I had to pay for that sin. I had to atone for what had happened in the past to care for Percy and his family.

I sat in silence for some time and eventually answered Percy's request. "I will stay here tonight and we will deal with this situation. Allow me to gather my clothing and prepare myself for this situation." I knew that Mary would wonder where I was on this night, but given all that had happened, I had little choice. I knew in the end that she wouldn't be happy with me leaving Percy and his family to suffer now. Though I still felt that I could not tell her anything about all of this, especially when she was with her family.

I stood from my chair and walked off the porch and out into the yard. I knew that I would have to be swift as Percy was eager to destroy this entity. Though I hoped that his eagerness would not jeopardize our fight against this being. I gathered all strength that I could in my mind and moved toward the clothesline. My bag still lay on the platform. I retrieved the bag and checked the inside of it for anything that would wish to crawl into the compartment. This search revealed nothing.

I began immediately gathering my clothes and folding them. I then placed them within the bag. My thoughts turned to Mary. I was not worried that she would be upset with me at this point, but that she wouldn't understand when I told her that I didn't wish to share why I was not present this night. I felt so strongly, however, that I had to protect her innocence in this matter. That she couldn't know why everything had to be this way. Why she would not see her husband on this night and celebrate our coming marriage. In my mind I could hear clearly, "A man must do as he is called to do."

I immediately felt an emboldening feeling. I knew now that I must be resolute in my actions on this night, or nothing would be accomplished. I knew that I had to not have any sense of frustration or negativity within my mind or it would be exploited by this demon. Percy would also come to know this as I would have to tell him as well.

I finished collecting my clothes and moved back to where Percy was sat. The day had now moved to the evening, and my watch had revealed the time of three o'clock. I was amazed that the time had moved so quickly. It was then that I realized that Percy was not sat in his usual position. He had now moved to standing on the edge of the porch and looking over his property. I was not sure why he was doing this, but I decided that it was simply his nerves. I moved closer and said, "I would like to share with you, Percy, that we must be resolute with this situation and not overconfident. We must be grounded in our convictions. Otherwise, the demon may be able to defeat us once again."

Percy nodded but said nothing. He continued to look out toward the barn. I could see that he was now focused on being the end of this evil within the manor. He wanted as I did for a resolution and soon. Though nothing could dictate how effective that we would be in this situation. After all, we were only two men that had stumbled upon an evil that was thought to simply be a metaphor. We could not let this be all that we were in this moment. We had to press ourselves to be something more than what we had been. We both now had to rise to this occasion without fear or hatred. It was these emotions that fed this being and allowed it to act in any way that it wished toward us.

I stood with Percy for a moment longer as he smoked his way to the bottom of the bowl. He never took his eyes off the barn in the whole time that I stood with him. He was poised to annihilate evil in any way that he could. Moment after moment passed as Percy cleaned his pipe and placed it within his pocket. He turned to me in one motion and said, "We won't be taking the wagon to the manor. Let's get going."

I nodded and followed him as he moved out toward the road. Eventually we matched each other's speed and walked beside each other. The road was dusty in the summer heat and seemed to billow around us as we walked briskly down the road toward the home. I could see now that Percy had gone into the home and grabbed his Bible while I was preparing my bag of clothing. We both were ready for this now. Nothing would be held back. We were on a mission that would allow us to finally defeat this demon, and we could feel it now.

We approached the drive of the manor and could feel the air shift. Percy wasted no time and began moving slightly quicker than me to the front porch. I followed as well as I could to the manor but feared that Percy would reach the door before me and be separated. The world seemed to dim as I entered the manor and could have a look around the home. Everything was quiet, but we could both feel a disturbance within the manor. Something was not quite right about this place, and we both knew what had to be done. I departed Percy's side as he prepared himself for our venture. I placed the bag within my bedroom and then returned to Percy's side. He held out the Bible toward me, and I grasped it in my left hand. With a few flicks of the pages, I had turned to the passages in the Bible that I had remembered that the minister had read from the day before. I then began to read aloud as Percy completed each sentence. I was amazed with his knowledge of the Bible as he didn't need any reference to speak with confidence. Though I could tell that some passages gave him a struggle.

He and I moved through the foyer and toward the stairs. Nothing could prepare us any more than we had already been prepared. The sun had now moved to a bright yellow and orange color outside the home as the day began to fade away now. We both could feel a great tension rising within this space, but it did nothing to slow our words or our movements to the stairs. I began to climb the stairs in front of Percy, and he seemed to lean from around me and announce my words to the other portions of the home. We both moved in unison and gave nothing to chance. Each step that we took saw us being louder and louder with our speech.

We now knew that the air around us stirred with a negative energy. It felt oppressive and didn't seem to stop. Yet we pushed on deeper into the upper level. I held out my hand now as I said these words, and Percy and I had begun to chant the Bible passages as if performing an intense ritual. I continued to make motions with my hands to guide the demon to remove itself from this home.

After a few moments, the floor beneath our feet began to shake as we moved forward. We felt the earth begin to tremble with our words. Our focus in that moment couldn't be defeated. Not one thing in this world would be able to stop us. We were both extremely determined to defeat this thing once and for all. My mind was all consumed with thoughts of Mary and the Lord above.

I could feel an energy rushing all over my body as I continued with my words. I felt protection and a fierce rush of energy fill me. The world around me was no longer present as I continued onward. I could feel electricity moving to the tips of my fingers and being collected there. My fingers and skin tingled with such energy, and I could feel a peace come over me. I knew that Percy and I were really collecting our emotions into one place and only projecting the love of God over this home.

The ground continued to tremble beneath our feet as we continued from the stairs and down the left hallway. All the doors swung open in that moment and began slamming back and forth. Percy and I could not be stopped. I could feel no fear in that moment, simply a holy rage that filled my body and continued to flood outward into the world around me. It was an immense feeling that emanated outward to the house. I was poised to meet with this evil now and gaze into its eye as holy fire consumed every last thing of it. I moved into the first room as the door had stopped swinging back and forth just as I had approached it. I entered the room and continued the incantation from the Bible. Our right was now to cleanse this home, and cleanse we did. We moved from room to room and paused for nothing. At one moment, a door had closed to separate Percy and me. I simply turned and continued to speak aloud. The door simply opened for Percy, and we were united again. I cast my hand outward again and continued to cleanse this room.

Time passed slowly within the home, and I could understand that this demon was being backed into a corner. Light was beginning to flood into the home, and Percy and I were continuing to focus on our words. I felt as if we were pushing the evil back. Farther and farther into the home we went until we had come to the other hallway. We didn't stop. We moved down the hallway and continued to chant the words of the Bible. This hallway didn't give us any doors that were slamming, but it seemed that the floors trembled even more now than they had before. It seemed that the home was coming apart as we continued. Percy and I were now moving into the far room that was large and had once bore witness to my aunt swiftly moving about the room.

Even this room didn't stop us. The door slammed behind us as we entered, and it seemed that the windows had grown dark and cold. Our breath was white and wispy as we continued to speak. Even the coldest day was not as cold as this was now. Percy and I continued to move in unison. We were prepared to deal with anything that would come toward us. Though I doubted that it would do any good as I could feel this energy welling up inside of me and moving all around us into the room.

Soon, Percy and I turned and began moving back toward the door. We approached slowly so as to stick together in this moment. Then I felt as if a wall stood before us. I could no longer move forward, and Percy seemed to turn to face behind us. He continued to chant louder and louder. This was the time that we had waited for in the home. This demon was determined to not allow us to reach its space in the attic. Eventually I broke my chant and yelled, "Free my passage, devil! In the name of God, I command you!"

With those words, the wall that blocked us moved away. I began to chant again and then started moving forward slowly.

Percy and I moved down the hallway and into each room again. Percy and I would move at a slow pace still. We moved past the door to the bedroom that held the passage into the attic and continued around the banister and out onto the balcony. I found it odd that even the balcony seemed cold and oppressive. The sun was blackened slightly now, and I couldn't see anything resembling life beyond this darkness. This did not deter me in any way as I continued onward with my chanting. I moved back into the home and around to the door to the bedroom. I was unable to enter at first as the door had slammed shut in front of my face. I still didn't stop. I touched the door with my hands, and it slowly began to open. Percy moved into the room behind me and immediately moved over and shut the door. We both anticipated that this thing would come out to meet us. Though we were proven wrong as nothing appeared and moved out into the room.

We moved into the closet and began facing up into the hole that led into the attic. Without speaking to each other, we both moved in one fluid motion. Percy braced the ladder as I climbed into the attic with the Bible still held in my left hand. My right hand was stretched out before me. My mind was focused on the attic and the darkness within. I didn't even realize that I had stepped into the attic without any assistance. I moved as if I were walking on a cloud. Percy seemed to do the same as I had not seen him enter the attic, but he simply rose into the attic space. We both continued onward into the attic. We went deeper and deeper still until we had reached the front of the home. I could see no light coming into the attic through the windows in the front of the home.

Percy and I were inseparable in this moment as we continued to move. I could see swirls of darkness hanging in the air all around us. When I would touch the darkness, they would simply dissipate from around us. Our chanting now had begun to grow louder as we seemed to be yelling out all the passages. The ground immediately began to shake as we neared the far corner of the attic. The shaking was so vigorous now that I feared that Percy and I would fall through the attic. As we grew closer and closer, there seemed to be a force that had begun pushing against us. I struggled to move farther. Then the force seemed to break, and I began to close in on the corner of the attic.

Just as we had reached the area and I had begun to reach out to touch the wall, there was a loud screech as if something were dying. The force returned and shoved Percy and me back to the opening to the attic. I quickly regained my footing and could now see this demon moving toward me from the corner of the attic. Darkness filled the space behind it as it moved along. I felt the darkness moving closer and closer. I held out my hand and resumed chanting as Percy moved to my right side and did the same. Our words seemed to be absorbed by this demon. We held our ground against all odds and didn't dare move from our positions within the attic.

In an instant this being held its hand above its head and swiped toward us as it reached our area. It then screeched again and broke into strands of dark clouds that flowed around us as if a bubble and enveloped us in protection. I felt power enter my body as this happened, and I continued to chant. We saw the darkness swirl all around us and moved back to the far corner. The demon materialized again and then began crawling across the ceiling toward us again. Percy held his hand out and upward as I continued to hold my same stance. The demon then dropped to the ground from above us and tried to break our concentration. We then heard a loud screech as it broke into more clouds of smoke and wafted about the attic.

We still couldn't be stopped. Our focus was now too great for the beast. It had no choice but to grow weaker with each attack. I could now feel my energy draining slightly, and I was sure that Percy's was as well. He looked to me and I nodded toward the corner. We both moved in the same positioning toward the corner. Hell would not stop us now. We were determined to be triumphant. The darkness backed farther and farther into the corner as we moved ever forward. I could feel some resistance but not enough to stop us in this moment. I continued onward until we had reached the corner of the room. I pushed harder and harder against the resisting force and reached my hand outward. I could now feel that I was reaching deep into a deep, frozen ocean. I could now feel the darkness that I had felt the night that I had been moved into that other realm. The feeling was wretched and horrible. I could feel nothing but hate and fear.

I reached deeper into this darkness until it broke apart and wafted about the room. I went farther and farther until I had reached the corner of the attic. Once I felt the wood against my fingers, the screeching started again but so loud that it felt deafening. I still chanted as I kept my hand on the wood. I could feel the hatred and fear lift from this place. I could feel that the home was becoming lighter and less clogged with emotion. My heart beat swiftly within my chest and seemed as if it would burst forth and into the room. I felt the darkness leave this place now, and I was not sure that I would be able to continue. The energy that I had felt was now leaving me. I closed my chant with, "I pray God cleanse this home! Amen!"

The power that I had once felt now left me completely. My fingers and body still tingled, and I was sure that I was feeling the energy of the Holy Spirit within me. I was consumed with a rage from God no longer. The attic was brighter than I had ever seen. I could truly feel peace at this moment. I could truly feel that I had been saved from this being once again. I removed my hand from the corner of the attic and turned to Percy. He was smiling now and seemed so relieved that we had been able to drive this demon out of the home.

He and I turned and left the attic. As soon as my feet were back in the bedroom, I could now feel all my energy leave my body. I collapsed onto the floor and didn't move at all. I could now feel that there was no longer a trembling to the floor now. Percy reached out a hand to me and helped me to my feet again. I was no longer capable as I once was. The room was warm and bright. The home was now leaving nothing to chance. There was no discernible evil anywhere within the home.

Percy and moved back to the foyer, and I bade him good night. Without any other words, Percy waved goodbye and moved out of the door and down the road. I knew that I would be hungry on this night, but I couldn't muster any energy to leave the manor again and return to the farmhouse. I would spend this night sleeping and resting for my wedding tomorrow. I was prepared for anything but now knew that I would have to relax to regain my own energy. I moved back into the bedroom and simply fell into a deep sleep without realizing anything else. I simply blacked out in my bed.

12

REVELRY

The next morning came swiftly. It seemed in my mind that I had only just fallen asleep. I didn't even feel the world slipping away as I drifted off into a deep sleep. I was also unsure what time of the morning it had been. Something told me that this rest was not a direct sign that this demon had been vanquished, but I was exhausted from thinking about it. My only thoughts on this day was that I would marry my wife tonight and we would return here and prepare for our trip to New York. Even if she was not prepared to do so, I could buy any clothing or other possessions needed. I still couldn't be sure that she wouldn't have many bags.

I needed to prepare for anything for tonight with bringing Mary here for us to start the rest of our lives. Our lives were about to merge in a very significant way, and I didn't wish to disappoint my wife on our first night together. I immediately climbed out of bed and dressed in my best suit for tonight. I had understood that I didn't wish to work outside or ever sit in the sun for too long so that I could be as clean and neat as possible for this evening. I continued to dress myself as I could hear the rumble of wheels turning and coming closer to my direction. I was not understanding why I was hearing this and decided that it was simply someone passing by the manor. I relegated these sounds to be unrelated. I slipped my coat to my suit on over my vest and made sure that my pocket watch was secure in my vest pocket.

I moved quickly from the bedroom and out onto the porch. My nerves were getting the best of me this morning, and I found my mind wandering to thoughts of Mary not being satisfied with our plans for the day. I knew, with all rationality, that this wouldn't be the case. Nothing could be further from the truth. Mary was a very realistic woman who didn't hold very many expectations of what her life should contain.

I only wished for the best for Mary and my life. I wondered to what end that we would be affected when leaving North Carolina and returning to New York. My worries were that she would be so put off by the distance we would need to travel. Though I was sure that she would enjoy seeing the countryside from the window of the train. I also knew that she would enjoy not having to take a much longer time to ride over dirt roads and small curvy pathways through mountains in order to arrive in the north. This would encourage a sense of wonder within Mary's mind. I held fears that I knew were due to my anxiety for the wedding this evening. I would have to continue to explain this to myself more and more as the wedding approached.

I could feel my mind sinking further into doubt the more that I thought about the day's events. Nothing would be worse than what I had already faced since arriving here in North Carolina, however. I knew this to be a deeper truth. I tried my best to focus on nothing else, but I would occasionally drift to the thoughts of losing my sanity over this wedding.

Eventually I heard a rapping at the door. The sound instantly brought me back into focus. I was now assured that someone had arrived and had not simply rode off in the opposite direction as I had thought before. Though I wasn't sure who it could be at the door. I hadn't alerted anyone to pick me up from the manor, and I knew that it couldn't be Percy as he would have walked around to the window. My curiosity got the better of me as I began moving to the front door. I wondered why someone would have been lurking around my door all this time in silence. Perhaps it was Mary's family that had sent someone to retrieve me from the manor and take me to their home. This would have been the best case that I could consider. The worst option would be that this demon and its spirits had infested the home again. I chuckled at this thought as Percy and I had seen a clear sign that this demon was now gone. I could now rest easy with this thought.

I opened the door and looked out into the day. I could see a man standing off to the right of the door. I had no idea who it could be as I had never seen this man in my life. He had a very clean-cut hairstyle with no facial hair. Nothing gave any indication that this man was even from this town as he was dressed far too well. He wore a fine suit that seemed to be made of silk or a high caliber of linen. I was confused by this man.

I opened the door the rest of the way and held out my hand to shake his. "Good morning, sir. May I help you?"

The man began laughing on the porch. I was now shaken. Who was this man, and why would he be simply laughing at me on my porch? I was a little irritated by this.

"You don't recognize me, Benjamin?"

I was now completely stunned. How did this man know my name? What illusion was afflicting my eyes? I had never seen this man in my life, but he acted as if I should recognize him at all. I was certain that this man could clearly see my confusion upon his face. Though I was not sure in this moment as he was simply bent over on my porch laughing heartily. Then my mind sprang into action.

I had heard this hearty laugh before. I wasn't sure, at first, where but I knew this laugh. I then realized what was happening and said, "Ben?"

He stood upright and wiped his eyes. "Yes, sir. I am sorry for laughing at you, but I told Mary and her father that you wouldn't even recognize me at all. Now I am certain of it." Ben continued to chuckle slightly as he regained his composure. "I thought that I would retrieve you well before the wedding so that Martin and I can speak with you."

I nodded and said, "Thank you, sir. I would gladly accompany you and speak with you and Martin."

Ben swiftly replied, "Great! Are you ready to go?"

I nodded and we moved out into the drive of the home. The door was firmly shut and locked. My bedroom in the manor was tidy and ready for sleeping that night as well. I was completely capable of leaving the manor without worry for any cleanliness.

Ben stood back from the wagon for a moment and said, "I am amazed that this manor looks so different now. I can see the beauty within the home. I have never noticed the grandeur and beauty of the home." Ben looked at me and nodded with amazement.

I smiled and felt a sense of pride in the fact that Percy and I were able to cleanse the home successfully now. I climbed onto the seat of the wagon that Ben had driven here to retrieve me from the home. He seemed to take the driver's seat gracefully as if he were an angel floating upward and on the seat. I was impressed with his silence and grace. He didn't say anything further to me in that moment and simply snapped the reins. The wagon lurched forward and then moved quickly toward the road. I looked back toward the manor expecting to see something within the windows, but I could see nothing in the window now. I felt a sense of peace about leaving the home and going with Ben to his home.

Nothing stood out to me that gave a sense of dread or worry about bringing Mary with me to the manor. I knew now that peace could truly be obtained while I still relied on myself to achieve something. I felt so much more capable than I had when I arrived. I had faced down evil and been able to conquer it and drive it from its home in the manor. I had succeeded in taking control of my destiny in this situation. I felt rather comfortable now. I could feel secure in leaving the manor and return later without worrying about being assaulted by an overwhelming negativity. This was the moment that I had been waiting for the whole of last week. Though I was a little irritated that it took the majority of my stay to accomplish this feat.

The wagon rolled slowly onward toward town now. Ben didn't even slow the horses as we took the left turn and began moving into town from the opposite side that Percy and I would usually enter town. I could see that Ben had a strong bond with his horses as he never really guided them with the reins but with clicks of his mouth and slight yelps. I knew this to be true as we took a right to move back toward his home. He let out a sharp yelp and the horses began gently and smoothly taking the turn. I didn't even feel a single bump in the road as we moved along. I was amazed to say the least. Nothing could have accounted for this in my mind. I was so used to Percy's wagon bumping along over the road that it was a welcomed sensation to feel the wagon smoothly rolling along. I could ride along in comfort this morning.

The sun had begun drowning the town in its light now. I knew that the time was approximately eight in the morning. I hoped that I would be able to eat at their home this morning as I was famished. Not eating dinner last night was not something that I had been used to in my normal life. I welcomed the change, but my stomach did not. I was now ready to drink my coffee and relax over a smoke. I also wished to partake in delicious morning foods. A selection fit for a king as I had had after eating dinner with Mary's family. Nothing could satisfy me more now than to have a breakfast banquet. I was sure that this would be the case to celebrate. Something told me that I would barely be able to stand by the time that we were being married on this day. The feeling simply told me that there would be enough wine to drown the state at our wedding. Not to mention the amount of wine that would be drunk before the wedding even began.

This thought gave me pleasure in itself. I would welcome the chance to celebrate many things on this day. After all, I could feel that my life had changed for the better in a broad way. Every aspect of my life had improved, and I could not help but feel that I should celebrate this as much as I could before things changed again.

These thoughts continued to control my mind as we rode farther out of town. Though instead of approaching the farmhouse directly, we took a left before approaching the property. The horses turned with a simple click of Ben's mouth and a slight whistle. We were now riding past the farmhouse and moving toward the back of the property. Ben asked, "Could you believe that I had to build this road before anyone would come by to drop off the lumber for the winery? I was outraged. It took weeks of tearing up the soil here and filling it in then packing it down. Another week went into pouring the gravel onto the surface and another week to dig a drain trench along the roadside."

I was confused about this myself. "What was the reason that they had you do all that for the lumber?"

He looked to his left for a moment then shook his head in frustration. "They told me that the ground would sink to bring it all in one load. I told them to bring it in several loads, and they simply refused. I was irate, and I am sure that my wife didn't appreciate having to hear about it constantly. Poor woman heard about it until it was completed. Then she heard about it until I had focused again on building the winery. Though I suppose that it is better this way. Now my customers have a comfortable road to ride upon as they approach the winery."

I nodded. "Perhaps it was supposed to happen that way so that you wouldn't have to do it all later."

Ben gave me a look that was filled with annoyance. I could see that having to do all that work for the road was much more of a process than he had let on. Ben then shrugged his shoulders and returned his sight forward.

The road was well built and seemed to be perfectly level amid the rolling landscape of the rest of the property. I could see that a gentle mist hung over the area and the sun had not risen enough to illuminate this area. There still seemed to be a gray darkness that filled the sky here. The mist seemed to waft about as if having a mind of its own. I was sure that this winery had been shrouded by the mist so as to keep it secret. The only thing that could be seen from here was the slight row of trees to the right of us. I saw this as a very relaxing sight even though it seemed as if rain would be sure to follow. I hoped that this was not the case and that the sun would clear up any clouds as simply a part of the mist that gently billowed about on the ground.

As we moved closer, however, it seemed that the sun just had not reached this area of the property. I was relieved to see that we rode through the mist and into a clearing around the winery. Ben pulled the wagon up to a large building that had been placed beside the winery and stepped down from the wagon as it came to a stop. He quickly unhitched the horses as he implored that he would be able to do it on his own. He then led the horses into the building and moved them into their own stall. He latched the stall and left the wagon outside of the building. I could tell that he was not worried about any rain that might fall in this place. Perhaps he knew all too well that this mist would hang over this area frequently. We moved back toward the winery and entered the main door. The building was huge and contained many large barrels of wine.

We stopped in the doorway as Ben pointed everything out to me. "On the right and left of the room, we have the fermenting barrels. We pour the mixture into these barrels and turn them into a sour. That is a word that means a pulpy liquid that we can use to begin the wine-making process.

"The sour is then poured off into smaller barrels and sugar is added. The whole process takes a while. Once we mix in the sugar, then the barrels are moved to the floors above in order to ferment over time. I started this whole process seven years ago. Our wine has not reached a pedigree yet, but we are quickly approaching such a state with the more wine that is made and not sold."

I gave Ben a puzzled look and replied, "I thought that you would like for the wine to sell."

He nodded and replied, "Some batches, yes. The other batches need more time to ferment and make a richer blend in their barrels. This will give them a richer bouquet over time until they reach a level of pedigree. Then we can bottle and sell them for more money as they have a more refined taste. Some wineries have been able to reach a pedigree over hundreds of years and have wines that have been in their stock for as long.

"This makes the wine highly desirable. Then they will sell for a much higher price. We rotate the stock and make sure to separate our pedigree batches with the quicker yield to make sure that we can keep a constant flow of money coming in. We also provide food here as a few of our servants here are very accomplished cooks. They usually prepare delicious courses that will pair well with the wines that we have chosen for the day. I have held many parties here and gatherings. I always sell a lot of wine.

"If I continue this way, then I would have enough money to retire from farming and allow someone else to manage the farm. This is my dream. I will then be able to market and sell much more wine to increase my business. I love farming, but I know that I don't wish to spend my whole life slowly farming myself to death. It is a hard life, and I would be willing to allow someone else to live in the farmhouse and maintain the farm for free if I were to be able to receive some goods from the farm for the winery.

"Then I would be able to lift other farmers and their families up from poverty. Let someone else deal with the headache and sell the goods from the farm for their own. Nothing would be easier for me to do in several years."

I was simply amazed at the sight of Ben's operation within the winery. I could tell that this was his true calling as he seemed to have spent many years investing time and money into the winery and his farm. I welcomed the ability to one day travel here and partake of the wine. Though I was sure that he would be providing quite a selection of wine for my wedding today. I was excited to see that I would be able to try his wine further and hopefully be given a chance to taste his more pedigree wine. Nothing could make me happier. I would be able to marry the woman that I loved and also be able to partake in the best wine that North Carolina had to offer from Hillsborough.

Ben motioned for me to follow him up a flight of stairs onto the next floor. Once I reached the upper landing of the stairs, I could see that this winery was truly immense. Barrel after barrel of wine had been stacked neatly along the walls all around the winery save for the cooking and dining area that I now approached from the stairs. Martin was seated on the far side of the table from me. I approached the table and greeted him and shook his hand.

We all sat at the table as our breakfast was beginning to be delivered to the table. This setting was perfect to have breakfast. The lovely fragrance of wine hung in the air all around us. I was hungry, but now even more so with all the delicious smells. The cooks brought dish after dish out and placed them on the table. I could see that all the usual meats of breakfast were presented along with eggs and toast. Also some fish had been lovingly prepared and grilled over the fire. Everything smelled delicious alongside all the potatoes and bowls of sauces. I was overwhelmed with hunger now as I stared across the table as if I had never seen any food. I was now assured in my feelings that I had felt earlier. Wine was being brought out and placed upon the bar to my left in buckets of ice. There was a large selection of wine, and I desired to sample it all. I looked to my right and said, "Surely this wine is for the wedding."

Ben smiled and said, "No. We are going to sample some wine for your big day. Mary is at the farmhouse being dressed and pampered for her wedding, so I thought that we would drink until it is time to go to the wedding."

I smiled and said nothing. What could I say in a moment such as this? I had been given the opportunity to partake of all the wine that I could handle in one morning, and I was not about to disappoint my host. Though I didn't desire to be drunk, I was sure that I could drink until content. I am often never content.

Martin, Ben, and I began eating slowly. We immediately opened a bottle of wine and also began drinking. No time was wasted in celebrating my wedding on this morning. We couldn't resist to share stories about our past and to welcome ourselves to the idea of more wine. Ben had even taken the time to begin a collection of whiskey that had been given to him from a wealthy client of his winery. We held off from drinking such stout liquor until we had made a good dent into the wines. I was sure that I would either die from drinking too much or drink just enough to have no fear in front of the crowd of people that would attend.

I immediately moved to buttering some bread and crunching into it. I also ripped the sausage apart and chewed the soft meat slowly so as to take in all the flavors that had been lovingly cooked into the dish. This was the epitome of joy for my vacation to Hillsborough. I knew that this would mark a beautiful beginning to my betrothal to Mary. We all now sat in silence as we grazed upon the whole table full of food. We all would eat a round of food and then talk as we drowned the food in wine. I had the feeling that my stomach had begun to swim. Wine and food alike sloshed about with every move that I made. I could feel my body begin to warm a bit as we all shared our fourth cup of wine.

Ben chimed into the conversation with, "How is it living in New York?"

I smiled and thought for a moment and said, "I think that it is a great place to live for me. My life has been much easier living within the city. Everything is such a luxury. I don't have to grow food, I can walk to anywhere in the city on paved streets, the shops are always open during bathe day, and I am comfortable to walk in the parks any time that I wish for a more rural setting. I am pleased to have such a life."

Martin and Ben seemed enthralled. "Tell us more," Martin said.

"I have lived in the city for many years now. I have been able to have anything that I wish at a moment's notice. I especially enjoy having access to foods and goods that are not sourced in America. Things that we cannot grow or make domestically. There are so many different foods and ways to prepare foods. There are always spices that I have never seen at the market or vegetables that I have never tried.

"Restaurants are always preparing the best food. No one is able to say that we don't have a plethora of different choices when choosing something to do within the city. Public areas have games to play and sights to see that I have found nowhere else in my life. In a moment I can travel outside the city and move out into the country to enjoy mountains and rolling hills.

"A lot of my life has been exploring the city recently, but I have other things that I can do as well. I also have the freedom to charter a ship to anywhere in Europe that I wish to go. I love to live in an urban setting. It is a very different world than North Carolina. Though I have really enjoyed myself these few days."

Both men seemed to be amazed that I would have such a life. I invited them to come to New York when time allowed and see it for themselves. I was sure that a man as cultured as Ben would love to visit the city for a change and not be confined to this area of North Carolina forever. After all, he was a man that would enjoy traveling in order to market his wines effectively. Perhaps New York could provide Ben with a resource to advertise to spread his brand further. I had no doubt in my mind that anyone would love the lifestyle that one would find in a city like New York City. Though I was sure that Ben would still enjoy his way of life in North Carolina.

Breakfast was delicious and I could not want for more. Every dish was lovingly prepared in such a way as to make the senses overwhelmed. I could not properly describe the scents that I smelled. The taste was even more as I partook of the delicious food. Ben and Martin and I all sat around the table and continued to share stories. I could not even begin to understand all that Mary was facing now. I knew that she was excited and worried as well, but I could do nothing to ease her fears.

I knew that time alone would be able to ease us into this new life together. Though I simply wished that I had the power to do that myself. Martin and Ben, however, didn't seem to have any issues with these thoughts as they continued to celebrate. I was immediately struck by how quickly they had returned to drinking. I was sure now that I would not be sober for my own wedding. The thought crossed my mind to simply stop drinking, but I didn't wish to be rude or to refuse the hospitality of Ben and Martin in this case. I feared that they might find an offense with this and not give me their blessing. In that moment I reasoned that I would drink just a little more and then stop. If they were to be irate with my refusal, then they would simply have to be upset. How could I deny myself in the company of others? I drank another two glasses of wine then stopped drinking. This seemed to bother Martin and Ben after a few moments and a few more glasses of wine.

"You don't like the wine, Benjamin?" Ben asked.

I shook my head and replied, "No, sir. I simply don't wish to be drunk while at my wedding. I doubt that Mary would be too happy with me."

They both chuckled heartily. "Are you sure that you want to give into her demands this early in your life together?" Martin said.

I shook my head and laughed at the same time. "Nothing could be further from the truth. I simply wish to have class when I am in front of all of those people and accepting the love that I have so desired from Mary," I said emphatically.

Both men stopped laughing immediately. "We are sorry, Benjamin. This is your wedding day, and we shall not be rude to you since you have decided to take this noble path for love," Ben said.

Martin slapped the table and began to laugh again heartily. I could see that both of them adored hassling me in this moment. I also couldn't help but chuckle a bit myself. I didn't wish to push the issue further as I didn't know enough about either men nor their past to be able to make a witty comment.

Instead I simply sat silent for a moment and watched as they both continued to laugh and drink. Eventually both men paused their laughter and seemed to gain a tinge of seriousness. "Do you think that Mary will enjoy a life in the city?" Martin asked.

I thought for a moment and then said, "I am not sure. Even if I knew the answer, I don't think that I would take her word." Martin seemed perturbed with my answer as I added, "I mean to say that New York City is something that has to be experienced to know whether one enjoys living in the city. Mary has never been in that situation, so I cannot say."

Martin seemed to accept this answer as he didn't give off a hostile face. Relief washed over me in that moment. I understood the finer points of civility and didn't wish to cross either man, especially when they had consumed enough wine for three bottles to be empty. This was not small feat as all three bottles were the biggest bottles that I had ever seen in my life. I was sure that both men would have a harder time at the wedding because of the drink they still consumed.

"Thank you for the wine, Ben. I have enjoyed it very much. You truly know your craft," I said.

Ben stopped for a moment and then said, "Thank you, Benjamin. I am glad that you enjoyed the wine. Though I am not sure that I should let children drink anymore." Both men erupted into hearty laughter. I was not sure what to do in this moment save for the smile that sat upon my face. Nothing could be sure when these two men were drinking.

"That is extremely humorous, gentlemen," I said. "Though I am sure that you have forgotten that only children cannot control their own consumption of food and drink." My smile widened, and I started chuckling. Neither man knew how to respond. I thought for a moment that I had offended both men. They both looked down toward the table and then each other. Martin and Ben then began to laugh hysterically. I was sure now that they had both led me on. Nothing seemed to bother either man, and I truly understood that they loved their drink. Who was I to judge, however? I was sure there would be those who would criticize me for smoking as I did.

I could now see that the sun had risen quite a bit in the time that we had been drinking. The window to my right framed a most beautiful sight. The gentle hills beyond the road were basking and glowing in a flood of sunlight. Each blade of grass seemed to be a crystal refracting light back toward my eyes. I could not imagine a more beautiful sight in my life. I then produced my pocket watch and could see that the time was now approaching nine thirty. This made my heart race just a little more. I also knew now that I was beginning to fall into a drunken state as my hands felt numb. Then came the realization that I had not been able to share any information with Percy about what time the wedding would take place. I looked at Ben, who was now sipping down another glass of wine. "I am sorry to ask this now, but has anyone invited Mr. Merivel to the wedding?" I asked.

Both men looked up from setting their glasses on the table. "I invited Mr. Merivel the other night when you proposed to Mary." Ben was confident in his answer then added, "I also saw Percy standing on his porch when I arrived to bring you here this morning."

I was now confident that everything would go well this day. I didn't even have to worry about inviting anyone to the gathering. Though if Ben had invited anyone, then I wondered how many people would arrive for the wedding. Only time would tell now. I simply had to be patient and see the outcome. If something were to go wrong, then I could not be blamed as I was not the one to plan and put everything together for the wedding. This gave me some relief in itself, but I still felt nervous over the ceremony. I was aware that this thought seemed cowardly, but I was not going to hide my own thoughts from myself. I simply didn't wish to voice such things to anyone from Mary's family as I was sure that they had put a lot of time and energy into planning this wedding. I just knew that I would be happy with anything that had been prepared. The only thing that remained to be seen was how Mary would react. Though I was sure that she would be even more heightened today.

My mind stopped focusing on the wedding, eventually. I could not sit in the company of Martin and Ben and not have to worry about their impression of me. I knew that there would be no reason that they would wish to think anything less of me. I wouldn't wish to give them a reason, but I knew that I would not. The chair upon which I sat was comfortable in every way. I could really relax now and know that I was in good hands. Nothing would be out of place.

The chair was made of a sturdy wooden frame that had been curved backward toward the top of the backing of the chair. The cushions that gave the chair comfort had been prepared well. I couldn't even feel that the cushions had even given under my weight when sitting. I felt comfortable in a different way now. Not in a general manner, but I was completely relaxed in the chair. I was able to place all my trust in this sturdy furniture. Though I now noticed that this level of comfort and care had been put into every aspect of the winery. The winery might have been large, but there was a certain comfort with the building and everything in it. I was satisfied to know that I could have such a place to visit upon any return to visit Mary's family. I hoped that Ben's business would grow and allow him to achieve his life's work. I could think of no better outcome for Ben in this moment.

Time passed quickly as we all sat and talked at the table in the winery. Wine was being passed around the table and consumed very quickly. I simply didn't allow myself to be included in these actions. Though some of the servants had now begun to drink with Martin and Ben. I was content to allow the servants to take my place in the drinking. The day began to move quickly as I was being carried away by Ben's wagon toward the home once again. Martin was sitting off the back of the wagon and seemed to be holding on to the wood firmly. I could tell that Ben and he had been drinking too much. They both seemed to not be able to sit still in their seat. I was amused by this but wasn't sure what the other guests would think of this. I wasn't sure what I should do in this instance, but I surely felt that I should allow them to go to the wedding as they were now. Surely they would be able to control themselves enough to not be in the way of the wedding.

Ben steered the wagon toward the main entrance to the property and circled around to the front porch. He looked at me firmly. "Go in there and let my wife know that I am returning the wagon to the barn," Ben said.

I nodded and stepped off the seat quickly. I could see that Martin had simply leaned forward and tried to not fall as he thudded to the ground. He then staggered toward the front porch and through the door. I would have walked with him so that he didn't seem so drunk, but I was not given the chance. I just hoped that no one would notice, but it would be difficult for that to happen. I simply moved into the home as slowly and cautiously as I could. I didn't wish to see my beautiful wife until she had taken her place in the wedding. I walked across the porch and into the house. People had just started to move into place for the wedding. Everyone was being seated as quickly as possible. I wasn't sure when all these people had arrived or if they had been at the farmhouse since early this morning. I preferred to not think about it, however, as I didn't mean to not be here to greet everyone. I still was not sure of the customs for marriage in this town, but I was sure that I could have been doing something other than drinking all morning. I was just glad that I was not as drunk as Ben and Martin. That would not have been well.

Mary's aunt stood just outside the back door and motioned for me to come to her. I did as she was motioning. She pulled me off to the right of the door and said, "What in the hell have you three been doing this morning?"

I stood motionless for a moment. "I am sorry, ma'am. Ben wished for us to all share breakfast and a drink," I replied reluctantly.

Ben was now wandering into the backyard. He gazed at me, and I motioned for him to seat himself quietly. His wife was too busy scolding me. "Why would you three think it was acceptable to drink this heavily on a wedding day? I cannot believe that you would go along with this. What happened?" she exclaimed. Everyone was turning and looking in our direction.

"I do apologize, but I think that everyone can hear you. We had some wine and breakfast before we came here today. I am sorry that you weren't informed, but I am not drunk, nor should I be on this day," I replied sternly.

Mary's aunt now stood in silence. "I am sorry, Benjamin. At least tell me where Martin and Ben have gone," she said.

I could tell that she regretted speaking with me so harshly. I smiled and said, "Ben is being seated as we speak on the far side of the yard, and I have no idea where Martin is now. Perhaps he is visiting Mary."

The woman looked as if she had been witness to a ghost. Her face was pale, and she simply turned and walked away sheepishly. I had not raised my voice, but I now realized that I had been forceful in my speech and choice of words. I just hoped now that she would be able to forgive me. I also hoped that she wouldn't wish to deliver my actions to Mary's attention. This would have been the worst-case scenario. My future wife would now have another worry in her mind. I didn't wish to be more of a problem than a solution. My only true concern now was locating Martin.

I dared not enter the home again and move any further within the space. That really would startle everyone and leave cause for someone to say something. I just wished for my life to be peaceful now and for everyone to enjoy the wedding as I was sure that Mary and I would be doing the same thing. The one desire in my heart was that Martin wouldn't add to the problem. If he even realized that he had a problem.

Just as my thoughts had turned to that of finding Martin, he emerged from the home. He seemed much better now. I could tell that he wasn't staggering almost at all. "Everything all right, Martin?" I asked.

He smiled and moved out to where I stood. "My wife saw to it that I sobered up. Cold water over your face has a tendency to clear up any inebriation," Martin said.

I smiled and shook my head as I knew that he had fought with his wife. I was now looking at a man who had stated that he didn't worry about what his wife thought. This was a man who had been defeated when testing his own words. This gave me satisfaction. I stood in my same position until I could see that everyone had been seated. I then strolled out from the back of the home and took my place in front of the minister. I knew that I had to stand facing the home as I didn't want to miss the sight of Mary emerging from the home in her dress. I knew that she wouldn't be wearing anything fancy, but she was a woman who could wear the most simple things and still look stunning.

The sight of her truly stimulated my vision. I had no other desire than to see her in her most beautiful form than I had ever seen her. I could also feel that others were thinking the same as they turned their attention toward the back of the farmhouse. Three musicians sat off to the side of the minister. They all began playing their music, which sounded much more like a waltz than anything. It was an unconventional sound, but I enjoyed it. One man strummed a guitar. Another played an instrument that I had never witnessed at all. He played it similarly to a guitar but in a different way entirely as well. I was intrigued by this.

Before I could continue, however, I could see that Martin had taken his place on the back porch. He was poised to receive Mary into his arms and walk her toward her next step into destiny. I was ready to see her. I was ready to receive her commitment and love for the rest of my life. She would be the woman that I had waited all my life to meet. She would be the greatest companion that any man could know. I looked about to make sure that I was stood in the proper place. I even looked down to check that my feet were planted with the proper width. I also checked my positioning in relation to Minister Bryant.

Before any more time could pass, Mary emerged from the home and was guided to the back of the pews in which everyone sat. I dared not look at first but couldn't resist. Mary was beautiful in her white dress. It was a simple-made dress but had flowers stuck into the fabric that ran across her chest. The bottom of the dress flowed down and back with a thin fabric. The rest of the skirt was now shown to be much shorter. It barely covered her ankles as it flowed down from the rest of her. She wore a tiara of flowers and carried a bouquet in her hands. I could see a large smile stretched across her face. I had never seen Mary so satisfied in my life. Her beauty amazed me and truly held my attention. Nothing could take my focus off her for a moment. She walked slowly toward me with Martin wrapping his arm around hers. It seemed like an eternity for me to wait to receive my wife into my arms. Time stood still as Mary moved closer and closer to me.

My mind froze and focused in on the moment that her arm outstretched and she placed her hand in mine. I nodded to Martin and smiled. He did the same and then moved off to his seat beside Mary's mother. This moment held true love and passion as the minister began to speak. I held on to Mary's hands gently as we stood looking into each other's eyes.

I wasn't even sure that the minister had begun to speak. I was drawn deep into Mary's gaze. Her eyes had now changed to a light hazel color. She was so beautiful that I didn't wish to forget this sight for the rest of my days. I could also see that Mary felt the same toward me as well. Her eyes were glued to mine. Not a care in this world could break our concentration on each other. After a moment I heard her say, "I do."

Her words were so gentle and harmonious that it sounded as if she were singing them. I eventually heard the same question posed to me, to which I replied, "I do."

Mary seemed to jump slightly at my response. I knew that her heart had fluttered at the words that I spoke in commitment to our love. She was taken aback that I had spoken so quickly as well. I could see that she had doubted that we would move this far into a life together, but she was mistaken.

I continued to smile at her until the minister had closed his sermon. Everyone joined him in prayer for our relationship and our future together.

"Dear Lord, allow these two to share a beautiful and fruitful life together. May their hearts and minds be joined forever as their spirits have come to be on this day. May you pour down your eternal blessings upon these lovers in faithfulness and love forever. Amen!" Minister Bryant prayed.

Before anything else happened, Mary and I fell into a warm embrace and kissed each other again. No one could have told me otherwise in that moment or stopped me. I was dead set on setting our love in stone with that kiss. We were now married, and neither of us knew what that had meant until now. The world seemed different. It seemed that we had both begun to realize that this marriage was important to us. We both had to understand each other in all things. We both had to strive together in order to bring our world and love into one being.

I felt that it was important now for Mary to know something about the events over the past week. She needed to understand why I had been so distracted before, why I had been so distant. I also felt that she would need to know as my wife in case we were plagued by this being yet again. I had not wished for this to be the case but felt it better to leave nothing to chance.

I took Mary's hand in mine and led her back toward the end of the pews. A small cart had been moved in front of our path. We both climbed into the back of the wagon and began rolling toward the barn. I was confused as to why this would be. Mary informed me that this was where we would eat for our reception. Everyone would gather and eat with us as they all welcomed us into married life. We rolled up to the outside of the barn and stepped off the cart. Mary guided me into a shed that was beside the barn. She immediately shut the door and began taking off her flower tiara. I could see now that the cloth that draped behind her was not a part of her dress but rather her tiara. I found this very intuitive and ingenious.

She placed the tiara on a coat rack that stood behind her. She then fixed her hair into such a position that you could no longer tell that anything had been placed upon her head. Her dark brown hair was prepared beautifully and braided intricately into one large ponytail. The ponytail itself dangled down her back to her curvaceous buttocks. In fact, her back didn't touch her braid at all. It was her butt that seemed to hold on to the end of the very long and distinct braid. Two strands of her hair had been braided separately and dangled down from each side of her face. It seemed as if her face was framed in this way by her hair.

Mary was truly a sight to behold. I could see that she stood waiting for me to make a move toward her. I leaned forward and kissed her gently upon her luscious lips. I could taste her lips now with every moment that we kissed. I eventually began using my tongue to tickle her lips slowly. She chuckled and withdrew from our embrace. She had a catty look upon her face.

"We had better join the others, my love," she whispered into my ear. I nodded with a look that was sure to make anyone question my intelligence. My mind was empty and I could feel nothing but excitement. This woman was as devious as I was. I was overjoyed that we were able to see each other in any light that we wished, that I was free to partake of her love and guide her toward a place of ecstasy. We would both be free to enjoy each other's company without any restrictions. She of all people wouldn't wish that to be true either. I knew she was a woman that held back for the moment but would surely take advantage of anything that she could when pressed. I felt that she was calling to me in that moment to take part in her pleasure. I knew that this could not happen at this moment, but I could feel the pull with every fiber of my being. She was not actually calling to me, but it was more of a whisper from deep within my mind, a gentle breeze among the desperate cries of my psyche. I was indebted to her for so many reasons. This strong will to be a part of me was one of the reasons.

It felt like an eternity looking into her eyes until she took my hand and led me out of the shed and into the barn. I could now feel her lust fade from her. She was now more focused on the situation at hand. I knew this feeling all too well as I had been in front of many crowds of people during hurried hours at the bank. Your mind and emotions brace themselves for the onslaught that you are about to receive.

We rounded the corner of the door and moved into the barn. Everyone stood and cheered and threw seeds about the barn. Thankfully, the table had not been set yet. I didn't wish for anyone to have to eat seeds in their meal. I considered what I would do next but was quickly faced with the fact that Mary wasn't giving me a choice. She tugged upon my arm slightly and led me to the table where we would be seated. I pulled her chair back from her place at the table and helped her to sit down in her beautiful dress. I also couldn't help myself but to follow her curves with my eyes. Her body was a welcomed sight now. I almost couldn't help but reach out my hand and follow them to the end. I was ready now for anything. Though I was focused on nothing as my brain had all thoughts leeched from it. If I were to be shot in that moment, I would have never known what had killed me.

I waited until she was comfortable in her chair and pushed her underneath the table. I then took my place to her left and pulled my chair underneath me. I stared out at the crowd of people that were now waiting to be served dinner. After a moment, one of the servants walked over to us and set a beautifully prepared steak and potato. I could smell that everything had been covered in delicious spices. The potato held a sauce that I had never seen. It was creamy yet slightly green. I was curious to taste everything in front of me. I looked to my left and saw that Mary had been served a large piece of chicken instead. "Do you not prefer steak, my love?" I asked.

Mary shook her head. "I am not eager to chew a shoe at this moment," she replied. I could hear her chuckle quietly. She then gave me a playful look that made me obsessed. I wanted to know all her subtleties. I wished to learn all her quirks. I could only be satisfied with knowing how Mary worked. I wished to know all that drove her onward. All that caused her to be enthralled with any subject that she wished. These wishes of mine included what simple things she liked to entertain herself with in her spare time.

I was suddenly pulled from my deeper thoughts by a clanging sound. Mary's father stood from his table and said, "Thank you all for coming. I wish everyone to know that I have only just met Benjamin, but he is already a part of my family. I could think of no man better to care for Mary but him. Thank you for being courteous to our family in the past couple of weeks. I know that you have been a busy man, but welcome to our family, and we hope that you return with Mary before too long."

Martin's words rang in my mind. I was being entrusted with his own daughter, and he simply smiled and thanked me. I felt that he was either downplaying the severity of his emotions or that he was drunk enough to not care. Though I was unsure how anyone could be drunk at such a sobering event, I knew that I was not. I did feel, however, that I was being watched with reverence by the rest of the family. Once I had realized that Mary and I were something of a spectacle from her family, I focused solely on her. She ate so gracefully. It seemed as if I were watching an angel partake of this sumptuous meal. I was too distracted by Mary to eat quickly at all. I couldn't pause long enough to be able to cut my steak and taste its delicious flavor. My nerves had now reached a point of restricting me from doing anything save for paying attention to Mary.

She eventually noticed that I hadn't touched my meal and asked, "Is there something wrong with your meal?"

I shook my head and replied, "No, my dear. I am shy around large crowds of people. I feel awkward in this moment."

Mary smiled at me with her beautiful hazel eyes on mine. "I am sure that they won't care. I am also sure that my uncle will be offended if you don't at least try the food," she said.

I looked down at my food and began to eat. The steak cut so gently and seemed to fall apart. I could see now that the spices covered the top of the cut of meat. It seemed that the chef had charred the spices into the meat. The potato was also moist and delicious. The garnish that had been dribbled inside of the potato had a hearty, earthy flavor. There was also a slight sweetness at the end of the flavor.

I continued to talk to Mary as I ate this delicious meal. Wine was being poured in everyone's glasses liberally as I was given flashing memories of this morning. I could almost feel being back in the winery and talking with Martin and Ben as we shared our wine. I knew now that I would witness a repeat of those events. I would bear witness to everyone becoming inebriated with the bouquet of such a delicious selection. I, of course, wasted no time in accepting a large quantity of wine myself. I would continue my drinking from before. Now I felt accepted among fellow drinkers on this evening. I could now know that I was not being judged for any actions that could take place during the course of the wedding reception. I would simply blend in with the others of the event who had drunk too much. Though I also didn't wish to be so intoxicated that I would have to rely upon Mary to carry me into the manor.

I also held an unfounded fear that I would pass from consciousness and leave poor Mary to the demon. This was an idea that I didn't relish in any way. I could not bear the thought of leaving my beautiful and delicate wife to face something so heinous as a demon on our wedding night. If anyone would face what I had, it would not be during the most joyous evening of their lives such as tonight. I knew that if I held any suspicions that she would have to face this evil, I would not be taking her to the manor tonight. I would, however, be greeted by an empty manor that waited patiently for my arrival and warmth. Nothing would be frightful tonight other than the reaction that Mary would have toward her new husband. I chuckled to myself at the thought.

Mary and I continued to enjoy our dinner together. I eventually let the knowledge of others being present fade from my mind. I was now engrossed in spending this time with my wife. Mary seemed to be avoiding eye contact with those who attended the ceremony. She seemed to be focused completely on me. I knew that this was the best that we could hope to do as there were many people gathered in this barn. I never expected for our wedding to come together so well. Though I was also as to I would thank for preparing this event and putting all this time and effort into it.

Before I could finish another thought, Percy approached the table. He shook our hands and congratulated us both. "I am happy for you both. It took great courage for you to both marry so quickly and so young," he said.

I smiled and thanked Percy. He leaned over and whispered, "I'll be about in the morning with breakfast for us to all eat together."

I thanked him once again, and he strolled back to his family. Everyone was dancing and singing. The musicians had now moved into the barn and were starting to play music that seemed dear to the people of Hillsborough. I joined Mary in a dance as we all fell into the same dancing pattern. The revelry of this night would be remembered by everyone involved for some time.

13

MARY

The events of the evening had drawn the energy out of Mary and me. We both moved toward the farmhouse now. I held her gentle and soft hands as we walked side by side. I could feel her warmth and her love reaching out to me. In that moment, I felt that nothing could come between us. Nothing would change our love for each other. I felt everything between us now. I knew that my new wife would love to spend time together. Just the two of us, locked in a warm embrace, feeling the intoxication of our love. I could imagine her soft skin on mine, her gentle hands moving all over my body. I could feel the love that she needed to give out to anyone that was willing to receive it.

I wanted to be this man. I wanted to do what I could to make sure that Mary was cared for above all else. I was going to be the man that she leaned upon in trying times. The man who wouldn't judge anything that she would do or wish to do. I supported her in all things and in all aspects of our lives. Nothing would change that. Nothing would make me think any less of her or see her as a subject to my rule. I did, however, wish to teach her about life further, especially when it came to living in New York City. I could not prepare her enough for a life surrounded by people to meet and things to do. I feared that it would take some time for her to become accustomed to our new way of life. I also knew that it would be a shock to see how different my life would be from anything that she could imagine.

Mary seemed to float along beside me as we moved back to the back porch. A procession of people followed us into the backyard and began to celebrate more. There was even more dancing and drinking to do now. The sun had fallen behind the trees in the distance and only dimly lit the sky above. I could tell that Mary and I weren't ready to leave this place and all this laughter and joy. Everyone seemed to support our marriage. Each person older than myself wished to share life secrets about their marriage to us. The younger people seemed awestruck that we were married and ready to begin a life together. Though I was sure that the latter group of people didn't fully understand what we were experiencing in this moment. I knew that this would be the closest that I would come to being worshipped as a hero. I knew that this would be the only time in my life that I would have to deal with widespread fame. My heart was consumed with thankfulness at the realization that I wouldn't have to deal with this kind of attention for much longer. After all, I enjoyed a quiet and uneventful life. I wished to continue this kind of existence for much longer. This was my overall desire within my life. I wanted no more interruptions over some demon. Nor any ghosts that that infernal creature had controlled. I was dead set on cleansing my life of all evil from here on out. Determination dictated that I distance myself from any occult practices and only focus on God and his word. This would be my calling from all of these events. I felt only too sure that I was to cleanse my life forever and live a more diligent life in my faith. It was understood and evident by the fact that Percy and my faith had eliminated this demon from the manor altogether. At least it was in my mind.

I could see Mary standing with her mother in the distance. She gave her mother a hug and was undoubtedly receiving guidance on how she should care for her husband now. I could also see other women approaching them and congratulating my wife. This sight was so pure and beautiful. Everyone seemed truly accepting of our marriage and of our love. I only hoped that I would be able to live up to those expectations. Though I knew that I would. Mary's aunt had joined them and seemed to be looking about the party. This made me wonder if Martin had vanished again. I could only imagine he and Ben still in the barn sharing more wine. It would only be fitting for them to relax and celebrate on this night. Nothing else was to be done now, and I knew that they had worked hard all week.

I turned to look about the party and see if I could spy either man now. It was hard to distinguish individual people as everyone had started their dance over again. Now the movement of each dance was more spread out in this large yard. People had room to twirl each other and make much more distinguished movements in their art. Yet here I stood partaking in none of it. Just then my eyes caught Martin wandering about on the edge of the crowd. I could see that he was holding a piece of paper in his hand. This seemed odd, but I relegated it to Martin's behavior. Eventually he stopped pacing back and forth and stretched upward. He cupped his hands around his mouth and began to yell. After some, time the music had stopped and Martin had the attention of the whole wedding.

Martin stood for a moment and collected his thoughts. He then looked down toward his paper and said, "Thank you all so much for coming, once again. Please, begin making your way toward your wagons. I have received a notice from the sheriff that we are making too much noise for the other farmsteads around the area. Have a good night and thank you all for celebrating this marriage between Mary and Benjamin."

With his words everyone began saying good night to each other and to Mary and me. Everyone began moving away from the home en masse. I could see that some had left their wagons sitting behind the barn and began fetching their horses and hitching them to their wagons. It was truly a sight to behold. One by one, they all rode off into the night with torches held high above their heads for light. I had only ever seen a sight like this during funeral processions. The only people left at the farmhouse were Mary and her family. Even the servants had moved back toward their homes and began shutting up for the night. Though I couldn't see them now.

I looked about the backyard and decided that I would gather Mary and her things. This didn't take too long as Mary's family had prepared everything that she brought here and placed it all in her luggage. We then moved out onto the front porch to see Percy and his family sitting on the wagon. Before leaving, they greeted Mary and me and thanked her family one by one for the wedding and caring for us. Just as I turned to leave, Martin and Ben waved for me to approach them. I moved closer, only for them to look me in the eyes.

"Have a safe journey. Take care of Mary, Benjamin. It is your duty as her husband to make sure that she is safe at all times," Martin said.

Ben simply agreed and then shook my hand. He had a firm handshake now. It was as if I had earned both men's respect beyond all else. I then turned and moved over to the wagon and helped Mary into the back. She and I both sat on the back of the wagon and watched as the farmhouse disappeared into the night. I was not sure what the night would hold, but I was sure that I would be able to ward off any danger with a fresh torch in my hands.

Mary and I spoke to each other about the day. "I am so thankful for you, Benjamin. I have never seen my father this happy in his life. I could see that you bonded with him, and this was important to me," Mary said.

"Thank you, my love. I have had a very entertaining day with your family. I was not sure how this would all turn out, but I am thankful for you also. I have never been able to have this much fun with anyone. I usually keep my distance from others in that way, but tonight was different. Everyone was so kind and pleasant to be around at the wedding," I replied.

Mary smiled and leaned into my arms. I could see her being happy on a deeper level now. I had satisfied all doubts and worries that she held in her mind for this evening. I also had brought her closer to me than before and let her know that she could rely upon me for anything. Hopefully her family felt the same. I could only hope that Martin and Ben would trust me to care for Mary as they had. To love her as if she were my own daughter and nurture her into being a woman. This was the calling that I had answered. This would be my way to fulfill any expectation that either man could have toward the way that I treated and cared for Mary. I knew all too well that Mary could not have dreamed of a better wedding and reception. I knew that everyone had come together to give her everything that she had dreamed of out of the day. I loved Mary and I hoped that she would be able to say the same about my involvement in the day. I longed to be so beneficial to Mary and give her all that she craved in life. Though I knew that I was and that Mary would not wish for me to try so hard, I knew that I had to strive toward more every day. I would desire, above all, to make Mary's life that much better.

Mary and I laughed as we bounced along over the ruts in the road. I held the torch above my head so as to see everything that the night would hide in the forest. The light from the torch flickered violently in the wind. I could see shadows dancing alongside the wagon as we rode through the night. Mary and I seemed to be free from all worries now. We both could exist outside the normal realm of others. Our lives had become one, and it seemed that we felt entitled to all that this life would offer us together. I could no longer say that I had any doubts about how Mary felt toward me or our marriage.

It felt amazing to know that I could be free with another person, to really allow Mary to see who I really was and could be. I knew that she found comfort in this. She was a woman who truly knew that she needed a new start. I could see it in her eyes when she looked at me on this night. I could see her true intentions now. She only wished to have a life that called upon her to life differently. She was truly a woman with a gentle and pure heart. Nothing could change that at all, but I knew that she would need to address her trusting of others too much. I could see that this would be a problem upon living in New York City, a city like that would be no place for a girl who trusted everyone.

People seemed to not allow innocent people to thrive in an urban environment. I found this to be the biggest drawback of living within the city, but it was my home. I felt that this would not always be the case, but for now it had to be the case. Mary would have to adapt to that way of life, and I knew that she could. She was a remarkable woman in every way. She would not shy away from anyone that wished to do her harm. She had a strength that I knew that no one else possessed. I was obsessed with her, but I could not allow that to get the better of me. My goal was not to be consumed by her, but to be equal to her.

This was my only desire, and I knew that this was not the way of the world. No one could be happy anymore. No one would be able to live a life that benefitted themselves and others around them. Mary had not realized this yet, and I didn't wish to see the day when she did realize this to be true. I would never wish for such a pure heart to be hurt by careless individuals. She was mine to protect and love, and I would do this until my dying breath. Mary was my soul mate. Even now, we both seemed to be talking as of good friends. We both felt that we had known each other for a long time. Now this was even more evident by our marriage and ability to be around each other in a compatible fashion.

This would not be the end, however, to strife. We would know our fair share of heartache between each other, but this would not stop our love. I would make sure that I did everything to not take more than she could give. I would learn to be happy in every way with her and want for nothing more. Not as others had seemed to live for excess, especially those within the city who had carved out their own world among the streets of New York. I would not allow the world to consume our bond. I only had to trust that Mary saw everything the same way.

My only worry now was toward our first night together. I would have to move us into a room upstairs in the manor, but it was safe to do so now. The demon had been defeated, and I was no longer ashamed to allow anyone to buy the manor from me. The only caveat would be that I would have to broker a sale from New York and entrust the sheriff to transfer any documents that would be needed between myself and another. I had come to know that I could also trust Percy to be able to handle anything else that was needed. I would set aside the money for Percy when I arrived to my apartment within the city.

The wagon ride was swift. We all seemed to separate ourselves from each other. That or Percy and his family didn't wish to be involved in our lives just after being married. I had worried that they were able to see the love and lust that clouded around Mary and me. Nothing could be more embarrassing than to realize that they had understood the looks that Mary and I had given to each other. She would gaze into my eyes deeply, and I would run my eyes over the curves of her body in her dress. I knew that she was a well-figured woman and needed the attention that only her husband would be all too happy to provide. I longed for Mary more now as I knew that she longed for me.

Each bump in the road served to remind us that the world around us still existed. Otherwise, we would have remained in this state of longing. Though I was sure that she and I never wanted to leave that state. We knew it all too well now as we gave each other looks that would make a preacher blush. Mary and I would have to wait until reaching the manor as we were both too drained from the long day in the summer heat. The exhaustion was tangible from all who rode along within the wagon. Though I would not venture to say that anyone would have done anything differently. We all seemed to be in an upbeat demeanor. Most of all, Mary and I seemed to carry the excitement for everyone else around us.

Mary and I now moved into the manor as we bade Percy and his family a good night. The children didn't seem to move at all, and Chloe just waved a hand without caring about our departure. I approached the door to the manor and proceeded to open it. I peeked through the doorway first, expecting to see something horrid waiting for Mary and me. This was not the case, however. I simply carried Mary's belongings in from the wagon and set them on the floor by the door. I then allowed Mary to come into the home since I was sure that it was safe now. She thanked me for gathering her luggage and bringing it all in. I left the door open for moonlight and moved to a desk that was to the left of the door. It held only two things on its surface, a small candle that I had used before and a beautiful plant. I had only engaged the plant twice since arriving in Hillsborough. Something gave me the understanding that I would not have to care for the plant as much as some. I quickly felt around on the surface of the desk for the candle until my hand bumped against the plant. It shifted on the table and seemed to push the candle off the side of the table. I bent down as far as I could and began moving my hands across the floor. I was embarrassed, to say the least, but I was determined to not allow this to stand in the way of Mary and my first night together. Still, I felt that I was losing some sort of magic by awkwardly feeling about in the dark for a candle. Just as I felt the embarrassment wash across my face, I found the candle and immediately lit the wick. In one smooth motion, I turned back to Mary and smiled as if nothing had happened. I could see that she was not bothered at all. She seemed to have enjoyed waiting in the night air for me to light a candle for her. She was a most appreciative woman.

I smiled toward her and said, "I am sorry, dear. It took some time to find this candle in the dark." I smiled and raised my eyebrows to make her laugh. She giggled and hid her face slightly. I knew that she was just as nervous as I would be in this moment. I moved back to where she was stood in the doorway and closed the door. I suavely locked the front door and latched the upper lock. Nothing would disturb our passion tonight. I quickly picked up her luggage and began leading her into the upper floor of the manor. I was not sure which room that I would pick for the night, but I was sure that it would be on the left side of the upper floor. There was a bed big enough for two people, and the door was able to be locked three times. I had no plans of allowing this evil to ruin all aspects of my life.

I looked back to Mary as we both climbed the stairs. I could see that she seemed uneasy. She was hesitant to walk farther up the stairs. At first it was not as noticeable, but now it seemed that she only followed because of her trust for me. I was worried that she would be able to detect that something had once happened within the home. That is, if that was a reasonable ability for one to possess. After a moment, I decided that this was something that I need not concern myself about. If Mary could detect something, then I would confer with her after we had sealed ourselves within the room for the night. Though I was sure that she would not wish to remain on the upper level while I returned to my room and fetched my luggage for the night. I wasn't even keen on that idea either. I decided that I would lay her luggage within the room and move downstairs while carrying on a conversation. This would attract her attention to follow me. I was not sure that the demon would not wish to follow Mary and me downstairs or harm us, if it still resided within the manor.

Eventually I reached the bedroom and decided that I was panicking over nothing. Mary didn't act as if she had detected something odd at all. She seemed quite normal, and I simply was seeing what I wanted to see in her as we moved into the upper floor. I set her luggage in the room and to the right of the bed. My only condition for this night was that I would sleep closest to the door of the room. I would stand between Mary and whatever wished to do us harm in the night. Though I fervently hoped that I wouldn't have to worry about such things. My mind raced with thoughts of what might be tonight as I tried my hardest to choke down my fears. I felt odd now and didn't wish to show this to Mary. I could not ruin our night together by acting as if something was wrong in this place. I wanted her to be comfortable. This could only be achieved if she was not to know about the demon until tomorrow, at least. I was not ready to have that conversation tonight before we would lie down to sleep.

I turned to face Mary and said, "I have some things to fetch—" My words were stopped immediately as she threw herself into my arms and began passionately kissing me. I spun her around while still kissing her and holding her beautiful body in my arms. Nothing else mattered now save for making sure that the door was sealed shut. I slowly moved her to the door with my back to it. I was not sure that I had reached the doorway until my back ran into the door and it shut firmly. I then reached behind me and began latching the door locks. Three locks were all accounted for in my mind. With this knowledge, I was finally able to focus on Mary and me.

I pulled her close to me and held onto her tightly. I was ready for all that she had to give to me. I moved my hands gently up her right arm and to her dress sleeve. I pulled gently until I felt the fabric begin to slide down. I pulled and pulled until the sleeve had lodged itself against her skin. I then followed these movements with my left hand on her left arm. I knew now that I would not be able to control myself. Mary would become a woman tonight, and I would not hold back any of my passions for her.

I leaned over and began moving her toward the bed. I could feel her hand brush against my face as she continued her passionate advances. I then placed my hand on her left butt check and squeezed. I could feel her gentle yet firm buttocks in my hand. My right hand had now moved to the small of her back as I caressed her back with my hands. She didn't seem to pause or even hesitate in this moment. She moved her hands up and rested them on my broad shoulders. I could feel her push as hard as she could to try to lock her hands together in the middle of my back. This was futile as we moved into another position. I had grasped her right hand with mine and turned her around until her back was against me. I slid my hands down her sides until I could feel her luscious butt begin to take shape. I grasped onto this part of her body and pulled her backward against my groin. Her butt was firm against me now, and I could feel that she was not going to stop me from anything that I desired. She simply threw her arm behind her and began feeling my neck as I kissed hers.

The skin just below her jaw was soft and supple against my lips. I moved along her neck and then began working my way down. I could hear her gasping for air as I pulled her butt as tight as I could against my groin. She let out a slight moan as I moved my right hand from the middle of her stomach down to her hips. I grasped her hip firmly and pulled her back again. She simply held on to me and moved as I moved. The passion rose now to a fever pitch, and I could not help but remove my shirt. I then ran my right hand down to her thigh and began pulling up her dress. Her skin was soft against my hands, and I longed to feel more. I slid her dress up and pulled it slowly over her head. I paused to see what she would wish to do with her dress, but she simply tossed it to the side and wrapped her leg around my waist. I reached down with my left hand and grasped her butt firmly again. I could now feel everything in much more detail. This didn't stop me from tasting her delicious breath as we kissed, however. I could taste a sweet flavor, something that I would liken to a tart candy. I tasted all that I could and concentrated on rubbing her tongue with mine.

I could feel Mary writhing in my arms as I lifted her up from the ground and pushed her pelvis against my groin. She once again let out a moan that was unmistakable. I could feel the passion in her heart for me. It grew until she could no longer restrain herself from my touch. She was losing her control, and she was doing it with me. This gave me the feeling of power. It was a pure energy that overwhelmed both of us as we continued. I pulled my right hand up to her waist and held on to her firmly for a moment. She then took my hand in hers and pulled my hand down her underwear. I lifted my hand slightly so as to pull her undergarments off her body. I was not certain how this was working as she had a full underwear on. Little did I know, she had begun removing the upper portion of her underwear from her body so as to allow me to slide everything off her. She then put my left hand on her butt cheek in such a way that I could feel all her butt. She then placed my other hand on her most sensitive area. I could feel that she was ready for our night together and she longed for my love. We kissed like this for a moment as I could feel her hands undoing my belt and unbuttoning my pants. Before I could do anything else, we both stood naked save for Mary's stockings. I felt her move to slide off her stockings, but I stopped her. I could not allow her to remove this clothing. I desired to feel her skin in such tight cloth.

I lifted Mary into the air and then laid her gently upon the bed. I began immediately kissing down her body as I moved my head closer to her legs. I could feel the soft skin against my lips now. She was ready for anything that I could give her on this night. I moved my lips back and forth over her until she couldn't take any more. With her taste on my lips, I moved upward and entered her. I could feel her pulsating underneath me as I continued to kiss and thrust myself deep into her. I felt as if nothing would stop me now. I could hear her moaning loudly into my ear as I continued to push. I kissed her neck as she wrapped herself around my body. She was consuming me as of a wild flower consuming a bumblebee. I was being accepted within her and her heart. I knew that no one had ventured to be this intimate or close to Mary. I also knew that no one else would have the chance now. I would be her one and only. I would be the man that made her sing on a lonely night. I reveled in this face as I could feel her tightening herself upon me. I then felt her tense up and then relax again as she screamed loudly. Her eyes were opened wider than I had ever seen before, and her face was flush with red. I could feel her physically, emotionally, and mentally. She was a fruit that was ripe for me to enjoy on a hot day. She was a cool drink of water in a long walk that never seemed to end. She was my sanity and my comfort. Now she was much more than anything that I had ever felt before. She was my desire, and she nurtured me with every kiss and every touch. She would touch me gently and give me goosebumps every time.

We both had become extremely sensitive as we continued to become one. I could feel her sliding against me ever more with each thrust. She was completely accepting of all that I was and would be. My heart, mind, and soul belonged only to her. She accepted them with a loud scream followed by a passionate moan. I could not stop myself from pushing deeper and harder into her. I could no longer think of anything except her satisfaction. It would no longer be acceptable to stop at pleasing her. I wanted everything that she could give and more, and I knew that she wished for the same from me. I pushed more and more and continued to move closer to climax. I could feel that she had become so moist that I was now covered in her. I could smell her now. All her desires and dreams were being expelled onto my flesh. She was reliant upon me allowing for her dreams to be achieved above all else. She trusted me now in her weakest moment, and I could not say no. I breathed her deep into my lungs and smelled her fragrance all around me. She was perfect to me and even more so now. Her love for me swelled, and I felt myself slip deeper into her. Her warmth was so inviting, and I could no longer help myself. I released myself for her and could no longer continue.

I knew that we had become one and nothing could have been more special to me now. I had lived my whole life waiting for a woman who would share everything with me and make things better in every way. I had no idea or dream that I would find a woman who fulfilled every desire within me. I could not hold back from her at all. She had everything that I could provide her. I lay beside her now and felt her gentle touch as she moved her fingertips across my skin. My head rested on nothing but her ample but supple breasts. I could think of no better place to be in this moment. Tonight would be the most special that I could experience with anyone. Our lives had now began, and I could not hold myself back from accepting her love wholeheartedly. I could now hear Mary's heart beating within her chest. She seemed to be overcome with relaxation now and relief. She simply lay back on the bed and didn't move at all. I could smell her gentle yet inviting fragrance even more. I knew that she gave off a scent that made me lose control over my actions. She always knew what to say and exactly what I wanted in the moment.

Eventually we found ourselves changing positions as she now lay her head upon my chest. I knew that she was listening to my heart beat as well. Mary was special to me, and I had given her an idea of how I had felt. She closed her eyes and said nothing more for the rest of the night. I could not know what to do now as I didn't wish to disturb her slumber.

After a few moments, I worked myself from under her. I tucked her into the bed on her side and then moved over to the candle. I gently blew out the flame and crawled back under the sheets. The darkness had overcome every part of the room as I could feel the coolness of the sheets tickling my skin. The only other warmth that I could feel was that of Mary's body against mine. She was beautiful and still as she slept. I wrapped my arms around her body and pulled her close. The moment that I had blown out the candle that lit the room, I felt a rush of energy. Everything in me called for me to tempt Mary into being together again. Though I knew that she would not likely awaken at any attempt by myself to tempt her into anything. She was fast asleep now, and I simply couldn't disturb her peaceful slumber.

I lay there thinking to myself for a moment about all that had happened. I still couldn't believe how quickly my life had changed without much effort at all. I welcomed this change to my life if it meant that I would be able to share my time with Mary and truly love her. I could think of no better way to spend my time now than with her. I swiftly began to calm myself and feel rest calling to me to lay my head back and sleep. I immediately thought of the demon that plagued this home no longer. I wondered if this being had been called back to hell as it should have remained. It didn't matter now, however. No demon would be able to stop the rest that I would begin to fall into now.

14

RETURNING HOME

The day broke through the small window in the room and illuminated the whole bed. I had awakened before Mary this morning and was content to lie next to her and watch her sleep. I felt comfort as I had never felt before in the manor. My whole world had went back to normal now, and I finally understood what it would have been like if I had been able to rest on this vacation. I had imagined this moment for a long time. Now it felt as if I had waited for an eternity to feel this relaxed within the manor.

What I once had thought would be an easy and relaxing trip had turned to a nightmare, but had now redeemed itself. I could not be happier with my new wife in a house that finally held silence. I no longer felt that I had to worry that this demon was defeated. I felt peace that I no longer had to worry about Mary and how she would be able to receive this demon. I had reasoned now that I would not trouble her with ideas and notions of demons and spirits. This was a malevolent factor in life that I could not live with myself to bring this to Mary's attention, especially now that I was watching her sleep so peacefully.

I could see in her expression on her face that she was in a deep and peaceful sleep. She didn't hold a smile or a twisted and evil expression that one might give when having a nightmare. Her beauty was now more evident than ever. I had never seen a more beautiful and amazing woman in my life. Her beauty was such that none could compare. I knew that others would say that I was simply smitten with my wife and there were other women that were much better-looking and gifted. I would disagree with this statement. My wife meant the world to me and even more so now that we had been together. No, she was a beautiful woman whose whole life I wanted to share.

Just as the sun began to shine through the window brighter than before, Mary opened her eyes. I turned my head and tried to not allow her to know that I had been watching her sleep. She took in a deep breath and exhaled slowly. I turned to face her as if I had just noticed that she had awoken. "Good morning, my lady. How did you sleep last night?" I asked.

She held a wide smile upon her face. "I slept well, my love. Last night was wonderful!" she replied. I felt a tinge of pride wash over my mind. I could see within her eyes that she was telling me the truth. I had indeed brought nothing but satisfaction and pleasure to my wife. Reality had now shown us that we were compatible in every way. I felt more comfortable around Mary now, and I could understand that she only wished to understand me. This gave me a sense of belonging and calm as I had never felt before. I knew now that she was truly happy with me and I was truly happy with her. Though I was not sure how I would put any of that into words at the moment. I was more awestruck by her beauty and the fact that she was my wife, that I could attract such a magnificent woman into my life and care for her as no other could.

I could feel my heart burst every time that she whispered into my ear, every time that she would speak to me in that sheepish way as she had many times before. Mary was a gift to me in every sense of the word, and I longed to make her happy in every way. I had felt what life was like with no one by my side that I could count on or trust. I never knew what it was like to have anyone close to me in any way. Now this young woman had impressed upon me the need to have her contact in every way. I was far too open to Mary than with anyone else in my life. My feelings indicated that this was what Mary needed and longed for, but I would have to adjust to this way of life. I was not a man to express himself easily or without more thought than was needed in any situation.

I looked at Mary as the sun gleamed off her face. Her skin appeared to hold a halo around it, and I could not look away. She was as of an angel sitting beside me. Her beauty was unlike any other, and I felt that I could not look away from her in this moment. I tried everything that I could to move my gaze toward something else, but she and I seemed locked in this moment. She slowly began smiling and moved toward me. Her lips were soft and gentle upon mine. She kissed me in the most passionate yet proper way that I had ever known. Once I had barely felt the euphoria of this moment, she moved back toward her side of the bed and began putting on her clothes. This upset me in many ways as I never wanted that moment to flow away. Though I was not sure what I could do to hold on to that moment.

Mary had now begun to refocus on what our day would hold, and I was still caught in a moment that never ended. Each passing second was as special and as intense as the one before. I could feel her mind moving from topic to topic quickly as if she had to process the night and the day before. It almost gave me the impression that she had finally realized that she and I would now be together forever. Something inside me was disturbed with this thought, but there was nothing that I could do about that now. I simply pushed it out of my mind and let go of that moment. I had to do so now and begin to work toward readying myself for the rest of the day.

I climbed out of bed and began dressing myself as well. I could see that Mary now had her back to me and sat in front of a mirror to the left side of the room. I could feel her doubts and worries now, and they seemed odd. Her face gave me the impression that she was trying to cope with her new marriage. Her heart gave me the impression that she worried that she would not be enough for me to love. She was second-guessing what kind of wife she could be to me and how much I needed her to be only that—a wife. Mary had contemplated the thoughts of marrying me, but that was as far as her thoughts had traveled. Her intuition said to her that she would have to be more than she had ever been before, that she would have to change her mind and heart to accommodate mine. This disturbed me deeply until I said, "Don't worry, Mary. I don't expect anything from you except to love you and for you to love me. I care about nothing else. Please don't make yourself unhappy because you worry."

Mary paused instantly and looked down toward her lap. I could see that she was not crying, but was thinking instead. She hid her identity from me, and I could no longer look into her eyes. Her defenses had been put up against me, and I dared not find a key to open that door. I feared what her reaction would be to any questioning or further words. Mary seemed to be a woman that was recovering from something terrible, but I knew nothing about it. Perhaps it was that she worried about her family and their ability to care for themselves and the farmstead. Whatever she was pondering, it was not a comforting thought. I felt how disturbed that she was as well. It was far greater than I. I moved over to her and kissed her on the top of her head. I had placed my left arm on her shoulder and whispered, "I love you, Mary. Nothing will change that." She didn't react, so I simply put on my coat and left the room quietly. I knew that this was something that she would be dealing with until she was ready to talk about it.

Everything in me screamed for me to enter the room again and talk to her about it. I longed to force her to understand where I stood in all of this, but I felt worse about that idea than any other. Instead I strolled down the stairs and began moving to the back bedroom. I lit my pipe as I walked and inhaled deeply. I could feel the tobacco entering my lungs and soothing me in every way. My mind was at ease now, and I no longer had the worries that I once did. I could taste the delicious tobacco with all its sweetness and earthy tones. This was complimented only by the harshness of the smoke. My pipe had a long stem and large mouth piece, so I didn't have to worry about too much heat in the smoke. Though sometimes it was inevitable.

I continued to walk until I had reached the doorway to the back bedroom. I looked inside and noticed that the door stood open. I distinctly remember the door being shut last night. I found this quite odd but relegated this to just me misremembering the night. After all, I was focused on other things. I leaned into the doorway and looked about the room. My belongings didn't seem to have been moved in any way. This was also odd as I was sure that the door was not opened last night. My only idea for a rational explanation would be if Percy had come by last night and couldn't find us in the back bedroom so he left. This made sense from the idea that Percy would have avoided the upper levels at all costs. He had been the one to be most attacked in the upper floor. I finally decided to put this out of my mind and continue into the room. I gathered my bags and moved them out to the front door. The coach would arrive for us tonight, and I would have to explain that Mary was my wife and that I would need to pay them extra for her travel as well. I was sure that this wouldn't be a problem, but I knew how greedy traveling companies could be in these times.

I set the luggage by the door and then moved back up the stairs. I quickly reached the upper landing and moved over to the door to the room that we had utilized last night. I opened the door and peeked into the room. I could see that Mary was now putting on her rings and a necklace. She was always the one to dress importantly. The first time that I had noticed this about her, I thought that she was a part of a well-to-do family. Though I had kicked her in that moment and feared that I would be sued. I was happy that everyone had come to an understanding and that I would not have to appear in a court. That would have been a damper on my trip. I moved into the room and shut the door behind me. Mary turned to face me with a look that was very distant.

"Is everything okay, my love?" I asked. She nodded.

"Yes, dear. Everything is going well," she replied.

I gave her a troubled look and said, "I am sorry, Mary, but you look as if you are upset with me or worried about something that takes all of your focus."

She looked up at me and said, "No, Benjamin. Nothing is wrong. I am simply readying myself for our journey home."

I decided to accept Mary's words in that moment. I didn't wish to push her into anger or frustration with me. I moved toward her luggage and began collecting each bag. I then carried them out of the room and down to the front door. I placed all her bags beside mine. I then opened the door to find Percy standing on the porch. He stopped immediately. "Chloe and I would like to invite Mary and yourself for breakfast on your last morning in Hillsborough," Percy stated.

I nodded and smiled. "Thank you, Percy. Mary will be along soon. She is finishing up her preparations for the day."

Percy looked about for a moment. I could see that he was agitated.

I found it strange that both he and Mary were in a different mood than I had imagined that they would be on this day. "I am sorry, Percy. Is there something wrong?" I asked.

Percy looked down to the ground for a moment and then replied, "Last night was not good for our family. My wife and I could not sleep at all. Chloe saw something in the windows of the upper floor of the manor last night. It was the terrible and twisted face of Caroline moving from window to window. Though Chloe said that she couldn't see the body. I gazed through the windows as well and saw the same. The sight was horrid. She was not sure what to make of it, and I came clean about everything that we had experienced. She was immediately rather coarse with me for some time. I tried to tell her that you had decided to stay in the manor anyway. She seemed better when this finally sank into her mind, but she is still worried about what she had seen last night."

I nodded and continued to smoke my pipe. The realization set in that the house had not changed. Nothing had changed at all. I was still dealing with the same issue. My mind rejected the idea though that the manor was still infested with a demon. This thought was refused outright. I could not fathom how anything could have survived within the manor after Percy and I had cleansed the manor. I stopped Percy before he could say anything else and said, "Please try to hide this from Mary. I suspect that she knows that something happened last night, but I don't wish to alarm her as to the reality of the situation."

Percy nodded and seemed to gather his thoughts. I continued to smoke as Percy and I sat in silence. Neither of us seemed prepared to face anything like this again. Everything in our minds had pointed to the fact that this demon was gone for good and anything trapped with it in the manor. How could I explain this to Mary? What would she say? My mind instantly moved to the stance that I could not tell her anything at all. No matter what happened now. We would leave and say nothing about it to each other. Even if she did see something, I hoped that she wouldn't wish to talk about it and bring it into reality once more. I would block off these thoughts and memories, never to be spoken of again.

After a couple of moments, Mary emerged from the manor. She seemed ready for the day. She even smiled as she always had done when I introduced her to Percy. I could tell that something plagued her mind but that she didn't wish to speak of it. I hoped, of course, that she had seen nothing and that she was simply worried about our betrothal. I could work with her to find common ground in marriage, but I could not fix anything relating to the trauma of seeing something so horrid.

Percy, Mary, and I didn't waste any time in getting into the wagon and leaving the manor. I worried about our bags for the day, but I was not keen to the idea of entering the manor again and retrieving them. I simply focused my mind on breakfast and moved on. Percy and I talked in the short distance to his farmstead as Mary remained quiet. I was not sure if she was simply shy or didn't wish to add anything. I found this to be odd also because of the fact that she had always been a very outspoken woman. Before I could get the chance to bring her into the conversation, however, we had arrived to the front porch of Percy's farmstead.

I began to step down from the seat of the wagon and assist Mary when Percy said, "I'll take care of the horses. You and Mary go inside and relax." I nodded and helped Mary down from the wagon. I could tell that Percy didn't wish for us to be involved in the situation anymore as he seemed that he was having trouble not bringing it up. I knew that Percy was a good friend, but I didn't know how far he would be willing to go. I wondered if he longed to mention all this to Mary so as to warn her about the manor and for us to not stay there any longer than we had to stay.

I took Mary's hand and guided her into the home and to the seats to the right of the door. We both sat down together and leaned against each other. The only thought in my mind was that she too felt drained of all energy to deal with anything. We both didn't move for several minutes as we felt comfortable together like this. I turned my head to the right and kissed her. She smiled and breathed out slowly. I didn't even wish to imagine what she might be experiencing after potentially seeing something as scarring as what Percy had described to me this morning. I worried that this was causing her suffering and she couldn't tell me. Either she could not say anything for fear that her new husband would think that she was insane or that I had not witnessed something as disturbing as that.

No matter which it was, she must feel so isolated in these happenings that she could not bring them into words for fear that she would further isolate herself. This was an existence that I would never wish for her to have ever. We continued to sit in the dining area for a moment until Chloe and her children emerged from down the hallway. They all approached us and congratulated us on our marriage. I could see that Mary was very appreciative of them thinking of us in such a way. It wasn't every day that someone would think to honor us in such a deep and emotional way. After this, Mary was welcomed into Percy and Chloe's home with open arms. I could see that there was a connection already forming between both women. My mind seemed to not be bothered with the idea that I might not see my wife today if we were to visit with the Merivel family for some time.

After all, Mary was entitled to be away from me and her normal life to visit a friend if she wished. This was a futuristic thought process, but it was the way that I was taught from a young age. My father would often discipline me for being rude to a girl or woman.

My mother would often slap my mouth for being rude at all. This was my upbringing, and I could no longer be ashamed to have lived that sort of life.

Mary had now moved off into the kitchen with Chloe and her children. No doubt they were talking about being married and what life would be like. That or they conversed about common interests. I welcomed this idea as I knew that Mary was young and she would need all the guidance that anyone could give her. Percy moved through the door and sat down to the right of me. He produced his pipe and began lighting it. I did the same. After a moment or two, Percy motioned for me to follow him out to the back porch, and I did as he requested. I could not understand why this would be happening again after all that Percy and I had done to cleanse the home. Perhaps it was not enough for normal men to cleanse a home. Perhaps it was the way that we had done so in the manor. I took a seat on the back porch and continued to smoke as Percy spoke.

"I am sorry to say this, Benjamin, but that manor will never be the same. After all that we have done to cleanse the home, but there are still odd happenings. Maybe you will never be able to sell the home. Perhaps you should consider simply keeping the manor and letting it rot in place. I could purchase some of the land from you and you could simply keep the manor," Percy said adamantly.

I nodded and thought for a moment. This was the best proposal that I had heard in a while, so I was inclined to accept. I didn't wish to jump into any agreements, however, as we still didn't know if this haunting affected the whole property or just the manor. Perhaps it was that when my aunt died, the demon was simply locked inside the home. I could accept Percy's offer but felt that I should add one thing to this agreement.

"I will only allow you to purchase the property if you entertain the possibility that this demon may not allow any livestock or crops to be raised within the property bounds. I am sure that you know that this would be devastating to you and your crops," I said.

Percy nodded and said, "Then I shall purchase the property and see. That is if you are offering a fair price for the land."

I smiled and replied, "You know that I will be fair in the purchase of the land."

Percy nodded again. I could see that he too was troubled by this demon and the possibility that he would be purchasing cursed land. I knew that I could offer Percy the deed to everything, but only sell the property to him at land value. I thought for a moment on a price that was comfortable for me, but I could not decide. I looked up to Percy and said, "What price would you be willing to offer for the manor and property? I will only sell at property value minus the manor."

Percy thought for a moment. I could see that he was tempted to take my offer, but he too didn't wish to jump too early in our negotiations.

Eventually I spoke up and said, "I will tell you what, you purchase the land for two hundred dollars and I will give you the deed outright to everything in this area that my aunt owned."

Percy continued to think in silence. This seemed to be a tempting offer to him, however. I knew that he wished to own all the land for his farm. What a farm that would be. The immense size of all the property would mean that he could compete with Ben and his wife for the most wealthy farm in the area. This was Percy's mindset and had been since I had met him. He would be able to afford much more than he could now and be able to entice others from Raleigh to visit and pay what he asked for crops and raw goods. Percy was not a stupid man and would know the overall value of all this land. It would also mean that he would be able to attain much more land for his servants to live upon and tend to the farm. Though I was sure that he knew the dangers of having too much land to cultivate. I could see that he was reaching a conclusion quickly and simply said, "If you are so inclined, then I will offer you the rights to the manor as well for no cost. After all, it isn't of use to me in any way."

Percy seemed even more intrigued by this prospect. Eventually he simply looked at me and said, "I will need to think about this. I trust that Mary and yourself will be leaving for New York tonight as planned?"

I nodded and replied, "We will be, but we have a lot to do today. I was supposed to ask if I could have you take Mary and me over to her uncle's home as her family will be leaving for their farmstead today as well. She wishes to say goodbye to everyone."

Percy nodded. "I could arrange for that. In the meantime, I will think of an answer to your offer."

We both shook hands and agreed. I determined that I would need to write a letter to the sheriff so that Percy would be able to receive the deed on Monday. I knew that this would be acceptable to every party involved. The sheriff would be able to disperse the deed to Percy, and I would be able to leave knowing that the property had been sold to someone that would use it.

I puffed harder on my pipe and continued to enjoy the morning air. Percy and I discussed a lot of different ideas. I knew that he would be more than willing to assist Mary and me today, but I still felt that I owed Percy something in all this. I would also continue to think about my offer and make sure that there was nothing else that I would be able to do in order to make sure that I would sell this property. This would be my focus on this day as well as saying goodbye to everyone that I had met in this enchanted place. I also wished to thank Mary's family as well as Percy and his family for assisting me with all that I needed to do in this town. Because of all of them, I would be able to leave knowing that my business was concluded in the area. This gave me great satisfaction and happiness for my future.

I knew now that I was on the cusp of resting easier. I just had to allow my life to transition in whatever way that it would choose into my future. I had learned a lot of lessons in this town, and what was a vacation had now shown itself to be an adventure. Though I still thought that this was an adventure left deep into my past and not following me about my life in New York. I was sure that this would only mean a disaster. No one else that I knew would wish to be dragged into a life of torment and darkness. I was sure that I would be the only one affected, but I could not be sure if anyone else would attract such evil. Worst of all, it might prey upon others in the building in which I resided. This was something that I was sure to avoid altogether. Nothing I knew about this demon or what anyone else had indicated was to show that it would be able to haunt anyone at random. This gave me comfort as it was my burden to bear because of my mother and aunt being filled with contempt for their father. Perhaps they were using the demon to trap his soul and my grandfather would be tormented forever. In some ways this thought gave me comfort, but I still didn't like the way that it was done or the outcome that was affecting my life.

Once I had settled my thoughts, Percy chimed in, "So where did you and Mary sleep last night?"

I looked over at him and replied, "We slept on the second floor in the left hallway."

With these words, Percy's eyes widened to show the complete eyeball. He was shocked at my answer, and I had not known why yet. "Your aunt was running about on the second floor terrifying us and you didn't hear anything within the home?"

I shook my head as the conversation died there. I was sure that Percy didn't wish to implicate that we were being tormented in our sleep last night, but that was the first thought that ran through my mind. Could this be the reason that Mary was troubled on this morning. I immediately turned to the idea that I must now ask her again what was going on inside of her mind. After all, anything that she would experience would be my fault. No one else would have allowed such a fine woman to wander into a life filled with torment and demons.

This was not the way to keep a woman such as Mary, and I knew it. Though the one thing that was not clear was her reaction to all this. Would she simply tell me that she didn't wish to remain in my life because of such evil and hardship, or would it be that she would stay and assist me in understanding and fighting such evil? The solutions to these questions were not known to me, and I had to find an answer. I relegated that I would need to talk to her when we could be alone again.

Just then Mary and Chloe emerged from the home and asked

Percy and me to come and eat. We all moved into the dining room of the home. I was amazed at all the food that was upon the table. Everyone had been seated including the servants. We all seemed amazed at this large spread. I had never seen so much food in my life for one breakfast. Everything from sausage to chicken was present on the table, each food representing the best of their dish. I was feeling more like royalty this morning than a simple banker or farmer. I took my seat beside Mary and thanked Chloe profusely. She smiled widely and accepted my thanks. I turned to Mary and kissed her on her cheek as she blushed. We all ate and seemed to get to know each other on a much deeper level. I now learned all about Mary and her background as well as Chloe's background. I welcomed this information as now Chloe and Mary weren't so much of a mystery to me anymore.

Time passed slowly as we all continued to talk and eat. The morning sun had moved into a much higher position now. I produced my pocket watch from my vest as we had all concluded breakfast. I was now faced with a time of ten o'clock in the morning. I thought that it had been earlier, but Mary didn't seem to be worried about anything at all. I approached her and asked, "The time is ten o'clock. What time would you like to visit your family today?"

Mary thought for a moment and said, "Would Percy be able to take us now? Or would you rather go for lunch?"

I shrugged my shoulders to indicate that it was her decision. I quickly felt that this was a mistake as I didn't even get an answer. Mary simply thought and thought about the situation. Eventually I said, "Let us go for lunch then."

Mary smiled and agreed. I could see that she didn't wish to bring this news to Percy as she was not sure that he would be happy to spend lunch with another family apart from his own. I ignored this, however, as I wasn't sure that I should say anything. Nothing I could offer would be able to change her mind without Mary becoming heightened.

I moved out onto the porch again and left Mary to converse with Chloe once more. Percy had already taken up his position in the rocking chair. I moved over to the other chair and sat down. I said nothing at first but eventually asked, "Would you be willing to take Mary and me to Mary's uncle's house for lunch?"

Percy nodded but added, "I will but I will return here. My wife is already on my back about not being around enough in the past two weeks." Percy then turned his head to me. He had a very serious look upon his face that indicated that he was irritated with the outcome of my visit.

I apologized to him and accepted his offer. We would at least be able to visit Mary's family for lunch. We would simply have to ask her family to return us to the manor afterward. I knew that this wouldn't be a problem, but I feared putting her family in the same position as Percy. Percy's words had put me in a place to be hesitant to converse with him. I was not sure that he would be in a good mood today, but I would not simply ignore him. I attempted to talk to him, but he stood from the chair and nodded. He strolled off to the barn and left me sitting upon the porch. It was now clear that something had happened during breakfast. Perhaps he didn't like my words toward his wife this morning. That or her witnessing what happened in the manor last night was affecting her more than I could know. I worried now that Percy was blaming me for all that had happened.

To tell the truth, it was all my fault, but I had nothing to do with my aunt or mother at such a young age. Unless I was to have been involved in these rituals without knowing. Then again at that age I would be dead. Those cultists would have surely sacrificed me to this demon. Though the question that I had to entertain was why they had not. Perhaps my mother had not wished for this to be so and my aunt would not talk her into it. The idea that she would be sacrificing her son to a demon for power was not something that any mother would just do. Then again, how was it that they were provided the boy in the visions that I had witnessed and the writings of the minister? Could it be that they stole someone's child and forced them to die for a demon's power? That would have been diabolical indeed.

Just as my thoughts had turned to this, Chloe emerged from the house with Mary just behind her. Chloe turned to me and asked,

"Where is Percy?" I didn't reply at first. "He is down by the barn. I am not sure what has happened, but he stopped talking and left."

Chloe seemed concerned. "I am sorry, Benjamin. I was harsh with Percy last night. It is my fault, Benjamin. I was out of my mind that he had not been around enough over the past two weeks," Chloe said apologetically.

Mary didn't seem any wiser to what we were really talking about, and I could not have the heart to tell her. I simply made motions with my eyes to let Chloe know that I didn't want Mary to know anything about this demon. She seemed to understand as she stopped the conversation there and walked out toward the barn. I was not sure what she would say to Percy or what she had said, but it must have been harsh indeed. Percy had never acted this way that I knew. He was always so upbeat and lively. Percy was a man who enjoyed his life and seemed to not have any issues with sadness or a longing for more. He was a simply man who wanted for nothing but simple things in his life. Though he also craved to create life and art. Nothing could be more evident in Percy's life and demeanor. Mary and I stayed on the porch in silence. I knew that she had questions that she wished to ask but would say nothing.

"What is it, dear?" I asked.

She paused and looked toward the barn. "I am not sure, Benjamin. I am worried about leaving all of this behind. I have never been outside of Hillsborough or the surrounding area. I know nothing of a life anywhere else. I have been trapped here in this rural life and could not possibly fathom a life anywhere else. Please understand that I am saying this because I am scared, not that I want to leave you or stay here," Mary said.

I could hear that she was fighting back tears from coming out. I put my arms around her and drew her close as I stood from my chair. "Nothing could be more acceptable in life, my love. Your family is special to you, and I would never wish to take that from you. I have never known a family such as yours, but I will be understanding if you would wish to remain and come along later," I said empathetically.

Mary shook her head and smiled. "I could not leave you when we have just begun. I will not abandon my husband to travel to our life together alone," she said with a hostile tone.

I could respect her wishes in all regarding this situation. Mary didn't wish to be scared and allow that fear to control her future. She only wished to remain at my side above all else. I could respect her in this moment as she spoke out for what she truly wanted. I knew of her desires and all that she wished for her own life. I also knew that she would not rest until she achieved it all. I wished for nothing else from my wife. My expectations could be nothing less. I would rather not limit Mary in her desires and needs. For who was I to tell a beautiful woman anything about her life? I didn't wish to have anyone do the same to me, so I could not possibly wish to put that upon anyone else.

Mary drew in closer and kissed me passionately. I knew now that she would feel my understanding for her in all this, that I admired her passions above all else. She seemed appreciative of the fact that I was allowing her to have an option other than just going with me to New York City forever. In her mind, she only thought of our return being after many years. This would not be the case as I could leave and travel whenever I wished, but I simply didn't. I had been far too diligent in my work to leave for no reason. With my wife, I would do anything to make her happy. Even if it meant leaving my world behind for a short time to visit with her family so that she didn't feel so isolated. Nothing would stop me from giving my wife the life that she had desired. No expense could tell me now, but simply push me to find a solution for her. She was my queen in all things, and I trusted her judgment.

A few minutes passed until Chloe and Percy emerged from the other side of the barn and began moving toward Mary and me. I could see that Percy was now much better in his actions than he had been when he left for the barn. Chloe was also smiling and seemed to be flirting with Percy. I looked away as to give them privacy and noticed that Mary was still watching them intently. I pulled at the fabric of her dress to get her attention. She looked down at me as if she had done something horrible. "Give them some privacy, my love. Do not share in their happiness for you may become lost in it," I said to Mary.

Mary smiled as if being accused of a crime for which she was guilty. I smiled at her innocence. She was beautiful and graceful as no other that I had ever seen. I was happy to just be in her presence. I respected Mary in what she wished, but she was still a young woman. She still didn't understand the ways of the world fully yet, and I would teach her. I also wished to teach her how to respect the privacy of others more conservatively than she would have been used to doing. She was not a woman who had grown into adulthood in a place like a city. The city was a place where no one had privacy, and it seemed to wear on others completely. I knew that Mary would have difficulty if this was the case. She would not be able to respect others while still observing their lives as they didn't wish. After all, respect was something that was slowly being lost within the culture of city life. I didn't wish to teach her to further this behavior. I quickly shut these thoughts out of my mind and returned to the present.

Percy and Chloe strolled onto the porch. Mary and Chloe retreated inside the home and continued to talk. Percy took his seat beside me again and said, "I am sorry, Benjamin, but this has not been easy on my family. We seemed to have been more prosperous in the past two weeks than normal, but the cost is put directly upon my family life. I don't wish to say any of this to garner pity upon my family from you, but it is the truth."

I nodded that I understood and continued to talk to Percy.

"I agree, Percy. You should never be called to put your family into harm's way for anything. I am sorry to you that I dragged you all into this. I would not be able to live with myself if I didn't apologize. Though I really couldn't have accomplished anything without your assistance," I replied.

Percy reached out and shook my hand vigorously. I knew that this would not be repayment, but it would comfort him.

It was to be known that this was all my fault. I released this demon upon Percy and his family for no reason. Perhaps I should have ignored the summons until the property was sold by the town or given to someone else. Though this thought didn't give me any comfort at all. Still, I would not be able to meet my wife or experience a life that I had longed to taste for some time. Percy and I continued to sit out on the back porch for some time. The sun had moved into a higher position in the sky. I checked my watch again, and it was now eleven o'clock. Mary and Chloe emerged from the doorway and beckoned Percy and me to ready the wagon for our trip over to Mary's uncle's house. We stood slowly from the rocking chairs. I could feel sluggish now as if I had been locked to the chair for days. I was not prepared to travel so much today, but I knew that I would need to in order for Mary to see her family. I only wished that I would be able to have more time between Percy and me. Maybe then I would have been able to spend time with Percy and his family without anything to do for the day.

I quickly followed Percy toward the wagon shed and began calling for the horses to come to the fence. I then assisted Percy in hitching the horses to the wagon after we dressed them in their harnesses. Everything was prepared now as Percy climbed onto the seat of the wagon. I was sure that we would be able to conclude our business at the other farmstead quickly and return so that I would have time to finish packing everything and loading it onto the wagon.

I assisted Mary in sitting in the wagon and made sure that she was secure before Percy snapped the reins and drove us out onto the road. The wagon bumped and lumbered along at first until we had reached the main road that ran by the farmhouse. We turned right and began heading back toward the manor now. Percy seemed content now and guided the horses gently and slowly down the road. I knew that he had a true desire to push the horses a bit and reach the other farmstead that much quicker.

The breeze blew by my face and cooled me off from the hot sun. There were no clouds in the sky at all today, so the sun gave no quarter against my skin. I was not pushed into sweating at all because of the breeze relieving me of the heat, but I feared the evening time. I knew that the day would rise in heat until my clothes would feel like they are burning. Then I would feel as if I could not escape the heat and humidity. This made me think of the horses and how cool they were under all that hair. Though I knew that they were walking along and feeling the breeze and shade as well. I just hoped that they would be able to drink water while we ate lunch. I had faith that Percy would tend to his horses in the proper manner as he always had. Now I was the one who was not prepared to talk to anyone today.

I could feel frustration now as we grew closer to the farmstead. It was not that I didn't wish to speak with Mary's family from hate or irritation, but I simply didn't wish to do anything but rest the day before we travel so far. I knew that tonight would not be easy to rest until we reach the train and could sleep. Though if we stopped off at Mary's home before we leave for Raleigh again, then I was certain to take a nap. I could see no other way that I would be useful in any circumstance. I understood Mary and all that she wished to do, so this was important to me as well. I could see no other way to thank her family than to spend time with them now before we left for the train. After all, if they had not stepped in and prepared the wedding, then we wouldn't have had an easy time doing so. I was also thankful that they understood that I had no parents or home to celebrate a wedding. My family was no more, and I would not be able to receive their help with anything now. Her family had also been very inviting from the beginning and allowed themselves to understand me and trust me. This was no small task, and I felt that it was worth some recognition.

The wagon turned right onto the road that connected to the farmstead of Mary's uncle. I could see that everyone had begun to escape the summer sun by hiding underneath the roof of their porches. No one simply strolled about the streets as they had done before. I was happy to see the town have less lively traffic as it meant that we wouldn't have to travel so slowly when going through the town. Time seemed to slow now as we moved closer and closer to our target area. Mary seemed to have a look around as if she was not surprised in any way. I knew that her family had traveled into the town many times in her life, but I thought that she would still hold wonder over this sight.

Instead, I was taken aback by the look on her face as if she wasn't surprised.

Percy took his time now as he turned right again toward the other portion of the road and headed out of town. The trees slowly surrounded us now to give us shade as we moved down this old dirt road. We rolled quicker now as the road had begun to turn slightly downhill. We then shot to the left and moved into the entryway for Ben's farmstead. Percy drove the horses past the house and to the corral. He stopped as Mary and I departed the wagon. I assisted Percy for a moment with the horses and then we walked toward the farmhouse. The whole farm seemed like a ghost town in the heat of the day. Even the animals were all hiding in the forest and resting in the shade of the trees. I felt that the servants would likely wish to do the same or work within the winery where the cool air would be able to assist everyone in not working until they were too exhausted. After all, the breeze seemed to blow by at just the right time.

Percy, Mary, and I all walked slowly through the blazing sunlight toward the farmstead. We reached the backyard and were greeted by Ben and his wife. Everyone had begun to sit for lunch, and we were invited to eat with the family once more. Ben put his arm around my shoulder and said, "How are things going, my boy?"

I smiled and replied, "Everything is going well. Mary and I are really bonding."

Ben smiled after he heard my words. I could see the relief wash over his face.

Mary and I took our seats on one side of the table as Percy moved to sit across from us. Everyone had already begun to say the prayer as we sat down, so we did so quietly. I could feel the happiness that was shared by all in this room. I was confused, however, by the lack of some of the usual servants that had sat with the family. I could see that Mary thought the same. Eventually, she piped up and asked, "Where are the servants, Uncle? Have they all left again?"

Ben laughed as he wiped his mouth.

"No one has left, dear. I simply gave them the day off. We decided to tell everyone to come for lunch with us, but they were already preparing their own food. Apparently, I forgot and it was too late to invite everyone out for lunch. The only people working are the cooks at the winery, and they are only meeting to build a new menu. You know that our busy season for the winery is approaching, and we all want it to be perfect," Ben replied.

I smiled at the thought that everyone was being cared for so well. I knew that Ben was a keen businessman and he was not allowing his greed to get the better of him. He had a taste for the finer things and for wealth, but he knew where to draw the line. He would not over-step his bounds and force people to work in such hot weather. I knew that some would, but to what end? That would only serve to make their workers suffer more in heat as intense as this.

Ben then turned to Mary and asked, "How are you, dear?"

Mary smiled sheepishly and replied, "I am well. Benjamin and I slept in the manor last night, and I have to say that it is beautiful. The rooms are so large and many. I was amazed at the size of the home."

Ben smiled greatly as he began eating again. He shook his head slightly. I understood what he was thinking, but I was not going to voice anything in this moment, especially in the company of so many women. Without hesitation, however, I chimed in with, "We came by today in order to see you all before we leave. Where have Mary's parents gone?" I asked.

Ben swiftly replied, "They all returned to their homes this morning. They ate breakfast with us and then departed for their farm. I didn't need their help for the past two days, so they just decided to leave after the wedding. They were both so happy for you two that they went home to celebrate." I could see Ben's smile widening on his face. He was jesting, but I could see that it bothered Mary that she was not able to see her family before they left. I leaned over and whispered in her ear, "We will see them on the way back to Raleigh. I will request that the coach driver take us there." Mary thanked me and smiled once more.

I knew that she had found her peace now. Her family was all that she had known. Letting go of anyone who had been around you for most of your life would be hard on any level. I knew what that was like all too well. I still remembered my mother and how she suffered. I would not wish to push anyone to simply leave people behind before they were ready. I just hoped that Mary was ready.

We all sat and ate for an hour or so as my watch read one o'clock as we stood from the table and began saying our goodbyes. Ben asked us to come back and visit the farm again, and we promised that we would. Percy seemed eager now to leave and return us to the manor so that he might go to his home. I understood this well and wished nothing more of Percy now. We all hugged everyone and began moving back toward the wagon again. Percy had left the wagon facing toward the main entrance so that we would not have to do much to hitch the horses and leave. I could see that Percy worked at a furious pace to retrieve the horses and attach them to the wagon again. He was a man who was determined to return home and be with his family. I just hoped that they wouldn't be plagued anymore by evil. When I left the manor, I knew that I would not disturb the demon anymore and cause the torment that Percy and his family had already felt.

I helped Mary into the wagon instead of helping Percy so that we would be ready to leave. I then rushed to the front of the wagon and hitched the horse on the passenger's side. I then tugged on the connections and made sure that they were tight. I didn't wish to have a horse leave one-half of the wagon behind. Percy finished hitching his horse and quickly climbed onto the wagon again. I followed his lead, and we began rolling toward the road again. I turned to Percy and thanked him for bringing us for lunch with Mary's family. He didn't respond. I feared that Percy was being distant because of his worry that his family would not be able to recover from the horrid sights that they had witnessed. What would be worse was if his children would witness something as they had last night. I knew that he would never be able to forgive himself for allowing something to frighten his children in this way. I would not be able to live with myself either.

Percy pushed the horses onward now as we moved back into town and took a hard-left turn. The wagon shuddered as it crossed the road and finally settled into a rut. We then rode swiftly out of town again and into the woods. With a gentle but sharp right turn, we began moving directly toward the manor. Percy didn't let up now. He was too intent on reaching his home soon that he snapped the reins again and brought us up to a higher speed. We moved quickly now toward the manor, and I feared that we wouldn't be able to stop before riding through the wall and into the foyer.

Mary held on to the wagon tightly where she could. Percy masterfully brought the wagon close to the drive and then slowed the horses again as he drifted right then left. We lost our speed as we gradually moved to the front porch. I thanked Percy once more and shook his hand. I gave him fifty dollars for all the trouble that he had been through with me. He then let me know that he would be here tonight to take Mary and me to the coachhouse. I thanked him again as he rode off. Percy was not a man to be nice to those that frustrated him. Instead, I understood now that he only rushed to be with his family on this day. Even though his wife had apologized to him, he still felt that something that she said was correct and sought to change that for his family. I knew now what this could be, but it was not my place to inquire.

I turned to Mary, who was already waiting by the door. I unlocked the door and we entered the home. I latched the door again once we were inside. I was sure that Mary and I would rest before traveling tonight. I turned to Mary and kissed her. "I think it would be best for us to sleep some before we leave tonight," I said.

Mary said nothing but followed me as we climbed the steps to the upper room. We both entered the room, and I lay upon the bed while watching Mary undress. I loved the sight of her removing her clothes and allowing her beautiful curves to be shown to me. She then took her place beside me as we kissed for a moment. I could not help but run my hands down her body and feel every bit of her. She was gorgeous in every way, and I could not resist the chance to let her know. Eventually, we both faded into sleep and held each other.

I awoke to the sound of the wind blowing through the trees outside the manor. The sun had slipped down toward the horizon once again as I climbed out of bed. I checked the watch in my vest to see that the time was five in the evening. I was not prepared for us to sleep this long. I knew that we needed the rest, but I also needed to rush to prepare for our journey now. I didn't even wake Mary but gathered my clothes and began dressing myself. I walked down the stairs and looked in all the rooms. I was sure that I would need to check for anything that I might have left out of place or anything that I might have left behind. I could not see anything that I had left but moved to straighten the rooms and close any windows that I had opened. I also wiped away any ashes that were left from Percy or me smoking within the manor.

I straightened the books on the shelves in the sitting room and moved the bucket for the well into the spring house. I made sure that I hadn't left any food behind or left any surface disturbed. Swiftly, I moved back into the foyer and began counting my bags to make sure that they were present to be taken with us. I then moved back upstairs and slowly walked throughout the upper floor. Nothing could be left out of place and nothing could remain dirty. I wouldn't wish for anyone to get a bad impression of the manor if Percy were to sell it for a large home. I knew that he would never utilize the home now, but perhaps he would be able to sell the home and the property that it sat upon. The last room that I came to was the attic access room. I looked in and made sure that we had closed the hatch to the attic then pushed the ladder into the closet. Perhaps this hatch would be enough to trap the demon in the attic for good.

Mary emerged from the bedroom and saw me standing outside the bedroom to the attic. "What are you doing, my love?" she asked.

I turned and said nothing at first. I walked over to her and said, "Just checking the rooms in the manor to make sure they're in order. Are you ready to leave, dear?" I asked.

Mary nodded and we both began moving down the stairs again. I heard a distinct knock at the door as I knew now that Percy had arrived. I practically ran down the stairs and opened the door. Percy entered the manor and immediately began loading the bags into the wagon. No one said anything much as we moved our luggage into the wagon. We then moved into the manor and talked for a moment. Percy thanked me for visiting and stated that he was glad that I had come down. He said, "I only wish that I could have convinced you to stay." We all laughed as I responded, "Maybe another time, Percy. Thank you for all of your help. I am glad that I came. Give your family my regards." Percy smiled at my words, and we all began moving toward the door. Just then I heard something from the upper floor. I turned to Mary and said, "Please wait for me outside."

She nodded and moved out onto the porch. Percy and I closed the door and looked upward. Nothing could be seen at first, but there was a loud boom coming from the bedroom. A candle that I had left at the top of the stairs toppled from its holder and fell to the floor. I tried to will myself to move up the stairs and put out the candle before it started a fire, but I could not. Fear had frozen me in place. Percy and I looked on in horror as great claws reached out of the bedroom with the attic hatch and began dragging the demon from the room. The demon's face emerged with a bellowing scream. Percy and I gathered our strength and willed ourselves to move again. Before I could move toward the stairs, however, the demon was intimidatingly walking toward the stairs. The thing was black, so black, in fact, that it drowned all light in its darkness. The eyes contained in the demon's head were a bright red and shone about the area.

I felt lost in the darkness that made up the demon. I was also amazed at the size of this dark being. It had to have been ten feet tall now and hunched slightly. The back of its head touched the ceiling of the manor. It reached out a claw and seemed to draw the flames to erupt. We then heard a terrible scream and a sound as if Mary were beating upon the door. Flames shot up the walls and moved with the demon as it slowly walked down the stairs. It then stopped and said, "Benjamin Price! I will be your end as I have been for your family! You will know fear and death before I am through!" With that, it raised its hands as the flames rose high enough to begin scorching the ceiling.

Percy and I rushed out the door and onto the wagon. Mary was left to pull herself into the back of the wagon and Percy snapped the reins harder than I had ever heard. The horses took off with all haste. Percy struggled against the reins as he guided the horses to turn out into the road. I yelled out, "My love, lie down!" Mary did as I requested as the manor erupted with a loud sizzling noise. The flames now shot out of the windows and stretched up to the roof. I felt nothing but the need to flee this town and never return. Percy pushed the horses harder than they had ever been pushed. We rode out into the forest that separated us from the town.

AFTERWORD

Go to hangaripublishing.com to learn more about the Author and stay up to date with their newest releases.

www.ingramcontent.com/pod-product-compliance
Lightning Source LLC
Chambersburg PA
CBHW061135120626
46546CB00005B/1788